Material Spirit

John D. Caputo, ***series editor***

PERSPECTIVES IN
CONTINENTAL
PHILOSOPHY

Edited by
GREGORY C. STALLINGS,
MANUEL ASENSI,
AND CARL GOOD

Material Spirit

Religion and Literature Intranscendent

FORDHAM UNIVERSITY PRESS
New York ▪ 2014

Fordham University Press also publishes its books in a variety of electronic formats. Some content that appears in print may not be available in electronic books.

Library of Congress Cataloging-in-Publication Data is available from the publisher.

Printed in the United States of America

16 15 14 5 4 3 2 1

First edition

Contents

Material Spirit

Introduction

GREGORY C. STALLINGS,
MANUEL ASENSI, AND CARL GOOD

The authors in this collection were given a simple invitation: to write on the topic—or paradox—of "material spirit." No limitations or parameters were specified for their contributions save a request that they speak to contemporary concerns in the study of religion and whenever possible take into consideration the relation between religion and literature by drawing on the language and concepts of literary and critical theory in the treatment of questions that might ordinarily be considered more proper to religion or theology. The authors responded with essays on an array of subjects, ranging from religious practices in early Christianity to global climate change. Although none of them wrote out of an awareness of what the others were doing, their reflections on material spirit share several interrelated threads that seem an intimate result of their literary-theoretical and paraliterary moods.

The first and most obvious commonality is a conception of "the sacred" as a question of immanence rather than transcendence—or perhaps of "immanent transcendence," as one of the writers, Richard Kearney, puts it, in an echo of the "material spirit" paradox itself, and as the subtitle of this volume seeks to mark with a verbal aberration, "intranscendent." A second commonality is the conviction that the reading of religion need not be oriented toward a renewal of religiosity but potentially has more subversive effects. And third, among those effects might be the continued possibility of a certain paradoxical kind of experience: of that which is not quite religious but which also is not entirely beyond the scope of the religious, perhaps even what could be called an experience of material spirit, though the gesture that would open the in-possibility of such an experience would not be a search for gnosis or contemplative serenity but an act of exposure to the displacements of language, an act that might in addition divest the traditional religious subject of some of its assumed foundations and securities.

The engagement with literature and literary theory in these essays on religion could be said to respond to a number of questions. How does literature (or the language of art in a wider sense) relate to religion or religious texts? What role can literature and literary theory play in contemporary reflections on religion, in particular for theorists who pursue more than epistemological claims, insofar as they also seek cognitive expansions in linguistic experience, as well as the possibility of effects, including political ones, beyond those of mere scholarly insight? Historically, has the employment of critical theory in literary studies pointed toward certain questions of the sacred in literary texts, even as those questions may have been invisible to literary critics themselves? Although theoretical literary scholars have often viewed religious traditions and practices with suspicion, is it not the case that the deconstruction of the binaries of faith and reason pervasive in contemporary critical literary theory and paraphilosophical critique since the work of Jacques Derrida, Julia Kristeva, Maurice Blanchot, Mikhail Bakhtin, Emmanuel Lévinas, and perhaps particularly Georges Bataille may have opened the door to conceptions and experiences of the sacred—or of material spirit—that not only are radically incompatible with the religious fundamentalisms emerging during the same era but whose possibilities and deterritorializations are only beginning to be explored? Or has what some consider the undecidability of deconstructive and related theories a priori led to an impasse in the use of these kinds of theories as contemporary critical tools for treating religion? The essays in this collection address these and related questions in often quite different ways, and certainly beyond the framework of a common project.

How could one speak of a "material spirituality" or a "material spirit"? Has not the entire Western tradition, among others, been founded on the irreducible *difference* between body and soul, between the sensible and the intelligible, between expression and sense? Would "material spirit" represent an audacious effort to overcome that difference? If one were to further claim that "material spirit" has emancipatory potential, wouldn't that send it off on a witch hunt against spirits, as Marx and Engels do in the third chapter of *The German Ideology*? What they call "an impure history of spirits" in that chapter is a pitiless, scathing, and ironic attack on Max Stirner and the entire Christian tradition that precedes and follows him. "Without realising it, Saint Max has so far done no more than give instruction in the art of spirit-seeing," read the opening words to the section precisely titled "The Possessed (Impure History of Spirits)."[1] If we were to look in another direction, such as toward the absolute idealism of Friedrich Schiller, even a brief examination reveals a spirit combating the body and taking its point of departure from an iron will. Wouldn't a call for material spirit in this direction seem paradoxical?

To look in yet another direction, it could be said that the concept and the idea of material spirit arise from an effect of deconstruction as it is articulated early on in the work of Jacques Derrida, particularly in those moments, from *Speech and Phenomenon* (1967) to *Specters of Marx* (1994), in which a new concept of materiality is announced. This concept encompasses not only the tangible, empirical, or palpable aspects of the field of reality but also those dimensions proper to the immaterial. It is not difficult to demonstrate this double reach of Derrida's concept of materiality: from the moment in which God, spirit, or soul are recognizable by a subject who could have an experience of them, they are repeatable—that is, identifiable beyond all the deformations that they can undergo in their avatars, apparitions, or manifestations. If Zeus is recognizable beyond the mere fact of showing himself as an eagle, water, or a bolt of lightning, it is because in all of his occurrences he preserves a common trace. It is this iteration that gives place to all the forms of immaterial materiality, among which doubt, spirituality, and the different forms of religion must be included. If the word "religion" is derived from the Latin *religare* ("to bind fast"),[2] what *religare* binds together is not one world that is material and another that is immaterial but two forms of materiality.

But the concept and the idea of material spirit also arise from a political effect, and if we turn our backs on this effect, we deny knowledge of a crucial dimension, the political uses of religion. Such uses are critical for understanding the struggles at the heart of religious groups. It is not by accident that Michel Foucault linked the "critical attitude" to Christianity. In "What Is Critique?," after defining "the critical attitude" as "the art of not being governed or, better, the art of not being governed like that and at that cost," he states that "criticism is historically Biblical": "To not want to be governed in that way was essentially to seek in the Scriptures another relation different from that which was linked to the functioning of the teachings of God, not wanting to be governed was a certain way of refusing, challenging, limiting . . . ecclesiastical rule."[3] This could be said differently but not more clearly: material spirit is also a way to comprehend political struggles at the heart of religious groups with an emancipatory end.

The articles in this collection propose a wide variety of formulations, yet they consistently refuse oppositions between body and soul or the sensible and the intelligible, or direct calls for new modes of theology and religious orientation, just as they also insist on lingering at the paradoxical border of material spirit itself, where hopes or claims of transcendence are always suspended in favor of heeding what might be called a language testimony to the latent agencies of immanence, to the orphaned letter of the sacred text, and even to the political as a subversion of the Enlightenment project.

In his essay for this volume, Richard Kearney reads the work of Marcel Proust and Virginia Woolf through the lens of what he calls anatheism, "the return to the sacred after the disappearance of God." Yet this return is something more than a negative echo of metaphysical otherworldliness, since it comes about through the consecration of "ordinary moments of flesh-and-blood *thisness.*" Thus Kearney relates modernist literature to a much older "complicity between mysticism and so-called atheism," the Eckhart-like phenomenon of a "mysticism *after God*" that testifies to everyday miracles occurring in the most quotidian events and things, "in the transubstantiation of higher into lower, extraordinary into ordinary, transcendence into immanence." In Proust and Woolf, Kearney finds the paradoxical realization that to live fully, one cannot exclude death from one's life, a concept that has Buddhist overtones. This realization entails an engagement with the world dominated by love—"where the natural universe of ordinary things is loved rather than abandoned"—and yet such an immanence is approached through a kind of transcendence of imperfect representations. In Proust's *In Search of Lost Time,* although metaphor seems to constitute a sacramental act that unites multiple moments of the past, Kearney stresses that these epiphanic moments are experienced (by Marcel) only after the event, across a gap of time, as essence is returned to contingency and metaphor becomes allied with metonymy. Metonymy thus constitutes the bridge toward what Maurice Merleau-Ponty in his last work, *The Visible and the Invisible,* described as a moment of chiasmus within the immanent "flesh of the world." As Kearney puts it, "this double trope of metaphor-metonymy is what we have been calling transubstantiation: the reversible translation of word into flesh and flesh into word." Such notions of the sacred seem far from today's Enlightenment-inspired phobia concerning the corporeal. Yet the Proustian character's chiasmatic moment of mystical dying, of moving from mortality to second natality, is nonetheless a kind of continual deferment in "a form of messianic repetition or remembering forward." Likewise, in Woolf's *To the Lighthouse,* the Buddhistic vision into the "emptiness" and "void," the nonhuman aspect of things that haunts the imaginations of her characters, is made manifest only through a deferral, through, in Didi-Huberman's words, "the failure of representation, not its success."

The following two essays focus on the excessive disposition of the sacred. Karmen MacKendrick traces in Christian confessional modes an expenditure incongruent with what Bataille criticized as the Enlightenment tradition's tendency toward rational project, to the detriment of sacrifice and process. She focuses her attention on an excess or extravagant waste, called expenditure by Bataille, that religious thought since the Enlightenment has sought to control or keep at bay in the attempt to rationalize the Christian tradition. At the core of Christianity and the other religions, MacKendrick writes, one finds an experience of sacrifice and the sacred "removed from the realm of project and productive labor to that of conspicuously nonproductive consumption and . . . intimacy." Confession, for MacKendrick, has to do with Bataille's notion of communication as mystical expression of woundedness, which most contemporary religions would seek to deny in favor of a "security of boundedness." Rather than leading toward such a security, confession involves a breaking of will associated with "pain and damage and incompletion." But as such it constitutes not a mere struggle against insubordination but a "struggle . . . against not-struggling" that involves the body's most intimate relation to language: confession is a "paradoxical willing against will by engaging in a kind of speaking and writing that turn language not only toward silence but toward its own more passionate inarticulation." In this emphasis on speaking and writing, MacKendrick examines the testimony and confession of passionate inarticulation in Bataille's literary as well as critical writings, in contexts where the literary and the language of the sacred seem to collude in their openness to the heterogeneity of the self in relation to an unpresentable alterity. In the work of Bataille and elsewhere, passionate inarticulation emerges out of the very multiplicity of the will in its breaking and in relation to alterity as a certain "resonance": "the multiplicity of wills 'within' a subject at a given time" opens to a relation with "the effective will from 'without,'" as the latter "resonate[s] with, catch[es] on to some inner will, however minutely represented among the multiple desires of the self." Such an experience of immanence—the woundedness and the breaking of the self that opens to something beyond the self—thus coincides with an excess of language, of an "expenditure of words."

In Manuel Asensi's subtly subversive analysis of a famous *villancico* (religious poem) by Saint Teresa of Avila, we again encounter a fractured subject of a certain kind of confession, this time a subject who has radically lost or ceded "her own, proper position" in relation to a God figure, which, as an effect of that loss, turns from a "transcendent" God into an "immanent" one. If MacKendrick places the emphasis on subjective fragmentation as a sacral/sacrificial gesture that opens to relationality with an undetermined alterity, Asensi stresses a kind of infolding of that relation into what he calls a "transverberation." He closely follows Saint Teresa's poem's complex play of competing and contradictory affirmations, setting his point of departure in the way in which the speaker in the work enunciates out of a death that is also a life ("I die because I do not die" [muero porque no muero]), out of an absence that becomes a form of presence. The poem's enunciation contrasts with the poetry of Teresa's fellow mystical contemporary, the more transcendental Saint John of the Cross, who longs for a mystical union from below. Asensi compares these two fifteenth-century figures as exemplars of thepositioned and thenonpositioned subject: "The subject in Saint John's poem *speaks* because the subject is present; the subject in Saint Teresa's poem *repeats,* because in actuality the subject has disappeared." Yet that disappearance proves to be radically more than the forced exile resulting from religious subjection or abjection. Asensi shows how the speaker in the work not only disappears in subservience to God but also reappears as the "master of God," the disappearance and reappearance manifesting a "destructured subject . . . that oscillates between the capacity to turn God into her captive and prisoner and the recognition of her own earthly abandonment." Ultimately, Asensi finds a political effect in that destructured subjectivity: Saint Teresa, so often co-opted for the cause of Catholic orthodoxy or for projects of Platonic aesthetic epistemology, turns out to be a radical saboteur of language, opening language to a "field of schizoid madness," as together "God and the mystic . . . have stolen the language of the world in order to give it back as a poisoned dart."

Burcht Pranger likewise intervenes in a context of Spanish ascetic mysticism with an exploration of problems in the interpretation of religious Baroque visual art. In images of the suffering Christ from seventeenth-century Spanish artists such as Francisco de Zurbarán and Francisco Ribalta, hyperrealism, or perhaps also hypermateriality, poses an interpretive challenge: what experiences of ascetic withdrawal could these works claim to promise when not only their realism, intense color, and sculptural effect but also their ways of representing human figures of asceticism in relation to the suffering Christ would seem to absorb the subject of contemplation rather than figure a mystical possibility? The stakes of this question are broad since, as Pranger observes, even in noniconic contexts of Christian theology, from the extremes of early monastic asceticism to Calvinism, a singular characteristic of Christianity is that its notions of spiritual withdrawal and renunciation have historically and theologically depended on the *presence* of Christ: the word continually made flesh. This becoming flesh, as Pranger puts it, "foreclosed any attempt at an ultimate withdrawal through vanishing into thin air," with the Calvinistic tradition even leading to a theological worldview in which "creation is . . . injected with a hyperrealism that allows for neither escape nor rest," inciting the faithful to "labor harder, to save more capital for better chances and higher purposes, and to postpone temporary enjoyment, not with an eye on more spiritual and ethereal possessions with fewer dimensions but going for the 'real thing,' Christ in heaven." Both the hyperrealist Baroque iconography and the Calvinistic celebration of Christ in heaven would ultimately seem to lead toward the Christian subject's "utter absorption," his or her substitution by the visual-religious object. Nonetheless, Pranger's analysis does not climax in this observation but takes it as the starting point for a further discussion that threads its way from consideration of a devotional text by Bernard of Clairvaux to a reading of Ribalta's painting *Christ Embracing Saint Bernard,* a composition in which Pranger detects echoes of the Bernardian text in visual language. In his commentary on both the visual text and the hyperrealist painting, Pranger offers an oblique and open interpretation that deviates materially and spiritually from the impasses of Christian theological absorption.

Kevin Hart also examines religious mysticism in the language of art, but with a focus on a much later context, that of nineteenth-century poetry. His essay elaborates a phenomenology of Christianity through a reading of Gerard Manley Hopkins's "Hurrahing in Harvest," a poem that points in a singular way toward "how to develop a theology of the senses and a theology of manifestation." For Hart, a phenomenology of Christianity "is not mysticism; it is everyday Christianity, *lived* Christianity, Christianity as *life.*" As in many of the essays in this book, this notion of an everyday faith entails a conception of the divine that differs from the new fundamentalist, noncorporeal notion of deity that insists on conceiving of the light of God as the fleshy manifestation of God in Christ. Yet throughout Hart's reading of Hopkins's poem, such a corporeal, immanent God can only be approached through a kind of indirect journey, an impossible transcendence in John Caputo's sense of the term: as an "experience" that is always in a certain sense under erasure.[4] Through contemplation, religious seekers may be detached—a term often used with Buddhist associations by other contributors to this book, notably Kearney—from a particular scene so that "they can be reconceived and attached elsewhere: in the clouds, in the hills, anywhere." This requires an active gaze to perceive hidden patterns of divine love—or the veiled manifestation of "the kingdom of God"—in the world around us. Yet the possibility of a displaced, reattached experience of kingdom is irreducible to the kind of knowledge one ordinarily associates with Christianity: "the kingdom is not given to us as a system of explanation of what happens in this world ('revelation,' 'miracles,' 'visions,' and so on) or so many items of knowledge but rather, as George Herbert so beautifully said, as 'the land of spices; something understood.'" Unlike the fundamentalist gaze of assurance, such perceptions require not only faith but also imagination. Like several of the other essays in this book, Hart's reflection on Hopkins offers a chiasmatic moment of immanence in which what we contemplate seems to be looking back at us: as we reinvent the world with our imagination, the world reinvents us: "Contemplation changes us, and we change the world." Such is the immanent kingdom of God that nevertheless remains to be fully manifest, still a messianic, transcendent promise as "Hopkins realizes that the kingdom has not yet fully come."

Virginia Burrus approaches Augustine's writings on miracle through the lens of what she refers to as Franz Rosenzweig's "postmodern retrieval of a premodern theory of miracle" in *Star of Redemption.* Her reading of Rosenzweig's enigmatic—and deliberately obscured—references to Augustine leads to a new and often surprising conception of the signifying power of the miraculous in the early saint's writings. The conception in question is not without its own performance of what Asensi would call "transverberation" or MacKendrick the "resonance of alterity" as Burrus reads in, across, and beyond the two writers, putting them into a conversation that opens beyond the progression of thought across time, thereby enacting in her own reading something of the temporal-figural conception of miracle that she demonstrates in Augustine and Rosenzweig. Through her dialogic coupling of Rosenzweig and Augustine, Burrus notes a certain temporal excess in the latter's *City of God:* "Spanning the gap by perching at the reversible pivot point of temporality, miracle is the call that responds and the response that calls from within the rupture of time—time gathering time to itself, and thereby spilling beyond itself." Furthermore, in exploring the signifying and paratemporal character of the miracle in Augustine, Burrus focuses on his often surprising emphasis on the corporeal: "The intensification of pain (as well as of pleasure) fuses body to soul while drawing time to a standstill." This awareness of corporeal immanence for Augustine corresponds to an experience of time itself as excessive, as the thickening of time proper to miracles: "To perceive bodies in their . . . plenitudinous excess and poignant finitude—to live fully in the eternity of *this* day—is already to see God," although such a seeing is also "the masking of becoming." As occurs in the other essays in this collection, the Augustinian miracle would seek a nontranscendent relationship to the material: "If miracle calls for belief in unbelievable possibility, it does so not by transcending the material but by turning back toward it."

Kate Rigby also focuses on materiality, and the materiality of language, as she turns to questions of ecology. She argues that it is only by acknowledging the impossibility of art or literature to adequately represent the "things" around us that one can hope to unsettle the spirit-matter dualism complicit in a historical legacy of ecocide. She observes that "writing is not vibrant life." And yet neither does it have to be "docile artifact," since it may inspire readers, in the words of Wordsworth, to "quit your books," to "close up those barren leaves." Rigby reads the latter phrase as foregrounding the material opacity of poetic texts, furthermore positing it as that on which a "negative ecopoetics" would hinge. The phrase leads her to explore the Wordsworthian line in her title, "Come forth into the light of things." Rigby reflects extensively on the unexpected force of this line throughout her essay, juxtaposing it with concepts from Silvia Benso and others, as well as extending it to a consideration of the work of contemporary ecologically focused poets such as Tim Lilburn. Through these textual affinities she reads the line as a call not to a sacred self-revelation of nature but to a displacement of the subjective grasping of nature, a "call to a risky proximity with things" that carries a burden of ethical responsibility to the possibility of encounter with "the other than human."

The final two essays in *Material Spirit* share both Rigby's ethical-environmental concerns and Pranger's interest in the often ignored effects of the materiality of the signifier. They do so in essays that draw on what Paul de Man referred to in his late writings and lectures as the material event. While Tom Cohen questions the turn toward religion in contemporary theory, he advocates a similar temporal—or temporizing—strategy to that found throughout the essays in this book when he calls for a return to Benjamin's imperative to "'blast' or activate a dormant trace or force of use to the present, and reinscribe the archive" (Cohen's term for recorded history), from which it would then emerge in order to effect a "politics of memory." He purports to subvert the mimetic humanism that continues to close off the possibility of such a politics, in an essay that also returns to—but also to a rather different version of—Rigby's ecopoetics. The material event for Cohen is a preoriginary set of marks, spaces, or traces, the madness of inscription or atomization repressed in the constitution of the Western tradition propped up by cult values of prosopopoeia and interiority. Ironically, the drive to implement these same values ends up causing their destruction all around us in a kind of cinematic slow motion of climate change, credit crises, and extincted life forms. Cohen's descriptions of these meltdowns may recall for the reader Georges Bataille's immanence of formlessness and expenditure that runs throughout many of the other essays of this book. Cohen shares with the other writers in this book a

God—more accurately conveys the complex paradoxes and ambivalences in play. For Proust and Woolf believed, along with Paul Claudel, that there is indeed another world but that it is inside this one. A sense of transcendence is alive in their work, but it is one inscribed in everyday immanence. Mystery is preserved, even celebrated, not as ecclesiastical dogma but as a mystical affirmation of incarnate existence: Word made Flesh in the ordinary universe.

I am suggesting, in other words, that these authors manage to eschew the received divisions between sacred and profane, religious and secular, transcendent and immanent, in favor of a retrieval of the sacramental in the sensible. What may be called the *eucharistic imagination* is no longer the exclusive preserve of high church liturgies but is generously extended to acts of quotidian experience where the infinite traverses the infinitesimal. Whether this mutual traversal of the sacred and secular in modernist fiction is a matter of sacramentalizing the secular or of secularizing the sacred is, of course, central to our discussion. What I am wagering here is that the anatheist paradigm allows it to be both at once: religion as art and art as religion. Not one or the other, though I am well aware that the relationship between faith and fiction remains a complex one.

Put hermeneutically, the question of a return to the sacred in these writers is carried out according to what I call "sacramental aesthetics." In formulating such an approach I am drawing on provocative insights by a number of continental thinkers, including Paul Ricoeur, Maurice Merleau-Ponty, and Julia Kristeva. This is not the place to elaborate the theoretical projects of these philosophers, but a brief word concerning their contributions to my horizon of interpretation is in order.

One of Ricoeur's hermeneutic focal points is the interchange between life and narrative. He argues that "the process of composition, of configuration, is not completed in the text but in the reader and, under this condition, makes possible the reconfiguration of life by narrative." He claims, more exactly, that "the sense or signification of a narrative stems from *the intersection of the world of the text and the world of the reader*" (which is already "prefigured" by the world of the author).[2] Ricoeur goes so far as to construe the double surrender of (1) the author to the implied author (or narrator) and (2) the implied author to the reader, as an act of kenotic service to the other that ultimately amounts to a transubstantiation of author into reader: "Whereas the real author effaces himself in the implied author, the implied reader takes on substance in the real reader."[3] In short, the author agrees to die so that the reader may be born.

In one of his last books, *On Translation,* Ricoeur refers explicitly to the act of eucharistic exchange in enunciating the process of translation as mutual hospitality between authors and readers: "It seems to me," he writes,

> that translation sets us not only intellectual work, theoretical or practical, but also an ethical problem. Bringing the reader to the author, bringing the author to the reader, at the risk of serving and of betraying two masters: this is to practice what I like to call linguistic hospitality. It is this which serves as a model for other forms of hospitality that I think resemble it: confessions, religions, are they not like languages that are foreign to one another, with their lexicon, their grammar, their rhetoric, their stylistics which we must learn in order to make our way into them? And is Eucharistic hospitality not to be taken up with the same risks of translation-betrayal, but also with the same renunciation of the perfect translation?[4]

In Derrida, the gesture toward what I call the sacramental happens by way of affiliated moments of refiguration. Derrida invokes Elijah, for example, as a messianic paradigm for the reader: the unpredictable other par excellence who calls the text forth and is in turn called forth by the text.

As we shall see, Proust the author calls to his future reader to discover in his work the book of the reader's own life. In so doing he invokes a sacramental idiom of transubstantiation so as to convey the miracle of textual composition and reception. The result is that readers are confronted with a miracle of *repetition* that *recalls the past forward*—an epiphany that explodes the chronology of time.[5] Such a readerly "repetition" is reminiscent of Kierkegaard's sense of *repeating forward* (kairological time) rather than recollecting backward (chronological).[6]

What Merleau-Ponty and Kristeva add to these touchstones of refiguration and repetition is a pointed philosophical return to the *sensible* realm—the textures, bodies, and moments in which lived experience evidences a "eucharistic" character. Like Ricoeur, these authors explicitly refer to the term "eucharistic," while adding the more Catholic (Merleau-Ponty) and Orthodox (Kristeva) meaning of "transubstantiation." This latter term has the general meaning of the changing of one substance into another, and a specific one when applied to the sacrament of the Mass: "The conversion in the Eucharist of the whole substance of the bread into the body and of the wine into the blood of Christ, only the appearances (and other 'accidents') remaining."[7] The term "sacramental" as used in this essay, and as explicitly cited by Merleau-Ponty, Kristeva, and Proust, refers primarily to the Christian sacrament of the Last Supper, but it also connotes the related meanings of deep communion between persons (human and divine), the consecration of ordinary material elements (such as bread and wine), and the power of certain words, images, symbols, and gestures to serve as outward visible signs of an inner spiritual grace received from beyond the self (for instance, from the other, nature, God).

Merleau-Ponty endeavors to locate the phenomenon of sacramental flesh in the marvels of the everyday. His use of sacramental language amounts to what I would call a eucharistics of profane perception. In the *Phenomenology of Perception* (1945), for example, he elaborates a profound connection between the *sacrament* as an operation of grace and the *sensible* itself as a "form of communion."[8] He writes,

> Just as the sacrament not only symbolizes, in sensible species, an operation of Grace, but *is* also the real presence of God, which it causes to occupy a fragment of space and communicates to those who eat of the consecrated bread, provided that they are inwardly prepared, in the same way the sensible has not only a motor and vital significance, but is nothing other than a certain way of being in the world suggested to us from some point in space, and seized and acted upon by our body, provided that it is capable of doing so, so that sensation is literally a form of communion.

Merleau-Ponty goes on in this same passage to sound the eucharistic power of the sensible as follows:

> I am brought into relation with an external being, whether it be in order to open myself to it or to shut myself off from it. If the qualities radiate around them a certain mode of existence, if they have the power to cast a spell and what we called just now a sacramental value, this is because the sentient subject does not posit them as objects, but enters into a sympathetic relation with them, makes them his own and finds in them his momentary law.[9]

Though working from a philosophically agnostic viewpoint, Merleau-Ponty offers an intriguing phenomenological interpretation of eucharistic embodiment as recovery of the divine within the flesh, a kenotic emptying out of transcendence into the heart of the world's body, becoming a God beneath us rather than a God beyond us.[10]

Numerous idioms of eucharistic empathy appear in the work of Proust and Woolf, and I discuss these as the chapter unfolds. It suffices for now to note the curious paradox that it is precisely when Merleau-Ponty traces the phenomenological return all the way down to the lowest rung of experience (in the old metaphysical ladder, the *sensible*) that he discovers the most sacred act of communion. It is here that we witness the crossing over of ostensible contraries, the most in the least, the highest in the lowest, the first in the last, the invisible in the visible. This amounts to a reversal of Platonism and idealism, returning to flesh as our most intimate "element," namely, that which enfolds and envelopes us in the systole and diastole of Being, the seeing and being seen of vision. Merleau-Ponty's phenomenology thus marks the surpassing of traditional dualisms (body-mind, real-ideal, inner-outer, subject-object) in the name of a deeper, more primordial chiasmus in which opposites traverse each other.

A linguist and psychoanalyst, Julia Kristeva likewise offers rich insights into the workings of unconscious tropes and associations in modernist writings about sense and sensibility. Raised in the culture of Greek Orthodox Christianity and educated by Catholic nuns in Sofia, Kristeva has a keen sense of the sacramental in a religious context (though she, no less than Merleau-Ponty, rejects the God of metaphysical theism).[11] She is attuned to those gestures conceived through a certain *sacramentality of the senses* found in works of art and literature. In *Time and Sense,* she identifies a certain grammar of "transubstantiation" at work in Proust's pivotal notion of involuntary memory. Kristeva relates the eucharistic aesthetic to the chiasmic liaison between the visible and invisible, the inner feeling and outer expression. Refusing the dualistic division of spirit and body into separate substances, Kristeva thus invites us to think of *flesh* more phenomenologically as an "*element,*" that is, as the "concrete emblem of a general manner of being."[12]

By way of response to and repetition of these notions of immanent transcendence, my own more limited aim is to sketch an aesthetics that illustrates how dying to an acosmic God may allow a God of cosmic epiphanies to be reborn. As novelists, Proust and Woolf epitomize a sacramental imagination that celebrates the bread and wine of everyday existence. I will focus primarily on Proust's *In Search of Lost Time* and Woolf's *To the Lighthouse.* In each narrative, ordinary moments of flesh-and-blood *thisness* are consecrated as something strange and enduring. These acts of transfiguration transpire in an embodied space and time far from the otherworldliness of metaphysical formalism. In this way my hypothesis is that the anatheist hermeneutic of incarnation may help discern a grammar of transubstantiation in these narratives of sacramental sensation. To this end, I will concentrate on certain eucharistic events in each novel, suggesting how they signal anatheist recoveries of the sacred in the profane.

Resurrection and Transubstantiation in Proust

Eucharistic idioms are central to the work of Marcel Proust. Tropes of transubstantiation, resurrection, and revelation occur in several key passages of *In Search of Lost Time.* They generally signal a grammar for recovering the timeless in time, as in the famous madeleine episode, but they also refer to a process of artistic transformation, as in Marcel's final disquisition on the writing process in *Time Regained.* If food and taste are sensible idioms that produce the quintessential epiphany of the first kind, it is another kind of epiphany, at the end of the labyrinthine narrative, that amplifies the second aspect of Proust's sacramental vision. I am thinking of the penultimate scene at the Guermantes when Marcel is left waiting in the library while a preprandial music recital is under way. Arriving late, Marcel experiences a cluster of epiphanies just before entering the Guermantes' salon. In this antechamber of remaindered time, certain achronic moments return to him. As we shall see, such encounters are emblematic of the manner in which the anatheist retrieval of the sacred in the profane is preceded by an acute acceptance of disillusionment and death.

Marcel's first involuntary memory is of entering the San Marco Cathedral in Venice. This is a site of eucharistic celebration par excellence. The flash of memory is triggered by Marcel's stumbling on some uneven cobblestones as he traverses the Guermantes' courtyard in Paris. Though he had been unable to take in the sacramental quality of the experience at the time (when he first visited Venice with his mother), he relives it now many years later here in Paris (after the event, through the lens of a second event). In this way the former "unexperienced" experience is finally reexperienced across the gap of time.

This "miracle of the courtyard" is followed by another involuntary memory brought on by the sound of a spoon striking a plate as a waiter in the dining room prepares the banquet table for the feast to come. Then we have a third quasi-eucharistic epiphany as Marcel wipes his lips with a starched table napkin, the sensation suddenly recalling a luminous moment in his childhood when he sat in the dining room of the Grand Hotel at Balbec. Finally, Marcel experiences a very formative (if forgotten) moment from his childhood: fetching a volume of George Sands's novel, *François le Champi,* from the Guermantes' library shelves, he suddenly relives an evening when Maman read this same book to him at bedtime in Combray. As we know from the opening scene of the book, it was this nocturnal reading that coincided with the inaugural moment when his mother left the dinner table with Marcel's father and Swann to come kiss her son, Marcel, goodnight. Reading and feasting are thus intimately associated with the maternal kiss—the kiss that set Marcel on his search for lost time, eventually culminating in the novel of that name.

Samuel Beckett has described this cluster of epiphanies as a "single annunciation," and this allusion to the miracle of incarnation is revealing. For in this scene Marcel comes back to the flesh. He is reminded, at the Guermantes' party, that most of his loved ones—Robert de St. Loup, Grandmaman, Maman, Swann, Odette, Françoise—are dead, that Charlus is dying, and that he himself has just escaped a brush with death in a sanatorium. Marcel is brought back to earth again and sees behind the masks of Parisian show and snobbery to the throes of mortal flesh—vanity, transience, and passing away. It is only then, the author seems to imply, that Marcel is at last ready to renounce the romantic pretensions of his youth and acknowledge that true art is an *art of flesh*—a literary transubstantiation of those contingent, fragile, carnal, and seemingly inconsequential moments that our conscious will is wont to consign to oblivion. Marcel can thus finally assume his vision of "Combray and its surrounding world taking shape and solidity out of a cup of tea."[13] The aesthete must perish for the artist to flourish.

Kristeva lays special emphasis on the San Marco epiphany, recalling as it does an earlier chapter in the novel and an earlier moment in Marcel's life, when he visited Venice with Maman. Kristeva interprets this pivotal episode as central to the understanding of Proust's eucharistic aesthetic, combining as it does the various epiphanies of Mamam reading, the madeleine, and the stumbling stone. Examining various drafts of Proust's novels and a number of notebook entries on John Ruskin, whose "religious aesthetic" greatly influenced him, Kristeva traces Proust's growing fascination with the liturgical terms of "transubstantiation," "real presence," and the incarnational mystery of "time embodied" and "time resurrected."[14] She herself uses these terms of eucharistic ritual to describe the way in which Proust's characters relate to themselves, each other, and the textual style of the novel, through a mystical crisscrossing of tenses: "As combinations of past and present impressions, the characters contaminate one another and fuse their contours; a *secret depth* attracts them. Like the madeleine soaked in tea, they allow themselves to be absorbed into Proust's style. These Proustian heroes and visions will eventually leave us with a singular and bizarre taste that is pungent and invigorating. It is the taste of the sense of time, of *writing as transubstantiation.*"[15]

Kristeva goes on to cite many scenes that elaborate on the sacramental process of transubstantiation in terms of "translation," "incarnation," "metaphor," and "superimposition."[16] For Proust, Kristeva notes, it is the task of the writer to "search for an object" in which "each hour of our life hides," and he believes that literature can resuscitate those hidden moments in the form of epiphanies. In his writings on the aesthetics of Ruskin and Male, for example, Proust identifies two particular such moments, a bit of toast that will become a madeleine and a Venetian paving stone—two of the key epiphanies in *In Search of Lost Time.* Commenting on the example of the paving stone in San Marco Cathedral, Kristeva writes,

> Tripping on the stone and then stumbling would thus be a way of having faith in the sacred. Indeed the sacred is made of stone: a 'living stone, rejected by men but in God's sight chosen and precious' (I Peter 2: 4–5). . . . The cornerstone, along with its manifestations in Proust's writings, is thus presented as a sign of the cult of Jesus, as the real presence of essence. The cornerstone appears to have been Proust's underlying motif, for between the cathedrals and the Mass . . . Proust wished to fathom the mystery of "transubstantiation." He managed to do so by . . . clearing his own path through everyday sensations, and by acknowledging an eroticism that influenced and increasingly overwhelmed the future narrator's involuntary memory.[17]

Or again, "In contact with the 'living stone,' he [Marcel] himself becomes a 'living stone,' a 'stream of light,' a participant in the sacred, in 'transubstantiation.'"[18]

Proust himself describes the coming together of different time scenes as "metaphor" and "resurrection." And for Proust these terms are curiously allied if not identical. Both involve the translation of one thing in terms of another. True art, Marcel comes to realize, is not a matter of progressively depicting a series of objects or events ("describing one after another the innumerable objects which at a given moment were present at a particular place"); it occurs only when the writer "takes two different objects" and "states the connection between them."[19] And here we return to Merleau-Ponty's logic of sacramental perception. For it is the identification of "unique connections" and hidden liaisons between one thing and another that enables the writer to translate the book of life (which "exists already in each one of us") into the book of art.[20] This is how Marcel puts it: "truth—and life too—can be attained by us only when, by comparing a quality common to two sensations, we succeed in extracting their common essence and in reuniting them to each other, liberated from the contingencies of time, with a metaphor."[21] That Marcel privileges figures of resurrection and transubstantiation in this work of metaphor is once again a confirmation of what I am calling a sacramental aesthetic. The textual deployment of metaphor as sacramental act articulates an artistic imagination that has lived through the agnostic "disenchantment of modernity" before daring to recover anew the sacred in the secular.

But let us take a closer look at the trip to Venice episode. This follows immediately after the death of Albertine and opens with a golden angel on the San Marco campanile "announcing" a certain "joy." Several themes are tightly woven into this short chapter, which reaffirms Proust's notion of "art as transubstantiation"—Combray and Venice, childhood and adulthood, France and Italy, and the two distinct temporal sensations of past and present "condensed into a metaphor."[22] The scene plays out a dream of death and rebirth: "Death plays a role in this condensation. A reference to the grandmother's death echoes Albertine's more recent disappearance, which is now ready to be internalized and transformed into the innermost depths of writing."[23] Recalling the mother's presence under the window, the narrator confesses an impression of "getting closer and closer to the essence of something secret."[24] Kristeva reads this visit to San Marco as pivotal to the entire development of the novel. It is, she claims, a crucial station on the initiatory journey between "The Death of the Cathedrals" chapter and the concluding volume, *Time Regained,* a journey constituting what she calls a "voyage toward a *living* meaning."[25] This is how she interprets the scene:

> The mystery of this incarnate Venice resides in the mother's presence . . . the incorporation of mother and city. . . . A strange fusion is established between the mother's body and Venice's body. Sitting and reading underneath the pointed arches of an ogival window, the mother inscribes herself in the beautiful stones of Saint Mark's. The window is identified with "a love which stopped only where there was no longer any corporeal matter to sustain it, on the surface of her impassioned gaze. . . . It says to me the thing that touches me more than anything else in the world: 'I remember your mother so well.'" Through the magic of this infiltration, the Venetian window becomes the matter sustaining maternal love—the window *is* the love for the mother. The same process applies to the baptistery, where we find devoted women who appear to have been taken right out of a Carpaccio painting: "She (the mother) has her place reserved there as immutably as a mosaic."[26]

The word "fusion" here is telling, I suspect, given the French association with brewing beverages, for example the infusion of linden tea in the madeleine episode. So we might say that mystical fusion and liquid fusion brush shoulders across memory and time. Nor is it insignificant that Marcel's anamnestic retrieval of the Venice baptistery in the epiphany of the Guermantes' paving stone is contiguous with the related recall of Maman reading the story of François le Champi and his foster mother, *Madeleine* Blanchet: a mystical-maternal association that Kristeva makes much of.[27] Kristeva concludes her psychoanalytic reading by suggesting that the Venice scene is best understood as an "incarnation founded on the love between a son and his mother."[28] She is well aware of the Catholic Marian connotations of this Madonna and Child imagery and deems it highly significant that Proust redrafted the chapter several times and was revising it right up to his death, as witnessed in certain deathbed notes to Celeste Albaret—such as "cross out everything that occurs before my arrival with my mother in Venice." Hurried by his final illness, Proust concentrated on communicating his own "aesthetic credo" in this pivotal episode, a credo that involves "the integration of the spiritual theme with the sensual theme, which includes the love for the mother in the celebration of Venice."[29]

Proust chose ultimately to highlight the "interpenetration between Venice and his mother, between the angel's light and the body," and this choice endured until the final typescript, inviting us to consider the trip to Venice "as an apotheosis of the madeleine and paving-stone episodes."[30] For Kristeva, accordingly, Venice powerfully assumes the mystical role of a "sensual and symbolic Orient," a city that becomes "maternal and thus stresses its own incarnation."[31] (I return to such "Oriental" allusions in my discussion of Woolf below.) This, concludes Kristeva, is the "cornerstone" of Proust's entire eucharistic aesthetic, treating Venice as a "world within a world" (Proust's words), the very character of "time embodied." In this manner the visit to Saint Mark's baptistery may be read as the crucial link between the "erotic *Bildungsroman*"—running from Maman and Ghilberte to Albertine—and the annunciation of epiphanies in the "final pensive pages" of the novel. But the all-important point is, once again, that Marcel can only experience the final epiphanies *after the event,* when the earlier sacramental moments—with Maman sitting in Venice, or reading to him as a child in Combray—are recalled and retrieved across the gap of time. *Après coup. Nachträglich.* If Marcel's visit with Maman to the Venice cathedral and baptistery is as pivotal to the novel as Kristeva suggests, it is not because Venice was where Marcel achieves his epiphany and becomes at last a sacramental author. If that were so, the novel would logically end with that chapter, and it doesn't. It is, rather, only after Marcel has experienced the "death of the cathedrals" and, by association and extension, the death of mothers (Maman, Madeleine Blanchet, and the surrogate imaginary love object, Albertine) that he can prepare himself for his ultimate awakening: the recovery in kairological time of what had been irretrievably lost in chronological time. In short, the first sacred fusion must be abandoned so that a second, sacred epiphany can be regained, and this time not in a triumphal basilica but on a simple paving stone. Venice is recovered in a Parisian courtyard.

Venice, in other words, is not the last station on Marcel's journey, and Maman is not the last object of his affections. On the contrary, by the end of the novel it seems that Maman has finally been accepted as the "lost object," prompting Marcel to move from an aesthetic of melancholy to one of mourning. As the novel progresses Marcel moves increasingly beyond the various transfers of amorous want and returns to the Madonna of the ordinary universe, Françoise. The menial maid of the opening chapters now reappears as "the Michelangelo of our kitchen."[32] (She is a quotidian creature capable of transforming a farmyard chicken into a delicious family feast of *poulet rôti.*) I would even suggest that by the final volume of the novel, *Time Regained,* Françoise—as everyday cook and seamstress—has become Marcel's model for writing the novel, his mundane muse. The narrator now confesses, after all, that he "should work beside her almost as she worked herself."[33]

This conjecture is confirmed if we recall how Françoise is compared to Giotto's *Caritas* in her being as well as her appearance (*pace* Swann) in the opening volume.[34] Replacing the endless litany of elusive metonymic loved ones—from Maman and Ghilberte to Mlle de Guermantes and Albertine—Françoise reemerges in the end as mistress of the everyday microcosm. The ethereal Albertine transmigrates back, as it were, into the Françoise of flesh and blood. The death of Marcel's exotic fantasy lover is the occasion for the rebirth of the forgotten scullery maid. Curiously, it is Francoise's very qualities of patient craft and endurance, grounded in a sharp sense of mortality and earthiness, that Walter Benjamin celebrates in his famous concluding image of Proust: "for the second time there rose a scaffold on which the artist, his head thrown back, painted the creation on the ceiling of the Sistine Chapel: the sickbed on which Marcel Proust consecrates the countless pages which he covered with his handwriting . . . to the creation of his microcosm."[35] Kitchens and cathedrals. Dying and creating. Earthly frailty as portal to art. Moreover, it is also Benjamin who would observe—whether thinking of the culinary seamstress Françoise or not—that "the eternal is in any case far more the ruffle on a dress than some idea."[36]

Where does this leave Mamam? I suspect that by the time Marcel recalls Maman in the final Paris epiphanies—which trigger the involuntary memories of both Venice and the bedtime reading of *François le Champi*—it is less a question of fusion than of transfusion. Or of "transversal," as Proust himself uses the term in Marcel's terminal musings on time regained. In other words, rather than embracing a form of immediate, magical union, Proust introduces the preposition *trans* to capture the sense of both identity and difference over time. Transfusion, transversal, translation, transferral, transubstantiation.

But a final word on Françoise. If Françoise is indeed Marcel's ultimate guide, it is perhaps no accident that the novel becomes fragmented in a number of different directions in *Time Regained* just when it seems on the point of reaching closure and becoming whole (in the manner of some Hegelian telos). Proust resists the Hegelian temptation. His book remains undecided as to whether Marcel's projected novel is actually the author's *In Search of Lost Time* or not. This is for the reader to decide. Indeed, it is curious how each philosophical reading of Proust—by Ricoeur, Deleuze, Lévinas, Benjamin, Genette, Beckett, de Man, Blanchot, Kristeva, Nussbaum, Murdoch, Girard—manages, in every case, to *translate* the novel into its own hermeneutic, making the work the ultimate exemplar, perhaps, of an open text, or of what we might call—taking our cue once again from Merleau-Ponty's model of eucharistic reversibility—a sacramental text. For again it is a question of the author sacrificing him- or herself to the text so that each reader can be returned—anatheistically—to a refigured existence.

We might conclude, then, by further considering the significance of how the once mocked Françoise is retrospectively restored as Marcel's most reliable guide. It was this housemaid, we recall, who was always the one pointing Marcel away from literature for literature's sake and in the direction of literature for life. She was the earthy servant who, "like all unpretentious people," had a no-nonsense approach to literary vainglory and saw through Marcel's literary rivals as mere "copiators."[37] It was Françoise, Marcel suddenly realizes, who had "a sort of instinctive comprehension of literary work" capable of "divining [Marcel's] happiness and respecting [his] toil."[38] And so Marcel ultimately resolves to labor as she did, stitching and threading from bits and pieces of cloth: "constructing my book, I dare not say ambitiously like a cathedral, but quite simply like a dress."[39] The fantasy persona of Albertine, the main source of Marcel's tormented jealousies and deceptions, is finally replaced by the seamstress of the real. Mystique is unmasked by a maid.

In this respect, Françoise might be seen as a refiguration of Homer's Penelope. For Proust, as we have seen, navigates a return from heroic wanderings to the weavings of the everyday. The marvels of literature are no longer to be sought in monumental basilicas of grandiose design but in the intricate weft and warp of ordinary existence. And in this embrace of writing as weaving we find the literary trope of metaphor being allied to that of metonymy. The transformative and synthetic power of metaphor, which turns contingency to essence, is here supplemented by a second moment, which returns essence to contingency—that is, to metonymy as a process of displacement and replacement, of humble stitching and restitching, of one thing ceding itself to another in the quotidian play of existence. This double trope of metaphor-metonymy is what we have been calling transubstantiation: the reversible translation of word into flesh and flesh into word.

This understanding of writing as a stitching of webs, tapestries, textures, texts leads Marcel to the insight that he is the "bearer" of a work that has been "entrusted" to him and that he will, in time, "deliver" into other hands (the reader's). The connotations of pregnancy and parturition are pronounced here. Such a recognition of the basic intertextuality of writing comes to Marcel as a sort of deliverance from his own long fear of death. Affirming that real literature is a form of messianic repetition or remembering forward—from natality to mortality and back to natality again—Marcel suddenly finds himself "indifferent to the idea of death."[40] Learning to perish is learning to relive. "By dint of repetition," he says, "this fear had gradually been transformed into a calm confidence. So that if in those early days, as we have seen, the idea of death had cast a shadow over my loves . . . the remembrance of love had helped me not to fear death. For I realized that dying was not something new, but that on the contrary since my childhood I had already died many times."[41] Invoking the classic scriptural passage about the seed dying in order to flourish, Marcel's authorial self now faces the possibility of being posthumously reborn as another, as one of those many harbingers of new life, epitomized by Mlle de Saint Loup or, more generally, by his future readers. A second natality thus reemerges from mortality. In this way the final passage of the novel—recalling the dead Albertine and the dying Charlus—invokes an enveloping movement of Time that swings back and forth, up and down, carrying us toward vertiginous and terrifying summits, higher than the steeples of cathedrals, before eventually returning us to earth again, "descending to a great depth within."

In short, if time is all too wont to raise mortals "to an eminence from which suddenly they fall,"[42] might we not say that the acceptance of this fall back into the ordinary universe enables fear to become love and literary delusion to become true writing?

The Cycle of Belief and Unbelief in Woolf

My second example of sacramental aesthetics is Virginia Woolf's *To the Lighthouse.* Woolf makes no bones about her atheism; indeed, a sophisticated form of brazen atheism was almost de rigueur in the Bloomsbury circle in which she moved and worked. But it was not her rejection of a traditional childhood God that prevented Woolf from rediscovering a sense of the sacred in the very midst of secular life. *To the Lighthouse,* I suggest, performs a passage from theism to atheism—the famous Interlude of death and dereliction—before reopening, in the third part of the novel, an anatheist option: the possibility of a second yes to the "real" at the heart of nonbeing. Here, I submit, we witness a move from first belief to unbelief to a second kind of belief: an affirmation of what Woolf calls, simply and mysteriously, the "it."

The novel's main protagonist, Mrs Ramsay, is another mistress of the feast. Like Françoise before her, though in somewhat more urbane attire, Mrs Ramsay is introduced in the first part of the novel as both cook and seamstress. She nourishes and sews. She has a singular gift for "summoning together," for bringing couples into liaison, for holding her brood of eight children in maternal connection, and her husband in marriage. On the day we meet her she has two tasks: first, to give her son, James, some hope that he may sail to the lighthouse, and second, to prepare a supper of boeuf en daube for her family and guests that evening.

But this is no ordinary boat trip, and this is no ordinary meal. Mrs Ramsay is frequently depicted by Woolf in mystical terms. Woolf's use of indirect discourse—*le style indirect libre*—to convey what is going on in her various characters' minds gives the reader the impression from the outset that Mrs Ramsay's soul is somehow porously interconnected with the scattered souls of those around her. And this sense of mysterious interbeing is confirmed in the last part of the novel when we find her devoted painter friend, Lily Briscoe, recalling the same thoughts and qualities of Mrs Ramsay herself (the term "unfathomably deep," for example, recurs in the minds of both, as do curiously sacred sentiments of "emptiness" as "fullness," or the three "strokes" of the lighthouse beam that Mrs Ramsay contemplates, repeated in the three "strokes" of Lily's brush on the white canvas). Woolf noted in her diary her use of this narrative voice as a "tunneling process" deep into the minds of all her characters, which might reach a point where they could all connect, have similar thoughts, and move to the same deep "rhythm."[43] This rhythm she describes as "resonant and porous, transmitting emotion without impediment . . . creative, incandescent and undivided."[44] Through the free indirect discourse Woolf experiments with a "multi-personal representation of consciousness" that has "synthesis as its aim."[45]

When dinnertime eventually arrives, the tone is subtly sacramental. The gong announces solemnly, authoritatively, that all those scattered about the house and garden should "assemble in the dining room for dinner."[46] The meal unfolds as a quasi-eucharistic ritual. Mrs Ramsay takes her place at the head of the table and assigns each person their seat. As she ministers the meal she presides over the assembly with a quasi-mystical sense of "being past everything, through everything, out of everything."[47] The convened guests and family unite around the candle-lit table:

> Now all the candles were lit up, and the faces on both sides of the table were brought nearer by the candlelight, and composed, as they had not been in the twilight, into a party round a table, for the night was now shut off by panes of glass, which, far from giving any accurate view of the outside world, rippled it so strangely that here, inside the room, seemed to be order and dry land; there, outside, a reflection in which things wavered and vanished, waterily. Some change at once went through them all, as if this had really happened, and they were all conscious of making a party together in a hollow, on an island; had their common cause against that fluidity out there.[48]

There are many antagonisms and rivalries between different people at table; but Mrs Ramsay contrives to negotiate and mollify these frictions, letting each person find their voice and making various marriage plans for various guests (Paul and Minta, Lily and Mr Bankes). By the end of the meal, everyone seems united in eucharistic communion. The messianic Mrs Ramsay has worked her gracious magic on the gathering. The eschatological feast is, it appears, at hand:

> Everything seemed possible. Everything seemed right . . . just now she had reached security; she hovered like a hawk suspended; like a flag floated in an element of joy which filled every nerve of her body fully and sweetly, not noisily, solemnly rather, for it arose, she thought, looking at them all eating there, from husband, children and friends; all of which rising in this profound stillness (she was helping William Bankes to one very small piece more, and peered into the depths of the earthenware pot) seemed now for no special reason to stay there like a smoke, like a fume rising upwards, holding them safe together. Nothing need be said; nothing could be said. There it was, all round them. It partook, she felt, carefully helping Mr. Bankes to a specially tender piece, of eternity . . . there is a co-

> herence in things, a stability; something, she meant, is immune from change, and shines out . . . in the face of the flowing, the fleeting, the spectral, like a ruby; so that again tonight she had the feeling . . . of peace, of rest. Of such moments, she thought, the thing is made that endures. . . . The Boeuf en Daube was a perfect triumph.[49]

Mrs Ramsay's credo—as Lily will remember it in the final section of the novel—was "of the nature of a revelation. In the midst of chaos there was shape. . . . Life stand still here, Mrs Ramsay said."

But it didn't. Life moved on, and many partaking of that meal would suffer terrible death and loss in the war years ahead. And so this inaugural scene of union is shrouded in irony. A sense of elegiac doom hovers over the proceedings. Indeed, already in the midst of her musing Mrs Ramsay is caught by the awareness that "this cannot be." She finds herself "dissociating herself from the moment."[50] And for us readers, it is equally short-lived. Within pages Mrs Ramsay is dead and the novel descends—in the middle section, "Time Passes"—into an unconsoling exposé of transience and collapse. We also learn that Mrs Ramsay's ideal matchmaking has come to naught, and that two of her most beautiful children have perished during the war. In retrospect, the "smoke" rising from the dinner table takes on the connotations of a sacrificial offering. The paschal feast seems less a Passover than a passing away.

Yet this is not the end of the story. And we are still left asking, in the third part of the novel, what Mrs Ramsay meant when she spoke of "the thing is made that endures." Was she thinking of the "perfect" meal remembered, after the event, by those who live after her and finally make their way back to the lighthouse? Or was she thinking of the work of art wherein Lily would resurrect Mrs Ramsay and enable her to endure in the "finished" portrait? Or of the novel itself, which invites us, the readers, to revive Mrs Ramsay's eucharistic achievement in the very act of reading? Is reading to be seen as a feat of anatheistic repetition?

The connection between things *lived* and things *made* brings us to the heart of the matter—the rapport between Mrs Ramsay and Lily Briscoe. Here we encounter a complex set of traversals at work. Mystical affinities abound. The two souls intersignify in all sorts of curious ways. To take a key example, Lily's final brushstroke in part three is a repetition of the "stroke" of the lighthouse with which Mrs Ramsay intimately identifies. The latter scene occurs in the first part of the novel when Mrs Ramsay sits down late one night, her children in bed, and, taking out her knitting, feels an uncanny peace as she unites with the world outside her window. A "wedge-shaped core of darkness" deep inside her, we are told, merges with the beam of light emitted by the lighthouse far out at sea. To the third stroke of light on water, her own "unfathomable deep" blends with the depths of the ocean. We read that "often she found herself sitting and looking, sitting and looking with her work in her hands until she became the thing she looked at—that light."[51] Losing herself in the things she beheld, leaving behind the "fret, the hurry, the stir" of her anxious self, there rises to her lips "some exclamation of triumph over life when things came together in this peace, this rest, this eternity." And it is in this moment of quasi-mystical communion with the surrounding universe, as deep calls upon deep, that Mrs Ramsay adds, "We are in the hands of the Lord."

No sooner has she uttered this prayer, however, than she revokes it: "But instantly she was annoyed with herself for saying that. Who had said that?" Who indeed? And why feel so ashamed to have fallen back into the fold of common prayer? Because, apparently, it is somehow unearned. Too easy, too quick. Too cheap. "She had been trapped into saying something she did not mean." A "lie," Mrs Ramsay calls it, referring no doubt to the lure of an otherwordly deity, some Supreme Omnipotent Cause aloof and detached from the world of flesh, adjudicating our destinies. Resisting the temptation to escape into the hands of such a convenient God, Mrs Ramsay embraces, I suggest, another kind of mysticism, a deeper sense of sacred space and time where one is "alone with the alone" (as the Upanishads say) and where the natural universe of ordinary things is loved rather than abandoned: "It was odd, she thought, how if one was alone, one leant to inanimate things; trees, streams, flowers; felt they expressed one; felt they became one; felt they knew one, in a sense were one; felt an irrational tenderness thus (she looked at that long steady light) as for oneself. There rose, and she looked and looked with her needles suspended, there curled up off the floor of the mind, rose from the lake of one's being, a mist, a bride to meet her lover."[52]

But what is this post-theistic mysticism that Mrs Ramsay incarnates? In a curious admission shortly before her death, Virginia Woolf spoke of the sudden shocks and surprises of life as tokens of "some real thing behind appearances." She intimated that "behind the cotton wool is hidden a pattern," and that all human beings are somehow "connected with this." In short, Woolf expressed the view that the "whole world is a work of art." But no sooner had she made this confession than she added, "But there is no Shakespeare, there is no Beethoven; certainly and emphatically there is no God."[53] In short, her atheism could not be more evident. But what kind of atheism are we talking about? What exactly does she mean by her triple denial, her three nos? It would seem that Woolf is implying that the "pattern," the "real thing," is not *made* but *given.* It is not the product of creators, human or divine, but an intimation of some deep unfathomable love that connects all beings behind and beneath the appearances of agency and artifice.

Here we confront the problematic role of art in the novel, especially as represented by Lily's attempt to capture Mrs Ramsay in a painting. For how can art—be it Lily's painting, Mr Carmichael's poem, or Woolf's own novel—ever hope to represent the miracle of ordinary life? How can the made record the given, the imaginary reflect the real? Facing her canvas, Lily, we are told, is aware of something not herself, some "other thing" that is "truth" or "reality," something both there in the lampshade and also timelessly abstracted from it, a thing emerging "at the back of appearances." There is, Lily realizes, something suspect in art's attempt to reduce the contingency and transience of life to "beautiful pictures" and "beautiful phrases." What Lily needs to get hold of is the "jar on the nerves, the thing itself before it had been *made* anything." She seeks to achieve that "razor's edge of balance between two opposite forces," namely, art and life.[54] The problem therefore arises, how can art imagine the mystery of flesh without betraying it? How can it achieve the razor's edge of equanimity recommended by the sacred Vedic texts that, as her notebooks show, so fascinated Woolf? Are we on the threshold here of another kind of anatheist wager, this time nourished by Eastern sources?

Let's take a closer look at Lily's final gesture. In the final sequence of the book, Lily is seeking a particular stroke of her paintbrush that will, in a "leap" into the gap between art and life, complete her quest. She is struggling to somehow bring art and life together, make the impossible possible. What Mrs Ramsay found in that special "stroke of light," beamed from the lighthouse at night, Lily will find in a stroke of paint: something that connects in a moment of repetition. Lily eventually achieves her "vision." She renounces the goal of some pure, transcendental aesthetic for an art of ordinary things, an art that recognizes "traces" as living gestures of the absolute. It is, in fact, just as her portrait of Mrs Ramsay is being completed—repeating in the third part of the novel the painting that she could not achieve in the first—it is in this very moment of re-creation, of anamnesis, of second epiphany, that Lily hits on the marvel of the everyday: "One wanted, she thought, dipping her brush deliberately, to be on a level with ordinary experience, to feel simply that's a chair, that's a table, and yet at the same time, It's a miracle, it's an ecstasy. The problem might be solved after all."[55]

Everything, it seems, revolves on this reversibility of upper- and lowercase *It/it.* The miracle consists in the transubstantiation of higher into lower, extraordinary into ordinary, transcendence into immanence—and vice versa. It is a moment both kenotic (the emptying of Word into flesh) and eucharistic (the celebration of the infinite in the finite bread and wine of quotidian experience).

Woolf recorded experiencing this same "it" in February 1926—while she was composing this section of the novel—as she crossed Russell Square in London. Her diary entry reads, "I see the mountains in the sky: the great clouds; and the moon which has risen over Persia; I have a great and astonishing sense of something there, which is 'it.'"[56] This "it" is, as she puts it, something "out there," some "other thing" beyond one's will and personality. It is at once "frightening and exciting," for it refuses to be humanized by our subjective projections and names—including the anthropomorphic name of "God."[57] But for Lily Briscoe to achieve this aesthetic vision, for her to effect the final brushstroke, draw "the line there in the centre" of her canvas so that she can finally say "It was done; it was finished," for Lily to do this she has first to acknowledge the reality of Mrs Ramsay's death and absence. She has to forgo her ideal *imago,* accept the cut of mortality, and leap into the gap.[58]

In terms of the novel's characters this means, among other things, allowing Mr Ramsay's atheism to cut through Mrs Ramsay's mysticism. In other words, a typically anatheist move. Lily has to admit what is "other" to her fused and nostalgic memory of Mrs Ramsay, which she has been invoking for solace and reunion: "Oh Mrs Ramsay, Mrs Ramsay!" Mr Ramsay is the "opposite force" that resists Lily's reappropriation of Mrs Ramsay and compels her to take a leap from the "narrow plank, perfectly alone, over the sea . . . into the waters of annihilation." Before she can finish her painting Lily has to accept that Mrs Ramsay is *gone,* passed away, irrevocably past. For only then can she recall her, posthumously, through the gap of atheism, across the caesura of separation, in the final stroke that cuts, like a sword blade, even as it reconnects.

But reconnects what? Reconnects Lily's project to memory, her present to the past in a way that liberates into a future, repeating a lost moment forward. Or to put it in other terms, Mrs Ramsay is the "lost object," the deceased savior-friend whom Lily must relinquish if she is to move from obsessive melancholy to a mourning that accepts the real and liberates new life. For Lily it is Mr Ramsay—atheist and empiricist, angular and exigent—who represents this cutting edge of the reality principle. Mr Ramsay is the alien in her world, the stranger to her vision of things. As Martin Corner deftly observes, "Mr. Ramsay is an unwavering witness to the non-humanity of the world; he therefore represents to Lily that otherness which must somehow be got into the picture if it is not to be false."[59] Mr Ramsay, in short, exemplifies the "thing itself before it has been *made* anything" (by knitting, cooking, painting, dreaming, fictionalizing). And this thing, it transpires, is a no-thing. It is that emptiness, that void, that "unfathomable deep" that haunts the imaginations of both Mrs Ramsay and Lily. It is the "wedge of darkness" that has to be faced and acknowledged before it can well up into fullness and Lily can say, "empty it was not but full to the brim."[60] But first the letting go. The renunciation of the illusion of Grand Revelations, be they of art, metaphysics, or religion. The refusal of any grandiose system that trumps the world of flesh and blood and denies the universe of little things. We read, "The great revelation perhaps never did come. Instead there were little daily miracles, illuminations, matches struck unexpectedly in the dark."[61]

Lily's attempt to incorporate otherness—the "jar on the nerves," the "wedge of darkness," the "marvel" of the singular—into her art finds interesting echoes in Georges Didi-Huberman's account of a certain mystical aesthetic that insists on "making a representation that abjures its own powers of narrative and optical resolution," attesting to a "sacred ignorance" where "God's presence is felt and known in the failure of representation, not its success."[62] This testimonial deforming or problematizing of the image so as to signal its unconscious and unassimilable "underside" typifies sacramental rather than mimetic aesthetica. Didi-Huberman links it to a particular iconography of the Christian doctrine of the incarnation of Christ, which emphasizes immediate "real presence: rather than legible representation (symbolism, allegory, mediation, mirroring). It calls, he says, for an art of self-negating and self-transcending images that, loyal to a certain "sacred nescience" or apophasis, function less as mimetic icons of the known visible world than as disruptive mystical indices of the invisible in the visible. Paradoxically, what is lost (as absence) is regained (as presence beyond representation). The renunciation of inappropriate expectations allows for the unexpected return of the sacred.

In Lily's final letting go we encounter, I suggest, an instance of such mystical aesthetics. But this is a mysticism less of fusion than of equipoise, less of triumph than of that razor's-edge balance between opposites, celebrated by the sages of the Upanishads and certain Jewish and Christian mystics. In this regard, what we might call Lily's—and Woolf's—mystical anatheism takes on another valence, recalling as it does the Asiatic features of Lily's countenance (those "Chinese eyes" the narrator frequently refers to). For the letting go of Mrs Ramsay—in the harmonious memory of the opening meal—is also a letting go of our notion of an all-powerful divinity who saves us, namely, the anthropomorphic deity of Western myth and metaphysics. It is only in the letting go—in the kenosis of "truth" emptying itself of godhead—that Lily can complete her painting at the very moment that Mr Ramsay fulfills Mrs Ramsay's dream of bringing their son, James, and daughter, Cam, to the lighthouse. This is the moment of anatheistic return. The passage is particularly telling: "He rose and stood in the bow of the boat, very straight and tall, for all the world, James thought, as if he were saying, 'There is no God,' and Cam thought, as if he were leaping into space, and they both rose to follow him as he sprang, lightly like a young man, holding his parcel, on to the rock."[63] It is precisely at this instant of *grounding* that Lily, watching from the shore, draws her final stroke and says, like the suffering servant yielding up to death, "It is finished." *Consummatum est.* This is a moment of death and rebirth, of letting go and gaining back. A time when, at last, "empty flourishes form into shape."[64]

The mystical allusions of Woolf's closing paragraph are resonant and deep, and appear to confirm Woolf's numerous mentions in her autobiographical writings of a reality that goes beyond God to achieve its epiphany of the ordinary. Such mentions recall Advaita and Buddhist mysticism, which refuses to think transcendence apart from immanence, a refusal echoed in Meister Eckart's notion of *Abgeschiedenheit:* the abandonment of God so as to recover a God beyond God. This mysticism *after God* is, I suggest, an affirmation of a eucharist of the everyday, of a sacrament of common reality, of an epiphany of the It/it residing at the core of Woolf's vision. Lily Brisco, it seems, eventually finds her miracle "on a level with ordinary experience," a world at once itself and yet simultaneously transfigured into what Woolf calls "a reality of a different order."[65] A world poised on a razor's edge where opposites balance without collapsing into sameness. A world of anatheism.

Converting Word and Flesh in the Language of Epiphany

Is it significant that Proust and Woolf, witnesses of sacramental imagination, are, on the surface at least, agnostics? And what does it mean that the characters who best embody their sacramental aesthetic, Françoise and Lily, are women? Is this not a different kind of eucharistic language from the one that informs the traditional male-dominated liturgies (in which no women featured for centuries)? This is surely a sacramental vision of a new sort, or at least of the old revisited otherwise. It deploys the poetic license of fiction to suspend accredited doctrines in order to offer "free variations" of transubstantiation, namely, the reversible "miracle" of word made flesh and flesh made word. Recalling the canonical definition of transubstantiation as the transforming of one substance into another, we may say in conclusion that we have identified three main hermeneutic modalities in our readings above: (1) *intratextual,* (2) *intertextual,* and (3) *transtextual.*

As instances of the first kind we may cite the numerous examples of one *character* being transfused into another (Mrs Ramsay into Lily, Maman into Françoise) or one spatiotemporal *moment* being translated into another (the madeleine epiphany, the involuntary memory of Maman reading in Combray and Venice recalled years later in the Guermantes' library). As examples of the second mode of transubstantiation (intertextual), we might cite the transmuting of one *narrative* into another (Homer's *Odyssey* into *Time Regained,* Georges Sands's novel into Proust's) or the transliteration of eucharistic liturgies into sacramental reenactments by Mrs Ramsay, or Marcel in his final epiphanies. And finally, we may cite numerous examples of transtextual transubstantiation, including the conversion of author into narrator, character, and reader. This third mode—involving the very process of writing and reading, of configuring and refiguring—is the one highlighted in the phenomenological analyses of Merleau-Ponty, Kristeva, and Ricoeur. And it is with this final modality, I suggest, that we encounter an opening of the world of the text beyond itself—both forward to the posttextual world of the reader and backward (by way of implied regress from character to narrator to author) to the pretextual world of the writer. This acknowledgment, however tentative and mediated, of some *extratextual* element—intimating a life of action before and after the text—is in keeping with the sacramental paradigm of transubstantiation, a paradigm that, I have been suggesting, testifies to the unbreakable liaison between the body of the text and the text of the body, namely, the sanctified bread of life, or, to deploy the language of epiphany, between Word and Flesh.

Our two novelists may well be apostates or atheists by turn, but this does not in the least prevent them from being haunted by a singularly mystical vision of things. It may, in a paradoxical sense, even contribute to such insight by predisposing them to something beyond the reach of many official religious conventions. (The history of religions evinces a deep complicity between mysticism and so-called atheism). Each writer, I hope to have shown, bears witness to a special sacredness at the heart of the profane. But in each instance the mutual transfiguring of the material into the mystical is anything but sacrificial; it is not about expiatory victims sacrificed to redeem sins and appease an omnipotent father. The sacramental aesthetic of Proust and Woolf is far removed from an economy of penalty and compensation. On the contrary, it bears witness to literary epiphanies of radical kenosis and emptying where the sacred unhitches itself from the Master God ("equality with the Father," as Paul put it) in order to descend into the heart of finite flesh, so that the birth of the child as incarnate historical being attests to the demise of the Immutable Monarch of the Universe. Unless the divine seed dies, there can be no eucharistic rebirth. Or, to put it in the words of the young Jewish mystic, Etty Hillesum, "by excluding death from one's life we deny ourselves the possibility of a full life." It is, moreover, not adventitious, in my view, that the novels under consideration feature a deep anatheist openness to the stranger as prelude to epiphany: in Proust the acknowledgment of Françoise by Marcel, in Woolf the reckoning with Mr Ramsay by Lily. Without this basic hospitality to the uninvited guest there would be no transubstantiation between self and other.

In our novelists we witness the abandoning of a *first naïveté* in order to recover a *second naïveté*. This offers a moment of anatheistic return, after the experience of death and nothingness, that signals a new kind of "miracle" or "resurrection," or "grace," this time in ordinary events ignored the first time around. For Proust these moments of sacramental remembrance occur when his literary hero, Marcel, comes to renounce his initial great expectations and acknowledges the muse of the everyday, Françoise. For Woolf the moment occurs when Lily finally recalls the failed painting of the "purple triangle" (which sought to depict Mrs Ramsay and James in the first part of the novel) as she belatedly applies the final stroke enabling her to rememorate Mrs Ramsay *après coup;* only then can she have her "vision" and declare the painting "finished." The bread and wine of quotidian existence are thus celebrated as eucharistic epiphanies—the touch of a table napkin for Marcel, Mrs Ramsay's empty glove (a hint of empty burial clothes?). Hitherto ignored moments are "resurrected" out of passing time into a life that assumes and subsumes death, impossibly retrieved for a new generation of survivors. They are resurrected here and now, again and again, for each new reader or community of readers. Unless the seed dies, the wheat cannot grow and the bread cannot be shared.

I am not, of course, suggesting that Proust and Woolf are religious apologists. They are by no means advocates of Christian liturgies and sacraments. There are certain confessional writers who might be said to fit this category—Gerard Manley Hopkins, Paul Claudel, Georges Bernanos, or T. S. Eliot, not to mention Dante and many traditional religious writers throughout the centuries. But my purpose here is not to engage in confessional apologetics or to proclaim our novelists cryptotheists *après la lettre.* Rather, my task is to explore the possibility of a certain anatheist aesthetic in which the secular and sacred conjugate and cross. Thus, while by no means excluding confessional writers from adherence to such an aesthetic, I deem it valuable in this secular era to consider how certain nonconfessional authors deploy an art of transubstantiation to explore a mysticism of *God after God.*

I have been suggesting that this faith after faith may be clarified by the application of a phenomenology of flesh advanced by thinkers like Merleau-Ponty and Kristeva. But the "after" of anatheism should not be read as privative but as an affirmative function of "ana," that is, of retrieving what was lost as found in a new way, *après coup*[66]—as in ana-logy, ana-gogy, ana-mnesis, ana-kephalaiosis. In short, I have no wish to endorse an empty secularism that merely aestheticizes religion by removing its sacramental or faith content. In moving from religion to art we do indeed replace a first belief in God qua God with a *quasi*-belief in a *quasi*-God. But this suspension of primary belief, as we enter the world of fiction, is not the last word. Rather, it is the opening up of a space of imagination where the anatheist option may be made anew, an option that allows us, readers of fiction, to freely recommit to faith if we choose, to return to a God beyond both the qua-God and the quasi-God. In other words, the anatheist analysis of modern fiction I am attempting here has little to do with secularist reductions of sacred moments to purely humanist equivalents: All Hallows Eve to Halloween, St. Nicholas to Santa Claus, or the Mass of Christ to the commercial holiday of Christmas.

For anatheism, the transition from religion to art is not a one-way street. As my repeated emphasis in this essay on the hermeneutic return from text to life implies, the anatheist wager involves a moment of refiguration from author to reader in which the reader welcomes the "estrangement" of the fictional text in order to recover his or her sense of the sacramental in everyday profane existence. Literary epiphanies might thus be said to arise within the text but point beyond the text. The sacramental is not confined to a play of signifiers. For as flesh becomes word in the text, so the word becomes flesh again in the reader. That is the ultimate marvel of transubstantiation as it relates art to faith and faith to art. If the composition of fiction can serve to aestheticize the sacred, reading can serve to resacramentalize the aesthetic in our everyday world. But I emphasize the *can;* it is a matter of choice. The movement from life to text is always supplemented by the option of a return from text to life. In sum, anatheism is not about evacuating the sacred from the secular but about rediscovering the secular in and through the sacred.

Impossible Confessions

KARMEN MACKENDRICK

In a roundtable presentation from 1944, published under the title "Discussion on Sin," Georges Bataille levels against Christianity the harshest possible condemnation: he declares it boring. As regards most of both Christian practice and doctrine, this criticism holds up pretty well. But there have always been other strains in Christianity, as Bataille himself sometimes acknowledges—when he isn't declaring himself purely hostile to all its versions[1]—and some of those strains have been interesting in very Bataillean ways—cruel, sacrificial, or perverse. Indeed, it is a Christian priest (well, a Jesuit) who declares in the discussion, "For me, spiritual comfort is itself sin" (DS, 43). It is in its refusal of comfort, and especially its deliberate discomfort, that Christianity is least boring, and it is on one mode of such discomfort, that of confessional obedience, which can only occur where the body meets language, that I want to focus here. In confession is a particular kind of obedience, one that emerges through the sacrifice of language and, with it, of the will of the subject obedient to the pastoral imperative of (narrative) self-construction. The language of confession turns language against itself, at once obeying and undoing its imperatives.

Generalized Obedience

Dogmatically, obedience is not mere incidental accord of will, happening to desire the same thing that God or the designated superior desires, but an active submission of one will to another. Appleton's *Catholic Encyclopedia,* my source of choice for dogmatic declaration, states, "It is . . . the moral habit by which one carries out the order of his superior with the precise intent of fulfilling the injunction. . . . Stress is put upon the fact that one not only does what is actually enjoined, but does it with a mind to formally fall in with the will of the commander."[2] Thus the obedient will ideally subordinates itself to the will of another—in the monastic mode, to the will of God or of the abbot—*because* that will is God's or the abbot's, and it makes itself as like the superior's will as possible (making its objects, its direction, resemble those of the superior). The superior, it seems, has all the power.

But power, as all good Nietzscheans know, is relational. One who displays perfect obedience, carrying out every expressed impulse of the commanding will, may be engaged in a perfectly interiorized struggle with his own will against itself, successfully keeping it away from any impulse contradictory to the superior's, yet be imperfect, *because* of the very struggle, in this obedience. Or else he may be will-less, all desire and struggle stilled in the empty purity of his heart. Yet in this case too, despite the appearance of pure perfection, he is not obedient, because his is not even a subordinated will; it simply isn't there, or is already so perfectly in accord with that of the superior that there is no need for obedience, with its salutary humbling effect. Obedience is self-undermining not merely in practice but in principle; it requires the subordination of a will that must subordinate itself imperfectly if it is indeed subordinating itself at all.

What keeps obedience interesting is precisely this necessary imperfection, the struggle not only against insubordination but also against not-struggling. Confession, as I shall argue, adds further layers to this paradoxical willing against will by engaging in a kind of speaking and writing that turn language not only toward silence but toward its own more passionate inarticulation.

Willful Sacrifice

To speak in more overtly Bataillean terms, obedience, in action or in confession, is the will's willful sacrifice of willing. As a sacrifice, it is removed from the realm of project and productive labor to that of conspicuously nonproductive consumption and violent intimacy.[3] In it, to quote Bataille from another context, "The will grasps the fact of its own conflagration."[4]

"Sacrifice," according to Bataille, "is the communication of anguish" (*IE,* 194). Knowing the peculiarities of Bataillean communication, we will not be surprised to realize that this communication is no *alleviation* of anguish, or form of closure; it is associated instead with the opened wound, with sustained pain; it "is not the solution but the introduction and the maintenance of rupture in the very center, in the heart of humanity. It is only in the midst of anguish that this being which you are maintains enough consistency and yet leaves gaping the wound through which, hastening from all points of the universe, deadly destruction enters" (*IE,* 195). This "introduction and maintenance of rupture" is at the heart of Bataille's fictional works, where the (in)famous pornographic element is more at the service of despair, or at least destruction (death is rather more frequent than one generally expects in pornographic fiction), than at the service of gratification.[5]

Like Sade, Bataille is, probably against his own best efforts, an irredeemably Catholic pornographer. Several of his books feature priests, while others include characters taken for clergy—the narrator of *Story of the Eye* is mistaken for a cardinal; Lazare in *Blue of Noon* is likened several times to a priest. In *Story of the Eye,* Marcelle's masturbation in a closed wardrobe (from which the "Cardinal" releases her) is echoed toward the book's end by Simone's masturbation in a Spanish confessional. In violently opening both the space of communication and the communicative subject, sacrifice has a more than etymological relation to the sacred (*G,* 34), opposed alike to the world of smug certainty passing for faith (the belief in a world completed by God) and to that of rational atheism (satisfaction, as Bataille says, in "a world completed without God" [*IE,* 153]). Instead, "The one who sacrifices is, on the contrary, in the anguish before an incompleted world . . . which destroys him, tears him apart (and this world destroys itself, tears itself apart)" (*IE,* 153).[6]

The ultimate sacrifice, for Bataille as it was for Nietzsche, is at once of self (particularly of the confidently rational self) and of God (*IE,* 134). He writes in *Guilty* of "a world in which I have no meaning unless I'm wounded, torn apart and sacrificed, and in which divinity, in the same way, is just a tearing apart or being torn apart, is executing or being executed, is sacrifice" (*G,* 45). Far from establishing securely our relation to God or to gods, sacrifice reveals the world in its ungroundedness. The sacrifice of God ensures the lack of assurance, holds the wound open: "God—to follow human custom here—is everything that might happen, taken as a whole. The act of breaking up this apparent whole itself takes place at the level of appearance. The crucifixion, for example, is a wound by which believers communicate with God" (*G,* 31).[7] The struggle to obey, and more, to keep obedience a struggle, is the struggle to sustain the absence of sustaining, to bleed guilt through divinely inspired wounds. Thus the struggle is sustained by impossibility, holding open the communicative sacrificial wound at the very heart of the possibility of selfhood. We are only completed, we only stop bleeding (and blushing), when we're dead.

Autonomy and Incompletion

For Bataille, the sacrifice of self begins as the sacrifice of self-willing. In the desire to be auto-nomos, self-ruling, we find as well the desire to impose ourselves on the world, to remake it into our own form, so that its rules don't interfere with ours. But this desire, as Bataille points out, carries its undoing within it: "The need for an attraction—the necessity, found in the autonomy of human beings, of imposing one's value upon the universe—introduces from the outset a disordered state in all of life. What characterizes man from the outset and what leads up to the completed rupture at the summit is not only the will for sufficiency, but the cunning, timid attraction on the side of insufficiency" (*IE,* 88). We are perpetually lured not only by the pleasures of irresponsibility but even, perversely, by incompletion and insufficiency: not only toward not-everything but also into not-enough. Bataille adds, "Our existence is an exasperated attempt to complete being (. . . become everything). . . . We don't dare affirm in its fullness our desire to exist without limits: it makes us afraid. But we are all the more uneasy at feeling within us a moment of cruel joy as soon as the evidence of our misery emerges" (*IE,* 89). The desire for incompletion, for feeling at once the narrow constraint of our own limits and the open space of our own possibility, doesn't merely oppose our desire for limitless dominance over all that is; it inheres *within* that desire, always implicated in it as the cruel, self-tormenting pleasure of our necessary failure, of impossibility. We are afraid not only of our desire to exist without limits but of our desire for our own desire's frustration, our desire against satisfaction.

The desire for completeness is the desire for perfect rule over self and over the world formed in the image of self—a desire for the completeness of God in, or as, oneself. "God," says Bataille, "is only an attempt to attribute being to a condition of autonomy (which appeared inaccessible to man)" (*G,* 131). The urge to be autonomous is our desire, then, to *be* God—but not, as Bataille himself intermittently realizes, to be God as ultimate sacrificial subject, to be the God on his knees who subordinates his will all the way to death. *That* desire, present in Christianity as the wish to be the god not only of humility (*IE,* 65, 81) but also of humiliation,[8] is a touch more complicated than the desire to be the god of completion, and, if only for that reason, quite a bit more interesting.

But, as I've said, Christianity has tended to refuse its more interesting options. Bataille is, again, mostly right to note, "Theology's principle that 'the world is complete' is maintained at every time and in all places, including the night of Golgotha. There's a necessity for God to be killed: to see the world in the weakness of incompletion. The next thought to occur is that, come what may, the world has to be completed, though this is what's impossible and incomplete. Everything real fractures and cracks" (*G,* 27). There at the very site of the communicative wound we have an immediate denial of any possibility of woundedness—and by this denial, divine completion is neatly closed away from suffering, from undergoing, and so from communicating with or within the world. Most theology stubbornly maintains the need for completeness (holding up God as the exemplar of autonomy), but everything real fractures and cracks and sustains only its insustainability, its incompletion. It is unlikely to be accidental that the "debaucheries" of Bataille's novels are so often linked with other ruptures—madness, for instance, or war, as well as death: Marcelle goes mad in *Story of the Eye;* much of *Blue of Noon* is set in the midst of the Spanish Revolution; *L'Abbé C* features a wartime betrayal by a member of the French Resistance.

It's obvious that Bataille senses clearly the paradoxes implicit in the practices and dogmas of Christianity. The most attended-to duo in the Trinity, the omnipotent Father and the sacrificial Son, present curiously oppositional—or perhaps paradoxical—options for either identification or worship. One can strive to be everything, but of course this striving is forbidden—it virtually defines pride. So one can want to be God, to be complete and rule the world—to be the unsacrificed God of complete autonomy. Or else, as Bataille puts it, "if he chooses, he can become humble, poor, and—in God—enjoy his humility and poverty. He pictures God and himself succumbing to the desire for incompletion, the desire to be human and poor, and to die in torment" (*G,* 27). And here, of course, the forbidden pride and enjoyment sneak into the quest for the agony of the incomplete; to identify with God is still pride, and to strive for the ultimate humility is, necessarily, to undo it.[9] At the same time, this can become an intensifying feedback loop: one can enhance one's humility by adding to one's sense of wretchedness the fact that one is pridefully identifying with God. And what makes this dissatisfaction interesting—satisfying, even, in its own painful way—is the pull of and against this desire for satisfaction, for completion.

To make another Nietzschean point, the strong will may thus will against willing, finding nothing else quite powerful enough to engage its interest; it may, by the act of subordination, also covertly identify itself with the will held to be strongest of all, sneakily proving itself stronger still by not only willing the same acts but even willing to will them.

To will in this way is of course to encounter further paradox, because the self that wills is the very self against which it wills. "The subject—weariness of itself, necessity of proceeding to the extreme limit—seeks ecstasy, it is true: never does it have the will for its ecstasy. There exists an irreducible discord between the subject seeking ecstasy and the ecstasy itself. However, the subject knows ecstasy and senses it: not a voluntary direction coming from itself, but like the sensation of an effect coming from the outside" (*IE,* 60; see also 42).

We must, of course, be aware of Bataille's Nietzschean heritage here. "Will" is never truly singular, and "subject" never stable. Yet it seems clear enough that we can, and do, label a particular collection of will and sensation and memory, roughly bounded by the skin barrier of a body, as a self, a self in the face of an other, or others. It is the multiplicity of wills "within" a subject at a given time, "within" a self, that allows the possibility of the effective will from "without": "The forces which together work at destroying us find in us such a happy—and at times such violent complicities—that we cannot just turn away from them as interest would lead us to" (*IE,* 96). That will from without must resonate with, catch on to, some inner will, however minutely represented among the multiple desires of the self: every Bataillean novel features some character whose role is to encourage, to draw out, the self-destructive pleasures of others.[10]

One must be temptable, seducible. The desires to obey and to confess manifest just such seducibility, such an eager drawn-out-ness of the will, such a disregard for the security of boundedness. We must not only be susceptible to temptation (we must experience it in order to resist it), we must also be tempting: "your life . . . streams to the outside as well and opens itself incessantly to what flows out or surges forth towards it" (*IE,* 94). We fight ourselves in a multiple will to self-containment, autonomous self-imposition, spilling over, and drawing in what tears us open; we are complicitous with the destructive forces that nonetheless always elude even our will to desire them. As Virginia Burrus has it, "One must want, at least a little, to be broken, to be exposed, or the confession is sterile: it makes no truth; worse still, it forces stillborn lies. One must also resist, at least a little, being overcome by this desire, or the confession, rendered glib by the promise of cheap grace, is equally fruitless."[11]

Confession requires a confessor, a superior, not only as the complicitous force in the breaking of the will but as witness: "If I had to be the only one having attained [the limit]," says Bataille, "it would be as though it hadn't occurred" (*IE,* 42). Seldom are eyes as unblinkingly bared as those in *Story of the Eye,* but they must, always, be watching.

Christianity persistently turns away from these possibilities, from its own cruelty and pain and damage and incompletion, to head straight into the reassuring totality or completion of salvation. Bataille argues that this urge for reassurance marks the distinction between mysticism and eros—"Mystical and erotic experience differ in that the former is totally successful" (*G,* 13; see also *G,* 20)—but of course, he himself often refuses this distinction.[12] The difference between the mysticism Bataille rejects and that with which he elsewhere identifies his own urgent erotic need is perhaps sacrifice itself; he is most likely to acknowledge mysticism where laceration is involved,[13] where, in fact, total success is not an option, because the directional pull of the will is in paradox.

Making and Giving the Self

The sacrificial element of eros, which Bataille claims to prefer to more overtly religious sacrifice, is not immediately obvious. Michael Richardson in his consideration of Bataillean sacrifice remarks,

> Bataille's linkage of sacrifice with eroticism may initially appear tendentious, for in eroticism there is no victim. Nothing is actually sacrificed . . . no gift as such is offered up. Yet the sacrificial element is contained within the relationship between the lovers, who mutually offer themselves to one another. The gift is that of their own identities. It may be an illusory offering, since the loss of identity is only momentary. But it is no less real for all that.[14]

Real or not, that transience presents a problem beyond the question of its reality: how powerfully effective is a sacrifice when we know, even as we offer it, that the sacrificed will return to us almost immediately? How widely open can a wound like this be held? It is this urge to go beyond the fleetingly sacrificial that leads us to the kinds of self-tormenting sacrifice exemplified in confession.

In confession as in the obedience founded on it is the effort to sacrifice the self in the very act of constructing it, and thus to create a kind of sacrifice that impossibly sustains and renews itself, yet always risks, precisely because of that, becoming a new kind of ground, a new completion. It is an erotic sacrifice, making the self the gift given, but with the eros peculiar to asceticism.

Confession is not simply obedience to the imperative to speak; it is central, as Michel Foucault notes, to obedience itself. Like the practice of obedience, confession as a regular practice emerges in early monasticism, as the command to speak oneself, to tell the story of all that one is and, most especially, of all that one has done. It is entangled with other ascetic practices and functions as, among many other things, a reinforcement of those practices: we are less likely to slip into self-indulgence if we have to admit it. But it is, more deeply, a practice by which the very possibility of a truth about the flesh can be constructed, by which the material in its recalcitrance is to submit to the transparency of spirit.

Foucault links the emergence of modern subjectivity to self-construction in confession, elicited by "pastoral power," the priestly power that includes the induction of confessional speech, in which and by which the body is relentlessly revealed. The Christian virtue of obedience is fundamental to this power: "To remain obedient is the fundamental condition for all the other virtues. To be obedient with respect to whom? To be obedient with respect to the pastor. One is in a system of generalized obedience."[15] In this play of obedience, "the production of interior truth, the production of subjective truth, is a fundamental element,"[16] but at the same time, the truth of the interior is created by exteriorizing processes—most notably by confession. Bataille declares, echoing Nietzsche, "I loathe monks. For me, turning away from the world, from chance, from the truth of bodies is shameful. No greater sin exists" (*ON,* 75). But I want to suggest that, on Bataille's own terms, the "truth of bodies" is precisely that *toward* which ascetic monasticism turns, tangling together self, language, and will in the very fracturing, slipping incompletion that obedience in word and deed and even thought might at first seem to oppose. And it makes of that turn a sustained and painful pleasure, a shattering of the self by the very means of its making.

The word is made flesh, and vice versa; the truth of confession is the truth of the body, but we self-construct, we construct that truth, in words. As Bataille puts it, "With respect to men, their existence is linked to language. Each person imagines, and therefore knows of his existence with the help of words. . . . Being is mediated in him through words" (*IE,* 83). Burrus points out that "however intensely incarnated it may be, confession seems to remain crucially a verbal act—or perhaps better, a verbalizing act."[17] And as Foucault has it, "the verbal manifestation of the truth that is hidden deep inside oneself appears as an indispensable part of the government of men by each other, such as it was put into effect by the institutions of monasticism . . . from the fourth century."[18] The body is made what it is, is made to *have* a truth, by the drawing out of that truth, at once a demand and a seduction, in obedience to the confessional imperative that makes all obedience possible, an imperative to remake flesh into word.

In the monastery, the role of the abbot is not merely, not even primarily, to command but to draw out, confession, and having him there to do so is one advantage that life in the monastery has over even life in the desert.[19] The monk's role is to make himself known; the abbot's is not only to hear his confession but to read his flesh. And the flesh *must* in turn be told—Cassian is especially concerned that his monks confess, with an eye to minimizing or even eliminating their erotic dreams and "nocturnal pollutions," the most hidden, most evidently unwilled, pleasures of the flesh.

Not only must the flesh be told but the body also *tells,* as in poker, when a small involuntary tic reveals the truth of a player's hand to those aware of its meaning; the body tells the truth of its own inwardness, its obedient or its insubordinate will. This is vivid in the opening to the nineteenth *Conference,* where Cassian writes of a young monk who, slapped soundly in the face by the abbot in the presence of a number of other monks, not only does not speak but does not even redden, providing a lesson in patience to all who observe.[20] We confess at once voluntarily and involuntarily in the words that fall from our lips and the rush of blood under the skin.[21] Insubordination is far more frequent than the monk's perfect impassivity: one might think the will wholly submissive to divine command, but the wet dream argues otherwise, as does the blush itself. Bataille's novels are full of flushed faces, signifying shame, but also shameless arousal, arousing shame, and even anger.[22] And yet the body cannot be left to tell alone: its truth must be drawn further into words, or into silence.

As Peter Brown notes,

> To receive from Christ the grace of a transparent chastity was to shatter the last weapons of the unsurrendered will. . . . So intense a preoccupation with the monk's sexual thought-flow developed in ascetic circles because the aim of spiritual guidance had been the total expropriation of the inner world of the disciple. The inner world must be turned inside out. Nothing must linger in it that could not be placed unhesitatingly before others.[23]

Hesitation becomes itself a sign; the ideal speech flows fluently, without shame—or is utterly silent. These come together: if speech could flow with perfect fluency, unhindered by any shame or reluctance, it would not flow at all; there would be nothing to say. Thus Bataille can declare in the afterword to *Blue of Noon,* "It has been my aim to express myself clumsily."[24] To speak the truth of the self must be always to stutter, to have one's speaking broken. As David Brakke points out, the wholly transparent and wholly chaste self that is the ostensible aim of confession requires constant disruption, division, by speaking;[25] one must divide oneself in order to observe and speak the self, to impose on and construct. The stuttering speech reflects, it says, this division.

The constructed self can be neither whole nor self-contained. Bataille makes, more strongly even than Brown or Foucault, the point that speaking, to which my existence is always linked, is also, always, a giving out. I cannot establish my boundaries, the lines within which my self is constructed, except by crossing them.

> And this movement of my thought which flees from me—not only can I not avoid it, but there is no moment so secret that it doesn't animate me. Thus I speak—everything in me gives itself to others.
>
> But knowing that, no longer forgetting it, undergoing the necessity of giving myself decomposes me. (*IE,* 128–29)

I cross the limit of myself by the very act that constructs me, that of self-telling. I cross the boundaries marking outside and in to give out what I experience as inward, without which that inwardness is impossible, yet in another typically Bataillean moment I also end—or rather pause, take note of this configuration of myself—in never having given out enough, facing that decompositional necessity as a constant demand. No one else has hold of me; no one hears me exactly or remembers me completely, no one "gets" me, sustains me perfectly. Listening to his lover speak, the narrator of *Blue of Noon* reflects, "No one can know her any less than I do" (*BN,* 149). Simone speaks "intimately" only once, following an illness that has left her, briefly, incapable of sexual activity (*SE,* 38). The characters in *Blue of Noon* spend most of their conversations at least evading one another, if not lying outright; the one moment of unequivocal, untheatrical honesty is the betrayal at the end. *L'Abbé C* is centered on the secret of such a betrayal, revealed only indirectly and only after the speaker's death. Language fails us, and reveals us, and reveals, of course, our failure.

In narrative self-making, then, by which I impose on myself the form of myself, is also a self-giving that is never complete, never (self-)sufficient. But self-making by speaking out still seems sneakily like a taking up or giving in to a project, the creation of a *work* (in this case, a subject) out of what might otherwise have been the pure expenditure of words. To speak is, after all, an act of will: "Language is an organ of will (action comes from it), and expressing myself is a function of the will, which continues on this path till the end. What would it mean to speak of relinquishing will in an act of speech if not—romanticism, lies, unconsciousness, and poetic messiness?" (*G,* 111). This is a will connected to work; it intends results. How, then, could it be a sacrifice—and especially a sacrifice of will—to speak oneself? And the answer must be, I think, that to some extent, speaking is sacrifice, is sacrificed, wherever it becomes that which is read or heard by another (thus it invariably eludes the project and purpose one had in mind for it), but it is most vividly, most intensely sacrificial—another of those quantitative differences that becomes a difference in quality—where it turns on itself to willfully sacrifice the very self it constructs: when it speaks under the imperative of confession. That is: when speaking and what is spoken are not led, at least not entirely, by one's own will but are drawn by the command of a will with which one finds oneself nevertheless in complicity or collusion, a will that one wills to obey. One must be drawn, at least a little, into this collusion, or confession will fail. But one must also be resistant, at least a little, or there will be nothing to confess. One must be drawn to that very resistance, and drawn to the chance that what resists can break. Telling oneself is both the autonomous power of self-making and the subordinating shame of revelation. In *Blue of Noon*, the narrator declares, "I told this virgin the story of my entire life. My telling it to a girl like her . . . was so impudent that it made me feel ashamed. Never before had I told anyone what had happened to me. Each sentence was as humiliating as an act of cowardice" (*BN*, 34). A few pages later he adds, "she was now calm as a priest hearing confession. She simply interrupted me: 'That's no explanation at all for your being impotent'" (*BN*, 38). The failure of emission and the nocturnal fact of it must alike be told, and the confessor must implacably draw out the truth of the flesh.

The traditional role of confession is the rehabituation of the will, with the aim of turning it away from the flesh until the latter is as stilled and inexpressive as the now unnecessary speech, until there is no more to confess, no more self willing anything but what is commanded, and then not even that; until neither language nor body tells, because there is nothing remaining to say. It is only thus—as Bataille, appropriately, does not quite say—that speaking most strongly resists becoming project. And it is only thus that confession is a multiple sacrifice: of will (as an act of obedience), of language (as a drawn-out speaking), and of the self (as constructed by language).

In monastic practice, the theory goes, all of this openness in self-making will ultimately make the self as nearly perfect as it can be (how near that is depends on whom you ask, and has been the subject of some vigorous argumentation).[26] But Foucault goes on to add a vital qualification to his sense that this pastoral power has as its aim the creation of the sinless subject: "But we must underline that this expression does not have as its end the establishing of a sovereign mastery of oneself by oneself; what is expected, on the contrary, is humility and mortification, detachment with respect to oneself and the establishing of a relationship with oneself which tends towards the destruction of the form of the self."[27] The subject is created *as* imperfect, as self-destructive.

Yet this sacrificial self, like the sacrifice of the erotic gift with which I earlier associated it, still risks vanishing too quickly into a false reassurance. To be certain of sustaining the wound, confession, like obedience more broadly, has the impossible as its ideal: to speak fluently toward the absence of speaking at all, to speak a self that flows without stuttering into the perfect silence of its own absence.

That is, the one who confesses stutters (confessional speech must resist itself) toward having *nothing to tell:* monastic purity, the perfection of obedience in flesh as in will, is an emptiness of desire told by the not-telling of word and body both. All must be told until the will is trained, the speech is unstammering, and the blood rises neither to blushing cheek nor to nocturnally aroused genitalia. The perfect absence of desire that is ostensibly the object of confession leaves nothing to subordinate any more than to tell. Cassian's ideal—an ideal he considers very rarely, yet genuinely, attainable—makes meaningless the obedience that founds it. For the pure of heart, no desire is restrained, no urge subordinated, no command obeyed that was not one's own will already. Yet obedience, he says, is to be a lifelong practice.[28] And obedience, we recall, means subordination of the will, means restraint of the flesh.

The ideal, again, is to speak oneself, to speak one's flesh, into silence. But if we make ourselves in speaking, we unbecome when we have ceased to speak. And it is not only we who are unbecoming: language is essential not only to self but to the sacred. To speak the self into being, especially in this monastic mode, is caught up in the possibility of speaking God. Bataille's sense of language makes this clear: "I think of the intimate operations of religious activity, of sacrifice, of the sacred: language, which knowledge makes use of, remains intensely charged with these operations" (*IE,* 84). The sacred is fixed—falsely, of course, for Bataille—in Christianity. Not only does he find in it an "essential reliance on speech" (*G,* 37), but "basically," he writes, "Christianity is only a crystallization of language. The solemn assertion of the fourth Gospel—Et verbum caro factum est—is in a sense this deep truth: the truth of language is Christian" (*G,* 134). All of the religions of the book are religions of words, but Bataille may be right in attributing a particular logocentrism to Christianity: only here is the Word made God itself.

And Bataille does get Christianity largely right in seeing a crystallization in it, a tendency to stillness and to stasis. Yet there remains in it a shattering impulse, the imperative to break one's own mastery in both action and in speech—the impulse at work precisely in those figures who draw him, women like Angela of Foligno or Teresa of Avila, whose extraordinarily powerful wills are willfully entangled in complex self-debasement—the ultimately discomforting Christian exaltation. Language says us, and is that in and as which we say (and make) ourselves, crystallizing, it seems, not only in the completions and totalities of theology but in the complete self-revelation of confession (the imperative to tell all, to completeness in saying)—yet never quite crystallizing at all, never setting, never arriving, never ceasing to fracture and slip. "Ideally" pouring forth without hesitation, it comes to stillness not in a final, fully fluent answer but in its own absence, the silence of any saying at all. If the word is made flesh, if speaking responds to the imperative to speak the flesh, if speaking thus makes the truth of the fleshly self, then flesh is made word as well, and both of them slip, and will not stay still.

And it is in just this movement, from the self made in sacrificial saying to the self sacrificed in stutter or silence, that the sacred can appear. As Bataille notes, "Particulars are required if there is to be loss and merger. . . . The difference between sacrifice (sacredness) and (theological) substance can be easily noted. Sacredness is the opposite of substance. Christianity's mortal sin is associating sacredness with 'generality creating particularity.' Nothing is sacred if it hasn't first been individual (although afterwards it's no longer that)" (*G*, 34–35). We must make our individuality if we are going to be able to sacrifice it; we must be willful if we are going to be obedient; we must stutter if we are going to confess.

We torment ourselves by obeying the imperative to speak constantly of the desires we are most commanded to repress (or in which, commanded to expression, we must humiliatingly fail), by training ourselves in fluidity and fluency of speech until we force it into its own negation, so transparent that there is nothing left to see. To confess oneself is impossible: confession is drawn into its own inexistence, and only its constant failure keeps it returning. In silence—the long absence of speaking or the short space of the stutter—we say ourselves as Bataille says God says himself, as negation, self negated along with the theological sacrifice. We come to a still point not in the fullness of completion but in the breathtaking emptiness left by the sacrificed speech. "The inevitable incompletion," writes Bataille, "does not in any way delay the response. . . . On the contrary, it gives it the truth of the impossible, the truth of a scream. The basic paradox of this 'theory of religion,' which posits the individual as a 'thing,' and a negation of intimacy, brings a powerlessness to light, no doubt, but the cry of this powerlessness is a prelude to the deepest silence."[29] Paradoxically, self-constructing confession sustains incompleteness in humility, humiliation, subordination, exalted abasement, the refusal of comfort. The only permissible peace is in one's own absence, and that absence cannot be sustained.

And into the silence of our powerful powerlessness, we go on speaking the perverse delights of the impossible. "And the moment of torment will always be there," says Bataille. "But all of being, ready and open—for death, joy or torment—unreservedly open and dying, painful and happy, appears then with its veiled light, and this light is divine: and the cry that being—vainly?—tries to utter from a twisted mouth is an immense *alleluia,* lost in endless silence" (*E,* 300).

Most of the tradition of confession, of obedience, *is* boring: it seeks to stabilize the wounded and wounding flow of the self in a system of rules and in speech crystallized in both transparency and stability. But there is always a resistant strain, as the curious yet constant entanglements of the confessional and pornographic suggest. The ecstasy of obedience, of the confession that grounds it, is not that of an easy or smooth subordination. What we seek in submitting the will is not self-improvement but self-breaking: the drop to the knees, the stutter in the breath that refuses speech; and in that shatter of words are the alleluia, and the silence, and the scream.

The Third Life of Saint Teresa of Jesus

MANUEL ASENSI

Vivo sin vivir en mí,
Y tan alta vida espero,
Que muero porque no muero.
Vivo ya fuera de mí,
Después que muero de amor,
Porque vivo en el Señor,
Que me quiso para sí.
Cuando el corazón le di
Puso en él este letrero:
Que muero porque no muero.

Aquesta divina unión
Del amor en que yo vivo,
Ha hecho a Dios cautivo
Y libre mi corazón.
Y causa en mí tal pasión
Ver a Dios mi prisionero,
Que muero porque no muero.

¡Ay, qué larga es esta vida!
¡Qué duros estos destierros!
¡Esta cárcel, estos hierros,
En que el alma está metida!
Sólo esperar la salida
Me causa dolor tan fiero,
Que muero porque no muero.

¡Ay, qué vida tan amarga
Do no se goza al Señor!
Porque, si es dulce el amor

I live without living in myself,
And so high is the life I await,
For [That] I die because I do not die.
I live now outside myself,
Now that I have died of love,
For I live in the Lord,
Who desired me for his own.
When I gave him my heart,
He placed on it this sign:
For [That] I die because I do not die.

That divine union
Of love in which I live
Has made God a captive
And my heart free.
And it fills me with such passion
To see God my prisoner
For [That] I die because I do not die.

Oh, how long is this life!
How hard are these exiles!
This jail, these irons,
in which my soul is bound!
Simply waiting for my escape
Causes me such fierce pain,
For [That] I die because I do not die.

Oh, how bitter this life
If it does not joy in the Lord!
Though love is sweet,

No lo es la esperanza larga.
Quíteme Dios esta carga,
Más pesada que el acero,
Que muero porque no muero.

The long wait is not.
God, remove this burden,
This burden heavier than irons,
For [That] I die because I do not die.

Sólo con la confianza
Vivo de que he de morir,
Porque, muriendo, el vivir
Me asegura mi esperanza.
Muerte, do el vivir se alcanza,
No te tardes, que te espero,
Que muero porque no muero.

Only trusting that I will die
Allows me to live.
For by dying, living
Assures my hope.
Oh death, where life is achieved,
Do not delay, for I await you,
For [That] I die because I do not die.

Mira que el amor es fuerte;
Vida, no me seas molesta,
Mira que sólo te resta,
Para ganarte, perderte.
Venga ya la dulce muerte,
Venga el morir muy ligero,
Que muero porque no muero.

Look, love is strong;
Life, do not bother me,
Look, for all you are left
To win yourself, is the loss of self.
Come now sweet death,
Come death, come softly,
For [That] I die because I do not die.

Aquella vida de arriba,
Que es la vida verdadera,
Hasta que esta vida muera,
No se goza estando viva.
Muerte, no me seas esquiva;
Viva muriendo primero,
Que muero porque no muero.

That life from above,
That life which is the true life,
Until this earthly life die,
Cannot be enjoyed.
Death, do not evade me;
Death, live dying first,
For [That] I die because I do not die.

Vida, ¿qué puedo yo darle
A mi Dios que vive en mí,
Si no es perderte a ti,
Para mejor a él gozarle?
Quiero muriendo alcanzarle,
Pues a él solo es al que quiero:
Que muero porque no muero.

Life, what can I give
To my God who lives in me,
If not to lose you
In order to enjoy him more?
Dying I want to reach him,
It is him only whom I love:
For [That] I die because I do not die.

—Saint Teresa of Jesus

In this *villancico* by Saint Teresa of Jesus,[1] the verb "to die" has three meanings: it designates the psychical and physical act by which the soul uncouples itself from the body in order to start heading down the way of dust (the physical death mentioned in the second half of the refrain, ". . . because I do not die"); it signifies the terrible suffering undergone by one who "experiences" God but does not die physically and thus definitively leave behind the prison of the body (the agony of this world, given expression in the first part of the refrain, "For I die . . ."); and it alludes to the supreme pleasure that intimate union with God causes in human beings (as expressed by and highlighted by the words, "I die from love"). What classical rhetoric designates as *derivatio* and polyptoton, the different morphology and the different function of the lexeme "to die" (dying, I die, death, to die), is not repetition of the same meaning with only slight variations through use of cognate words in close proximity but use of the same lexeme to express opposite and irreconcilable meanings. Or does a dead body have anything to do with a live body? Likewise, does a live body in pleasure have anything in common with a live body in pain? Can the body be both alive and dead at the same time, like Schrödinger's cat? Masochism aside, and although Bataille appears in my analysis of the poem, a body that dies from love is not compatible, according to what Saint Teresa herself has put into play, with a body that dies from intense suffering. It is clear that this is not just any word but the dominant word in this text, its hypogram, as represented in the refrain, "For I die because I do not die." Because of its importance, I have given it a certain primacy of place.

On this word, "to die," falls the responsibility of what Gracián referred to as the concept *(concepto)* in this poem and what this *villancico* denotes by the terms *villancico, cabeza,* and so forth. Furthermore, if "to die" and its cognates encompass contradictory meanings, it is not in the least strange that "I die" should also include the meaning of its opposite, "I live." In fact, when "life" is referred to as "this life," in which body and soul live together, then "to live" is the equivalent of suffering and death. However, when "life" designates the "high life," it describes a state of absolute happiness and pleasure. The result of the mystical experience is the impossibility of remaining within the binary and hierarchical logic that structures the opposition life-death. The beginning of the poem could therefore not be more telling: two diametrically opposed terms, "life" and "death," are accompanied by their negation, thereby unraveling the principle of noncontradiction: "I live without living" is the correlate of "I die because I do not die" and, even more concretely, "I live, do not live," "I die, do not die." This poem by Teresa of Jesus, following the mystical tradition that runs from Plato to John of the Cross, deconstructs the opposition between life and death, causing the semantic traits of death (the sadness of solitude and the absence of life) to cross over into life and those of life (happiness and joy) to be assimilated by death. Consequently, to live is in reality to be dead, and to be dead is in truth to live. Plato declared quite unequivocally that the philosopher should take leave of the body and should behave as if dead. Living in death, furthermore, is a recurrent theme in Teresa, who, for example, in the third mansion addresses God with these words:

> How is that You want us to desire so miserable a life, for it isn't possible to stop wanting and asking You to take us out of it unless with hope of losing it for You or of spending it very earnestly in Your service or, above all, of understanding that it is your will? If it is Your will, my God, may we die with you, as Saint Thomas said; for living without You and with these fears of the possibility of losing You is nothing else than dying often.[2]

This state of living in death is explored in the poem through its series of paradoxes: "sweet death," "death, come softly," "Only trusting that I will die / Allows me to live," etc.

Nevertheless, things are not as plain as the words just cited would seem to indicate, words that, in a nutshell, distill a number of the commonplaces attending the mystical poetry of Teresa of Jesus, John of the Cross, and the Platonic conception of the world. This can be noted simply by paying attention to the first verse of the poem, above all because it is where the poem's discourse is enunciated. The question at hand is, in what phase of divine relationship does the poem's speaker, whom we identify with "Teresa," find herself? "I live without living in myself" underscores a loss of self undergone by the witness. A split has occurred in the subject, a fissure that has taken the speaker to "live" not in herself but in another place, another sphere, another dwelling. The line points to a loss of her own identity, which was ripped away from her in the moment God chose her as bride. That is why she lives outside herself—or, what is the same, lives in the Lord—in that "spiritual marriage" that Teresa of Jesus describes in the seventh mansion. For that reason, she dies of love. If the poem is enunciated by a divided self, by a self that, as R. D. Laing would say, feels a distance, a disruption, in relation to his- or herself,[3] then who exactly is speaking? The phrase "For I die because I do not die" is not originally spoken by the person but is a sign placed by God on her heart when she was taken as bride. "He placed on it this sign" means that the words do not originate with Teresa but are the writing of God.[4] Furthermore, God does not speak for himself; rather, he places in the bride's mouth these words (*sermocinatio*). She says what the other wants her to say, and not only what the other wants her to say but also wants her to assume as her own.

Not only is "I die because I do not die" the hypogram of the poem, the object of analysis, but the entire poem is an amplification and a repetition of this motif. In the poem's opening tercet, "I live without living in myself, / I live expecting to live on high, / And I die because I do not die," we still do not know that in the expression "I die because I do not die" it is not the bride but the husband speaking. To the extent that this line forms a syntactic continuity with the following statement, "I live expecting to live on high," it seems that it is the bride who claims responsibility for these words, and this supposition seems confirmed in the third line, "For I die because I do not die." The repetition of that line at the end of the first strophe, however, which discloses the words as a sign from God placed on her heart, leads us to realize that there are many voices condensed into the apparent speaking voice of the opening tercet. Most obviously, these are the voices of the bride and the Lord—her voice "speaks" in order to repeat his letter and instruction; thus, it is his "voice" we hear—but behind these are the voices of every mystical poet who says, "I live without living in myself." The voice of Saint John of the Cross is the most notable and well-known example here, but Duarte Brito or Arnalte de Diego could also be mentioned, and even the much earlier voice of Saint Augustine. However, the difference is that in this case the phrase and what accompanies it are not enunciated by the speaker in her own name. Let us briefly compare this *villancico* by Teresa of Jesus with a similar poem by John of the Cross.[5] In his poem there is no doubt that the enunciating subject says "I live without living in myself / and thus I hope / to die because I do not die" (Vivo sin vivir en mí / y de tal manera espero, / que muero porque no muero) in his own name. He does not fail to stress the distance between himself and God, and for that reason he addresses the divine in the following manner: "Hear, my God, what I say," and a little later mentions "being away from you." Saint John's poem takes place in a present during which the bride is away from the spouse, and addresses the latter with the desire to reunite with him. By contrast, Saint Teresa's poem occurs in a present in which the bride finds herself in union with the divine: "For I live in the Lord." Saint John highlights his loneliness and the need for death so that what separates him from God will disappear. Saint Teresa highlights the pain of what is left to this earthly life-death, to this remaining-embodied, despite whatever communion she has with her husband. These are two very different positions that imply very different subjects.

The speaking subject in the poem by Saint John is a compact subject that maintains his own, proper position and from that place expresses his feeling of lack. The speaking subject in the poem by Saint Teresa is a fragmented subject who has lost her own, proper position and from that loss expresses her dumbfoundedness regarding the fact that she still retains the excrescence of her body, imprisoned in irons and shackles. The subject in Saint John's poem *speaks* because the subject is present; the subject in Saint Teresa's poem *repeats,* because in actuality the subject has disappeared. God is the ventriloquist of his bride; her soul is the tablet on which the husband has written and inscribed the essential nucleus of his words. When Saint John writes, "I no longer live in myself, / And without God I cannot live; / Then without him and without myself I remain, / This life, what will it be?" (En mí yo no vivo ya, / y sin Dios vivir no puedo; / pues sin él y sin mí quedo, / este vivir ¿qué será?), he signals the absolute desolation that overcomes him owing to the absence of the husband, a desolation that deprives him of himself and of God and turns his life into a barren wasteland. The difference between the two poems is notable in this respect. For Saint Teresa's emphasis is quite far from Saint John's: "I live now outside myself / Now that I have died from love, / For I live in the Lord, / Who desired me for his own." The line "I live now outside myself" does not describe the absolute desolation that fills the witness because of the husband's absence but rather expresses the fullness of communion with God and the transverberation that is suffered. In both cases the individual feels his or her most intimate self as something that is separated and divorced from the body, an object among objects, the appearance of a false "I," but whereas in Saint John the witness is unable to achieve—at least in this poem—the leaving behind of self, in Saint Teresa the leaving behind of the self has already taken place, and the sorrow is not that of the *pre* but that of the *post* ("Now that I have died from love"): that of the intermittent return to a body that, in the final instance, has been dispossessed.

This brief comparison allows us to situate Saint Teresa's poem in a more precise way. It is not only that Teresa's body is God's property, in the tradition of the Corpus Hermeticum, or that her voice in actuality is not her voice but that of the Other: her writings, like those of Virginia Woolf, are filled with moments in which the protagonist "hears" voices and receives signs. To this we must add an important distinction: Teresa's poem is a scene of negative dialectics and responses. The first two verses are opposed to the rest of the verses in that they describe a state of intimate communion between the bride and the husband. The witness says she lives in the Lord, that he desired her for himself; she affirms that she lives in divine union, in the passion that this union procures in her. However, she is not the passive figure of that action. She could have been so at the beginning, when the husband chose her, but immediately the bride turns into the dominant and active figure. The metaphor of the captive God does not trick us: God is captive and imprisoned, and that inflames her passion. The first masochism (to be God's property) turns into sadism (she is God's master). The transcendent God is turned into an immanent one.

Gilles Deleuze's reflection on classical painting could be applied to this case, *mutatis mutandis:* at first, the departure of the mystic toward the above ("such high life"), toward the husband, supposes—and in this Deleuze follows Bergson—a mad liberation, a total manumission, an entry into an order of heavenly sensations: "One must not say: If God does not exist, everything is permitted. It is just the opposite. For with God, everything is permitted. It is with God that everything is permitted, not only morally, since violences and infamies always find a holy justification, but aesthetically in a much more important manner, because the divine figures are wrought by a free creative work, by a fantasy in which everything is permitted."[6]

The "everything" that Deleuze refers to finds a historical precedent in that image-, vision-, and communication-producing machine that was Teresa of Jesus. There was always doubt as to whether these various manifestations were the work of the devil or of God; as we know, Father Daza decreed that Teresa had to have been the victim of satanic trickery (it was impossible, he argued, that God would bestow such extraordinary favors on a nun as imperfect as she purported to be). In fact, it is precisely in this liminal space between God and the devil where the political work of Saint Teresa is situated, both on the terrain of her actions (a persecuted woman who founded convents) and in the field of her writing (a woman scribe, composer of verse, belittled by critics, threatened in her own time by the Inquisition; one who opens language to the field of schizoid madness; a woman who constantly escapes: from her house, from the convent, from her gifts, from boredom, from the world, from grammar; a woman, in this sense, surrealist). From today's perspective, Teresa, like John of the Cross, represents orthodoxy, suitable even to be vindicated as a New Age figure and as someone who advances the cause of Catholic hegemony. Is it necessary to recall here that both John and Teresa had to escape from the clutches of both the Church and other Carmelites; is it necessary to recall that they both suffered cruelties, at times those of imprisonment, at other times those of disentitlement and marginalization? In Teresa's poetic writing, the political work emerges from the very start: first, because the nun writes as an act of obedience; second, because she writes only under the aegis of Horace's dictum of teaching to please. In regard to these two mandates, writing as obedience and writing as didacticism, what matters is not the mandates themselves but what she is able to sneak in under the cloak of obedience and in the guise of teaching and spreading doctrine, what she is able to sabotage under the pretext of the voluntary education of the nuns.

The poem exhibits a practically irreconcilable division. On the one hand, the first two verses concentrate on the mystical experience of the congress between the bride and the husband, an experience that, when viewed from earth-bound life (again: "For I live in the lord," "That divine union," "this love in which I live"), is an advance on—a divine trailer for—the high life that is to come. On the other hand, the rest of the verses, devoted to singing about that aspect of earth-bound life in which the body, pain, the shackles, the nuisances of life are felt ("exiles," "jail," "piercing pain," "this much too bitter life," "irons"), serve as a reminder that, despite congress with God, she is not solely and permanently at one with the deity. The poem itself underlines the irreconcilability of these two positions by splitting up the meaning of "life" in three different ways: bodily life lived in absence of the divine; bodily life when the soul is caught and wounded by the husband; and the high life, lived at the very limits of the body.

This division points to a destructured subject, a subject that oscillates between the capacity to turn God into her captive and prisoner and the recognition of her own earthly abandonment. This subject is split because it is in flight, whether the movement is upward, away from earth and toward heaven (when she dies of love), or downward, away from heaven toward earth (when she experiences the bitterness of life). However she might protest, this subject is in movement; she is both always building upward and escaping from any and all authority (who needs intermediaries between God and herself?), and also always relapsing into the long, bitter hope that "weighs more than irons." There are moments in this mad dynamic—those ecstatic raptures of which Bataille was so fond—when she is the medium through which the husband speaks; there are others, though, when she herself speaks and reveals herself. The key, again, is in the verb *placed.* If God placed his seal of ownership and his instruction on her, how is it that he has become the nun's submissive "subject"? Are we to say that it is only a "manner of speech" taken up and repeated by a tradition, as if metaphors and manners of speech were innocent? In the second verse, the roles are reversed: the husband ceases to be a husband with active and dominant attributes (he is now bride), and the bride ceases to be the bride with passive and submissive traits (she is now husband). If Saint John moves without problems from the masculine to the feminine, turning himself into the lady inflamed by passion (*en amores inflamada),* Saint Teresa moves with the same ease from the "she" to the "he" when she takes on the role of the jailer. Not only does she not need intermediaries (the problem all mystics have, regardless of institution), she has the audacity to declare that God is her captive, in a phrase, "God is my prisoner," where the possessive adjective is just as important as the object, "captive."

But of course, the captive escapes, the little bird flies away. Because what sense does it make for this man-woman that Teresa is to declare that she lives in an extraordinary love and, in the following verse, complain about how long this hard life is? The sense is that of a straying without purpose or end, a straying as deeply radical in its stumbling as the irony present in the words "death" and "life." What kind of trust can we place in language if it is able to make death mean life and life mean death? We are not dealing with apparent paradoxes, as is often said. To speak of apparent paradoxes is to reduce the power of paradox and aporia, it is to fail to notice that if the mystic turns language mad it is because he or she has become mad, because the political task of the mystic, his or her way of doing things with words and actions, is precisely through losing a stable subject position and shooting off into various directions: a movement from up to down, from divine union to the prison of the soul.

When the captive escapes Teresa's cage, it is she who becomes the captive, thus demonstrating—and this is one of the keys to the poem—that the different positions that the poem accentuates (woman, man, bride, husband, prisoner, jailer, love, pain . . .) are interchangeable, shifting, functional. It is more than evident that the love in which our witness lives will not disappear; in the middle of barrenness it will return—and vice versa. The movement from the second verse to the third is what demonstrates my argument: if from the first verse to the second the God that desired her is transformed into a prisoner, from the second to the third verse she no longer fulfills the function of jailer; rather, it is the life of the earthly body that assumes that function. It should be noted that the semantic field deployed by the second verse to designate the imprisoned state of God (captive God, prisoner God) is continued in the third verse (jailed soul, soul imprisoned by iron shackles and fetters). In the fourth verse, lines 27 and 28 condense the aporia I have been discussing here: "Though love is sweet, / the long wait is not." The proximity of the yes and the no (which Góngora would learn so much from) brings together in a very small space an affirmation and a negation, the affirmation of the sweetness of love and the negation of the bitterness of hope.

Teresa takes up the language of God, his command written on the sign placed on the soul; and that nucleus, spoken and sent out by the deity, is taken on, assimilated by her for the purpose of restating it, in order to change the direction of its meaning, to appropriate it. This appropriation of the divine language manifests a struggle for language, an all-out war between the nun and her husband. Nevertheless, the most important thing is not the struggle taking place between God and the mystic but that they have stolen the language of the world in order to give it back as a poisoned dart. The mystic is caught up in an autistic colloquy in which the deity and life are the interlocutors, but that autism, paradoxically, is the negation of the worldly, noisy, politics-laden circulation of language. Given all this, are we still surprised by Hélène Cixous's confession when she says she has been "Saint Teresa of Avila, that mad woman who knew a lot more than all the men. Whose knowledge came to her by virtue of her wanting to become a bird"?[7] John of the Cross possessed the virtues of the solitary bird, Teresa those of a bird who has gone mad in her desire to escape.

Translated by Jeremy Paden

Renunciation and Absorption

On the Dimensionality of Baroque Asceticism

BURCHT PRANGER

In 2010 the National Gallery of London and the National Gallery of Art in Washington, D.C., organized an exhibition on seventeenth-century Spanish painting and sculpture under the name *The Sacred Made Real: Spanish Painting and Sculpture 1600–1700*. The exhibition curators sought to show how the realism of the paintings of Velázquez, Ribalta, Zurbarán, and others had its roots in the artists' sculptural approach to rendering figures and scenes in a two-dimensional medium. In turn, the painted, polychromed religious sculptures of the era represented real life—the real life of Christ, Mary, and the saints, that is. The most popular topic represented in both religious painting and sculpture was, of course, Christ's (and, consequently, Mary's) suffering: Christ being flagellated, the *ecce homo* motif showing the man of sorrows, carrying his cross and subsequently hanging on it; or, for that matter, Mary as the lady of sorrows shedding real tears, the goal being to arouse an emotion or response in the viewer. As Xavier Bray, the curator of the National Gallery exhibition and editor of the exhibition catalogue, writes,

> Christ is vividly depicted moments after his death, his body rigid, his head down, his flesh color white. Hyper-real sculptures such as these made the sacred truly palpable. To approach this sculpture was to feel that one was truly in the presence of the dead Christ. In their original context such sculptures, whether positioned on altars and lit by candles or processed through the streets on religious feast days,

would have had a strong impact not only upon the faithful but also on painters' visual imaginations. Today, when the *paso* (float) carrying Juan Martínez Montañes's (1568–1649) sculpture of *Christ carrying the Cross* is carried on the shoulders of thirty men during Holy Week in Seville, the effect is astounding. The movement of the *paso* as it sways from side to side endows the sculpture with a disconcerting sense of life, as if the streets of Seville had suddenly turned into the streets of Jerusalem.[1]

Where painting of an earlier era lacked the real-life features of sculpture, in particular because of the limitations of a two-dimensional medium, an important step was taken by painters such as Zurbarán, who succeeded in infusing the flatness of figural representation on canvas with the suggestion of three-dimensionality. His *Christ on the Cross* of 1627, painted for the Dominican friary of San Pablo el Real in Seville, is a supreme case in point. Again, Xavier Bray:

> Nailed to the cross, Christ's lifeless body emerges from the impenetrable blackness behind, illuminated by bright light. The scene is entirely devoid of narrative detail and so the viewer is forced to focus his attention on the subject presented. Depicted with an extraordinary attention to detail, Zurbarán's painting takes the illusion of reality to a new level: it is as though the sacrifice of Christ is taking place right in front of us.[2]

Taken together, the painterly techniques in this work that help draw the viewer's attention also produce the illusion of three-dimensionality as the deep contours of the crucified Christ emerge out of the blackness into light. The force of the impression was so strong that contemporary visitors to the chapel could not believe their eyes, and mistook the painting for a sculpture:

> "There is a crucifix from his [Zurbarán's] hand," the Spanish art historian and painter Antonio Palomino (1653–1726) remarked after visiting the chapel, "which is shown behind a grille of the chapel (which has little light), and everyone who sees it and does not know believes it to be a sculpture."[3]

Admittedly, Christian "realism" in artistic renderings of religious topoi could never be allowed to proceed to the point that the image or representation could be confused with the real thing, nor could the handling of the real-life object be separated from devotional use and perception. Yet in

Baroque art the image and the sacral essence drew uncomfortably close, in the view of some church representatives:

> Sculpture was treading a thin line between the "representation" of a sacred subject and becoming the sacred subject itself, which according to the twenty-fifth session of the Council of Trent in 1563 was to be scrupulously avoided. As Saint Ignatius Loyola reminded his readers in his *Spiritual Exercises* (1548), statues should be venerated not for what they are but "according to what they represent." Perhaps this was the fundamental way in which painters "by implying" the real, defended the superiority of painting over sculpture; with a painting, the faithful were less likely to commit idolatry. In this respect, Zurbarán's *Christ on the Cross* is a supremely successful religious image: by fusing the arts of painting and sculpture Zurbarán created a convincing illusion of the reality of the sacred.[4]

The sense of the material presence of the divine produced by Baroque artists using techniques of realism to engage viewers thus created a problem for spiritual asceticism, and motivates the question I explore in this essay. How is the pictorial monumentality I have outlined above, with the help of Baroque painting and sculpture, related to asceticism? Confronting the overwhelming presence of the sacred object standing in for real life, the bloody Christ and weeping Mary, how can the faithful viewer move away from such captivating images into an inner self? In terms of the exhibition *The Sacred Made Real,* once an image has taken on a three-dimensional shape, whether in the reality of sculpture or in an illusionary perspective, how can the force of spaciousness—the force of realism—be negated at the very moment this image is received and interiorized by the believing and perceiving soul? Here a stumbling block becomes apparent, one that would seem to be squarely in the way of a Christian soul imposing an ascetic distance from both itself and the object of veneration in order to get closer to the divine. Moreover, this monumental realism with its focus on suffering would seem to distinguish Christianity from other religions. And if the veneration of objects depicting Christ's suffering and Mary's sorrow is to be seen as characteristic of a specifically Christian type of asceticism, affording the faithful a means of identifying with and so drawing near the divine, a dialogue with more subtle and less realistically pictorial forms of asceticism would fail to materialize because of this fixed, immovable imagery. Indeed, this epoch of hyperrealism in religious art turns out to have been ejected from any dialogue with modernity on scrupled grounds, a stance that is recruited as explanation in the museum directors' foreword to the exhibition catalogue: "The exhibition is designed to address a neglect that has its roots in the disdain with which the Enlightenment regarded these devotional works of art as objects of superstitious veneration, a disdain that was often mingled with the Protestant distaste for Mariolatry and martyrs."[5]

As I proceed to explore more broadly the subject of Christian asceticism, I hope to reap the fruits of having first introduced this strong, almost violent set of Baroque devotional images. For such imagery has not only been foundational for Roman Catholic piety on both a popular and a scholarly level to the present day. Hyperrealistic as it may seem to a secular beholder, it has also produced a peculiar kind of asceticism verging on self-annihilation, which raises the question of whether such a hyperrealistic life is realistically livable at all, a question I return to at the end of the essay. What requires our attention now is that throughout the history of Christianity, there has been no moment in which it would have been possible to address withdrawal and renunciation without in one way or another taking the problem of visibility and "realism" into account. Christ's becoming flesh—the incarnation—foreclosed any attempt at an ultimate withdrawal through vanishing into thin air. Paradoxically, it has never been Christ's remoteness that called for withdrawal but rather his real presence, once upon a time and thereafter continually renewed in the Eucharist and in the preaching of the Word, as well as in images and stone. Across the ages the presence of Christ has been at the root of conceits of absence and withdrawal, as manifested, for instance, in memes of darkness and the desert, as well as in the accompanying bridal imagery: dark night and the desert as the when and where of the lovers' meeting.

This tight, almost lockstep imagery remains in place if, moving away from the Baroque vantage point, we take a retrospective look at Christian asceticism and distinguish the various ways in which and the various levels on which it has manifested itself through the ages. Historically, what comes to mind first is asceticism as a means of bodily and in particular sexual renunciation, a practice brilliantly traced and described by scholars such as Peter Brown and Virginia Burrus.[6] Here we meet the apostle Paul, the religions of the East, Manichaeism, Greek philosophy, the desert fathers, the Greek church fathers, Ambrose, Jerome, and Augustine—in short, the variety of elements and personalities that went into the making of the Christian idea of asceticism with its (in the long run) distinctly monastic overtones. This very prominence of asceticism in the history of Christianity, including its withdrawal into the monastic, mainly Benedictine, life of renunciation, guaranteed its survival from late antiquity into the Middle Ages. Far from being distinctly Christian, it has proved itself to be a syncretic phenomenon, absorbing all kinds of influences along the way. But here again the imagery of a presence retained its hold, not permitting the historian to disentangle a more pagan, philosophical, imageless kind of asceticism from the more primitive aspects and the visibility of a God incarnate. What is more, the very problem of divine visibility appears entwined with renunciation, withdrawal, and the denial of images, as also with language, or any kind of articulation whatsoever. Negative theology and iconoclasm come to mind here as manifestations of an inner-Christian, cognitive asceticism insofar as a distance is established with regard to the divine object represented in language or imagery, a distance that in one way or another is intrinsically related to the moral and anthropological aspects of asceticism, such as physical and mental withdrawal.[7]

Before being able to say exactly what is ascetic about *The Sacred Made Real* I must take some detours, starting with what seems to be the opposite of this kind of realism, Protestantism, and specifically Calvinism, a movement whose disdainful treatment of Catholic imagery the exhibition curators hold responsible for the neglect of religious painting and sculpture of the Baroque. For despite Calvin's fear of images and condemnation of idolatry, the presence of his Christ is no less forceful, remote, and linked to asceticism. For the Reformers, real presence, in particular the real presence of Christ in the Eucharist, was no less problematic and ambiguous than it had been for the Roman Catholic theologians (despite the official declaration of the transubstantiation in 1215: declaring a doctrine does not mean resolving its ambiguities). To tackle the problem of Christ's simultaneous presence in the Eucharist and in heaven, Luther came up with the notion of a kind of dispersed omnipresence, ubiquity, a notion that covered too much and solved too little. Calvin's was a literal-mindedness, a bend toward realism that left his Christ both little and unlimited escape. This very realism prevented Calvin from mixing up or dispersing different presences of the incarnated and resurrected Christ, from giving up, in other words, Christ's three-dimensional status (no matter how sublime those three dimensions were supposed to be). Christ's real presence is in heaven; any other presence has a secondary, derived status. As a result, Christ's presence in the Eucharist is, without evaporating into a merely spiritual state, only real insofar as it is linked to, and brings us back to, Christ in heaven: *sursum corda.* In his *Institutes* Calvin presents his three-dimensional Christ as follows:

> The question here is not, What could God do? But, What has he been pleased to do? We affirm that he has done what pleased him, and it pleased him that Christ should be in all respects like his breth-

> ren, "yet without sin" (Heb. 4: 15.) What is our flesh? Is it not that which consists of certain dimensions? is confined within a certain place? is touched and seen? And why, say they, may not God make the same flesh occupy several different places so as not to be confined to any particular place, and so as to have neither measure nor species? Fool! why do you require the power of God to make a thing to be at the same time flesh and not flesh? It is just as if you were to insist on his making light to be at the same time light and darkness. He wills light to be light, darkness to be darkness, and flesh to be flesh. True, when he so chooses, he will convert darkness into light, and light into darkness: but when you insist that there shall be no difference between light and darkness, what do you but pervert the order of the divine wisdom? Flesh must therefore be flesh, and spirit spirit; each under the law and condition on which God has created them. How the condition of flesh is, that it should have one certain place, its own dimension, its own form. On that condition, Christ assumed the flesh, to which, as Augustine declares, (Ep. ad Dardan.,) he gave incorruption and glory, but without destroying its nature and reality.[8]

The implications of this suspended presence are far-reaching. In what has technically been termed the *extra Calvinisticum,* Calvin's literalness is so strong as almost to invert the image of Zurbarán's Christ, while maintaining its realism.[9] Rather than beginning with an earth-bound, three-dimensional image, such as Christ on the cross, Calvin starts with an equally three-dimensional image of Christ in heaven to be able to stretch its presence downward into earthly regions and visibility, spiritualizing the image along the way but never fully so. With this picture we find ourselves plunged into Calvinist asceticism, the *innerweltliche Askese,* as Max Weber called it. While Christ resides in heaven realistically, whence he reaches out to man on earth, all the faithful Christian can do is reach back, suspending (not denying!) the realism of his own earthly life and possessions and banking them, so to speak, in heaven. And with this suspension, Calvinist restlessness starts. Here we have no denial of creation, the body, or the real shape of things and minds. "Flesh must therefore be flesh, and spirit spirit." Creation is, rather, injected with a hyperrealism that allows for neither escape nor rest. Instead, the Calvinist faithful are incited to labor harder, to save more capital for better chances and higher purposes, and to postpone temporary enjoyment, not with an eye on more spiritual and ethereal possessions with fewer dimensions but going for the "real thing," Christ in heaven. Zurbarán's Christ on the cross, Calvin's Christ in heaven: what difference does it make, apart from the fact that one suffers and the other beams in glory? Both stand out for their hyperrealism, their utter absorption. Both are at the root of an asceticism of the most (three)-dimensional kind.

Utter absorption.[10] By that I mean that the sculptured image is so real and so aloof that it seems to blind the eye of the beholder or, more violently, to scorch the spectator's vision, such that the latter is almost substituted by the visual object. Here we are confronted with questions that are central to the nature of Christian asceticism. At first impression, viewing a picture, for instance of the suffering Christ, is not about withdrawal but about commitment and devout communication. Over the centuries it has been precisely the iconoclasts' argument that such a sweet to-and-fro between the sacred object and the perceiving soul made things too easy and tempted the spectator to mistake the image for the real thing, all of which resulted in idolatry. The obvious reply to this objection is that asceticism is practiced precisely by sharing and participating in the image in a way that is proportional to the latter's intensity and "realism." Thus Christ's flagellation and the *ecce homo* motif, his hanging on the cross, had as their second acts countless instances of self-castigation and renunciation on the part of the contemplative believer. Nor does it help very much to counter those scenes with images of the immaculate conception or Christ in glory if one wants to make the point that images of suffering may be fine as far as asceticism is concerned but that it is hard to see how more glorious imagery may incite to withdrawal and renunciation. It does. Virginity and divine glory being inextricably intertwined, the entire complex of Christian imagery is capable of playing a role in the service of ascetic exercise. Tellingly, in late medieval devotional literature *dulcis,* "sweet," is the key term covering both compassion with the suffering Christ and joyful adoration of the God-child being nurtured in the Virgin's arms. Underlying it all is the question posed by Aristotle in his *Poetics:* Why does tragedy give pleasure?[11]

With the notion of sweet contemplation as an ascetic performance, however, we seem even further removed from solving the problem of sculptural absorption, the question, in other words, of how to draw a line between the realistic force of a three-dimensional image—sculptural or one affording a deep perspective in the two-dimensional plane—and the perceiver, maker, or adorer, as well as the more urgent question of how our ascetic spectator is to survive this hyperrealism.

Ironically, it is the founder of "compassionate devotion," Bernard of Clairvaux, who with his usual playfulness cast this matter into relief by inverting, so to speak, any solid presence of a suffering Christ. Bernard accomplished this effect by emphasizing Christ's very absence (because of his ascension) while at the same time maintaining an oblique focus on the man of the cross:

> Why then should those solemnities concern me? Who will comfort me, Lord Jesus, because I have not seen you hanging on the cross, discolored by bruises, pale as a result of death. For I have not suffered together with him who was crucified, have not followed him into death so as at least to soothe with my tears those marks of his wounds. Why have you left me without greeting me, King of glory? Handsome in your shining dress you welcomed yourself in the high heavens. There is no way that my soul had been willing to be consoled but for the fact that the angels had been there first telling me with a shout of joy: "Men of Galilee, why do you stand looking up toward heaven? This Jesus, who has been taken up from you to heaven, will come in the same way as you saw him go into heaven."[12]

This is dazzling imagery indeed: the hyperrealism of Zurbarán's Christ hanging on the cross turned into absence. But this passage should be characterized as visually polyphonic, for it is more than three-dimensional, displaying a doubled or tripled asceticism. First and foremost—and in the center of the passage—we see Christ hanging on the cross. Next, keeping the pale image of Christ in mind, we see him in heaven and ourselves as bereft of our "ascetic" image, which amounts to a doubling of that very vision. The third dimension consists in the fact that reading this passage, we take in all its visual aspects at once.

This scene is exceedingly light and full of flexible imagery, which would seem to come down to saying that it is quite different from the monumental, sculptural presence of Baroque imagery. And it is different. Once we realize that Bernard's literary images are projected onto the barren walls of his austere, empty, imageless Cistercian monastery (asceticism all the way), we find ourselves in a theater conspicuously lacking the monumentality of statues or paintings. Yet so much is clear: we do not have a flat screen here. If ever there was multidimensionality in the air, it is to be discerned in the spatial and temporal focus on Christ on the cross, whose monumental absence is infused with dimensions of space and time as pictured by the writing contemplator designing an imagery play in which he, and he alone, is the principal actor. That being the case, what is left of Zurbarán's three-dimensional monumentality if the designer of the scene is so prominently present? Underlying this question is another one: is not any manifestation of asceticism bound to be self-defeating if it fails to annihilate the designer alias contemplator? Or, to look at the other face of the coin, is asceticism not by definition destined to be narcissistic and self-aggrandizing? And does not *The Sacred Made Real* actually come down to a (violent) competition for pride of place between the one who realizes and the one who is realized? All this can be reduced to the question, what is left of absorption? Admittedly, like Bernard's twelfth-century devotion, Baroque art also knew its implied maker and contemplator, as becomes clear from Zurbarán's *Saint Luke Contemplating the Crucifixion,* interpreted by art historians as depicting Saint Luke, traditionally known as a painter, "either in the act of creating a painted representation of Christ on the cross or contemplating a vision of it."[13] But in the end, it might be asked, who is absorbing whom? Does the maker-contemplator absorb his three-dimensional image? Or is it the other way around, and the image absorbs its viewer?

At this point it might be useful to recapitulate what we have so far. Calvin's Christ in heaven, who, because of his three-dimensional state, which prevents him from being spiritualized, so that he is available to anyone and everyone, elicits ascetic behavior in his followers on earth. Bernard's disappearing Christ, whose absence (as well as the absence of the contemplator at the scene of his crucifixion) intensifies a presence of sorts, keeps the self-same viewer in a state of unlimited ascetic suspense. With those pictures in mind, we are confronted with the following paradox. From the late Middle Ages and continuing in full bore into the Baroque period, the emphasis was on what images did *to* the spectator. Their increasing crudeness, bloodiness, and general realism served the purpose of "shocking the senses to stir the soul." Surprisingly, in the exhibition catalogue of *The Sacred Made Real,* little or no mention is made of this aspect, and the matter is referred to an accompanying lecture on this topic (apart from the passage on Ignatius of Loyola I quoted above).[14] And indeed, it is quite proper to single out Ignatius and, for instance, the writers of the École française, such as the founder of the French Oratoire Pierre de Bérulle (1575–1629), so thoroughly influenced by Spanish mysticism, who used what I have called "iron images," to be applied by the reader or viewer of devout scenes as a way to (re)organize the turmoil of the soul.[15] Here Calvin and the Catholic author converge: iron imagery is required to create distance; distance is required to be able to appropriate the image of a monumental, three-dimensional Christ. But can this act of (ascetic) appropriation be realized (through viewing an image) without the appropriating soul disappearing into the monumental image itself? In that case the human condition, from which, in one way or another, the ascetic act is supposed to spring, would seem rather bleak: in the beginning because of the "nothingness" of its confused and sinful state, at the end because of the "nothingness" of devout annihilation. If that were to be the net effect of *The Sacred Made Real,* one might wonder what kind of realism we are talking about.

I want to illustrate this point by turning to a painting by Francisco Ribalta, *Christ Embracing Saint Bernard of Clairvaux* (1624–27).[16] At first glance we seem to be presented with the opposite scene of Bernard of Clairveaux's absence at the crucifixion, Christ having moved to heaven. For the painting depicts Christ stretching out his arms from the cross (to which they are supposedly nailed) to embrace his favorite follower. Before we try to disentangle this paradox, let us hear the art-historical comment on this scene by the exhibition's principal curator, Xavier Bray:

> The practice of praying in front of sculptures and paintings, especially those depicting Christ and the Virgin, led some religious figures to experience a mystical union with them. Saint Catherine of Siena, for example, received the stigmata from a medieval painted crucifix, while Saint Bernard reputedly received Christ into his arms after praying before a sculpture of Christ on the cross. It is this vision of Saint Bernard's which is represented here by Ribalta, who was probably inspired by the account of the Jesuit historian Pedro de Ribadeneyra (1525–1611) provided in his 1599 edition of the lives of the saints: "The Lord so cherished Saint Bernard that one day when the latter was kneeling before the Cross, the Crucified Christ stretched out his arm and lay it on him, embracing and stroking him most lovingly. Immersed in this ineffable gentleness and deep silence, he united with the Supreme Being in an extremely chaste embrace."[17] To communicate Saint Bernard's rapturous visionary state, Ribalta shows him with his eyes closed and a smile on his face. Having surrendered himself to Christ, Bernard's body has gone limp and Christ bends forward to support him. What is remarkable is the way in which Christ has seemingly metamorphosed from a wooden sculpture into a living being. While Bernard's eyes are closed, Christ's are open and full of tenderness for the saint he embraces. The saint's body is swathed in white drapery whereas Christ is naked. The physicality of Christ is the most resonant and shocking aspect of the painting. His heroic and classical physique is bathed in a golden light as it emerges from the blackness behind.[18]

This commentary is interesting as much for its art-historical competence as for what it seems to ignore. Within the broad theme of sculptural painting, we have indeed a three-dimensional perspectival painting before us. But is it true that the physicality of Christ as a living sculpture is "the most shocking aspect of this painting"? Another question: if Zurbarán's *Christ on the Cross* looks so three-dimensional because "Christ's lifeless body emerges from the impenetrable blackness behind," do we not have as much impenetrable blackness here as well? Further, if Zurbarán's scene "is entirely devoid of narrative detail, forcing the viewer to focus his attention on the subject presented," what about Ribalta's *Christ Embracing Saint Bernard*? Do we not have a narrative here? Is there not at least something going on between two persons? If so, can we still take in this image in its three-dimensional size? In other words, what about absorption? What about the viewer? If I were asked to specify the various dimensions in Ribalta's painting, I would start by maintaining the description of Zurbarán's *Christ:* it is devoid of narrative and full of focus, a double focus, that is, not only on Christ but equally on Bernard; or, more precisely, the focus is not primarily on Christ but on the vision of the ascetic Bernard, who, blinded by ecstasy, "sees" Christ stretching out his arms. Admittedly, Christ is "bathed in a golden light," but the light falling on Bernard is a few shades stronger. From that viewpoint we can move upward and reduce the painting to its sculptural shape. It is Bernard who "sees" with his blinded eyes; it is also Bernard who, in a sense, while being embraced, embraces the slightly darker, shaded Christ, whose eyes are wide open. And if we move a bit upward still, we get to the most dramatic part of the painting, the almost invisible cross from which Christ slightly detaches himself while staying on it. What is so moving in this painting—in my view, at least—is that we still find ourselves squarely within the parameters of *The Sacred Made Real,* with its emphasis on the solid, sculptural dimensions of paintings, while at the same time the elements that go into making this solidness start moving a bit in a semidetached way: the cross remains in place, though now almost invisible; Christ does not come down from the cross but stays on it while slightly bending. Only Bernard is immobile, his body "gone limp," and it is this very immobility that deprives this painting of a narrative. Accordingly, what is shocking about this painting, starting with its almost invisible cross, is that it could as much be taken for a sculpture as Zurbarán's *Christ on the Cross.* If that is correct, an important fourth dimension could or should be added to the "sacred made real." No longer do we exclusively witness the transformation from painting to sculpture. Once three-dimensionality is established, the picture starts moving, talking, extending, shrinking. It starts, in other words, to become, very much in the Baroque mode, more realistic than real. At the same time, the still figure of the statuelike object strikes back. At first sight all dynamism of theatricality seems to stay in place.[19] For all the differences from the "original" of Bernard's text, with its moving figures, echoes of the latter can still be heard.[20] If in that text Bernard is at the same time the producer and adorer of his Christ on the cross and the deserted lover alias contemplator, those mobile elements together constitute a pictorial theater, though only in appearance, but an appearance that gains in intensity in Ribalta's painting moving upside down, from the invisible cross, and back. For once focus sets in, absorption replies, as a result of which all moving elements contract back into the integrity of one hyperrealistic, sculptural object.

Have we come any closer to the nature of Christian asceticism? So far we have considered two divergent aspects: the distant, "three-dimensional" Christ, on the one hand, and the embracing mystical closeness, if not identification, on the other. Both expressions are indeed about asceticism because stretching and absence are preconditions for absorption and (mystical) union. But if we look at Ribalta's *Christ Embracing Saint Bernard* with an iconoclastic eye, what are we to make of this twofold presence? Do we not have a kind of double idolatry here, an idolatry of both the object of adoration and the adorer? Narcissism to the utmost degree? And what about absorption? Does the presence of the adorer, however "unified" with his Christ, reinforce or weaken the power of absorption (so majestically present in the single image of Zurbarán's *Christ on the Cross*)?

Before answering this question, let us first take a look at the theoretician of the adorer's presence, Pierre de Bérulle (Charles de Condren), the founder of the French Oratory, so deeply influenced by the Spanish Carmelites. In his main work, *Discours de l'état et des grandeurs de Iésus,* Bérulle indefatigably—ad nauseam, even—presents his reader not only with the grandeurs of Jesus but also with the uninterrupted presence of his adorer.[21] In fact, Christ himself is the prime example of the perfect adorer—of his Father, that is:

> As of all ages there has been a God who is infinitely adorable. But there was not yet an infinite adorer. There was indeed a God who deserved to be loved and served infinitely. But there was no infinite man or servant able to respond with an infinite servitude and love. Now, you, o Jesus, are that adorer, that man, that Servant, infinite in your power, quality, and dignity, in order fully to fulfill that duty and pay this divine homage.[22]

From this state (*état*) of the divine adorer the presence of his human counterpart is derived. Quite statically and one-dimensionally, it would seem, since what we see sketched here is one point (the adorer) stretched out ad infinitum toward the adored. Next, the story of this divine adorer comes into the picture in the guise of his self-abasement, his self-annihilation even through his incarnation, Christ "abasing in himself the infinite and supreme being of his Divinity up to the point of the nothingness of our humanity." This abasement is doubled by yet another abasement: Christ's giving up, and his abasing of, his very humanity through his suffering on earth, on the cross. All the human contemplator of this human-divine action can do is follow suit by abasing and annihilating his own humanity, his self, that is.

> In honor, therefore, of this double [*double*] state and this double form of Servant in which I see your divine Incarnation, your laborious life and humble Cross reducing your supreme *grandeur,* I offer and present myself to you. I dedicate and consecrate my life both of nature and grace to you and I want to serve you, not only through my vows and actions but also through a state and condition that bring me back to, and give me a special relationship with, you, hoping that, as you are always mine, I may be always yours and that a permanent quality will reside in me that pays you a perpetual honor and homage. And seeing you as doubly turned into a Slave of our Love through your double debasement made for the love of men, I also want to be a Slave of your *Grandeur,* of your Debasement and of your Love. And I want my life and action both with regard to nature and grace to belong to you, as the life and actions of a Slave, yours forever. Thus I give up myself entirely to you, o Jesus, and to your Humanity that is sacred thanks to the most humble and submissive condition I know of, and that is the condition and relation of servitude that I acknowledge to be due to your humanity because of the *grandeur* of the State to which it is raised by the hypostatic union, as well as because of the excess and voluntary debasement with which it has given itself up and annihilated itself for my salvation and my glory, in its Life, in its Cross, and in its Death. To this intention, to this end, and to this homage I offer and establish, now and forever, my soul, my state, and my life, in a state of subjection, and in a relationship of dependence and of servitude with regard to you and your humanity altogether thus deified and thus humiliated.[23]

Do we not have a pretty accurate description here of what is going on in Ribalta's painting *Christ Embracing Saint Bernard,* and do we not, as a result, have a solution of sorts here to the problem of the double focus, the presence of both the contemplator and the sacred object to be contemplated, the one melting into the other? On the other hand, one might also ask, is there an end to this peculiar kind of self-abasement and self-annihilation, or should we admit that what we observe here is Christian asceticism getting caught in the self-destructive web of its own making, the inevitable result of which can only be nothingness and void? Not surprisingly, Roman Catholic authorities have panicked a bit at this radical type of self-annihilation and rebuked Bérulle for his radical stance. But what sense does that rebuke make if the train of thought and view, once set into motion, and owing to the overwhelming interconnectedness of imagery, can no longer be stopped in its course of realizing itself to the full?

The Sacred Made Real. If ever the shakiness of realism made itself felt, it is here in Baroque imagery as the realization of Christian asceticism. Little wonder that the expansiveness of three-dimensional space and the massive presence of sculpture are needed to counter the violent truth of it all being illusory. If Zurbarán's *Christ on the Cross* "compounded the question of what was real and what was an illusion," Ribalta's *Christ Embracing Saint Bernard* puts the finger on the weak spot of this particular kind of realism. Tellingly, this problem is hidden from view in the title of an exhibition on illusionary art, *The Sacred Made Real.* "Made" may point to the problematic state of ascetic realism, but in doing so it conceals the fact that we are basically talking about one big trompe l'oeil. At this point Bernard's mystical blindness may be seen as the key to understanding this specific brand of ascetic realism. I, for one, would hesitate to call this scene mystical (as the culmination of Christian asceticism), and much less still "mystical union." It is the other way around. We are dealing with absorption here. But for absorption to be effective it must be not only three-dimensional but, at least, four-dimensional. That is what Ribalta's painting tells us. Whereas Bérulle's literary rendering of this scene falls flat, the painting, not unlike Bernard's literary experiment of *his* Christ hanging on the cross, absorbs the viewer neither by annihilating the latter nor by the aloofness of its sacred realism. Rather, it is the cross staying where it is, "emerging from the impenetrable blackness behind," that both frames and frees, freezes and moves the embracers, catapulting them into the temporal space of Bernard's vision, in which absence and presence, seeing and not-seeing, coalesce to blind the eye of the beholder.

“For the Life Was Manifested”

KEVIN HART

What is it to hear with Christian ears, to see with Christian eyes, to touch with Christian hands? It would be, first of all, to live in a full, rich interpretation of the first epistle of John, to live in response to “the life” that “was manifested” (1 John 1:2), that “was from the beginning, which we have heard, which we have seen with our eyes, which we have looked upon, and our hands have handled” (1 John 1:1).[1] It would be a matter of “bear[ing] witness” to that life, of showing others “that eternal life, which was with the Father, and was manifested unto us” (1 John 1:2). It would be to live in the truth of what is preached in this epistle: “Hereby know ye the Spirit of God: Every spirit that confesseth that Jesus Christ is come in the flesh is of God: And every spirit that confesseth not that Jesus Christ is come in the flesh is not of God” (1 John 4:2–3). To hear with Christian ears would be to hear differently now that one has heard and accepted the *kerygma*, namely, that Christ, the Son of God, has come “in the flesh.” To live in an interpretation of 1 John would be to devise, haltingly or more fully (and both only through gifts of the Holy Spirit), a theology of the senses and a theology of manifestation, and—for those who work in systematic theology—to be able to hold the two together.

One approach to living deep inside the words of 1 John 1:1–2 would be by way of the spiritual senses. For Origen, Saint Gregory of Nyssa, and Saint Augustine, all the way up to Saint Bonaventure, and continuing in the contemplative orders, the spiritual senses have provided a means by which we, material creatures often at odds with spirit, can be in partial contact with the spiritual world: the outer man signifies the reality of the inner man, and the inner man signifies the reality of the divine. The author of 1 John speaks of the phenomenality of Christ in his mortal life and perhaps also after his resurrection. He was seen "by the fleshly eyes that see the sun," as Saint Augustine says.[2] But those of us who have come after the manifestation of the Christ can at best feel his spirit by way of the spiritual senses.[3] That there are competing interpretations of what these great theologians thought goes without saying, though each proposed that the spiritual senses are distinct from the corporeal senses. That there are arguments as to the rightness of what they thought is also plain. Whether the spiritual senses act best when the corporeal senses have been put to sleep or whether, once purified, they act in concert with them is a fault line in modern debate.[4]

There is also disagreement among the advocates of the spiritual senses. Origen, for one, speaks of the prophets who "tasted and smelt, so to speak, with a sense which was not possible," and Saint Gregory of Nyssa says that "the soul will see God in a divine watchfulness," while Saint John of the Cross holds that the spiritual senses do not give access to the divine but must be rendered inactive before God can be encountered.[5] We must pass from the light of *intellectus* to the darkness of *affectus.* For Origen and his school, "being human" means, as Saint Paul said, being "spirit and soul and body" (1 Thessalonians 5:23), with the spiritual senses mediating the outer and the inner person.[6] By the time the Alexandrian school was flourishing, Christian theology had overcome the idea of the soul as "material spirit."[7] That was the description that Tatian gave it in his *Oratio ad Graecos,* written in the late second century, his point being that we should pass from a material soul to an immaterial, divine soul. In the patristic age a doctrine of the spiritual senses is attained only when the human being, considered as a whole, can be seen as material spirit.[8] The spiritual senses help us ascend from the material to the spiritual world; they are to be cultivated as ways of taking us on a journey into the darkness of unknowing.

That vision of "being human" has mostly faded under the intense glare of successive philosophical criticisms, mainly circling around the rejection of a self-sufficient inner life, although the words "material," "soul," and "spirit" have survived, with different denotations and connotations.[9] "Material spirit" would be a self-contradiction within programs of naturalist reductionism, while in phenomenology it need not be, in part because here "spirit" (*Geist*) is not a substance but the intentional activity of consciousness, not just a matter of cognition but, as Eugen Fink makes clear, the very movement of life.[10] "Soul" and "spirit" name different things for Husserl: the soul is the bearer of my experiences, the spirit is the life of my consciousness. There is no Cartesian "inner life" for Husserl; our statements about the world are about the world, not about mental representations of the world. The "inner man" is transcendental life.[11] And yet it still makes sense to speak of imagination, memory, and understanding, the staples of the doctrine of the "spiritual senses" as usually considered.[12] "Experience teaches us," Husserl writes in the second book of *Ideas,* "that real spirituality is connected up with material Bodies only," and he later observes, "The unity of Body and spirit is a two-fold one, and, correlatively, a two-fold apprehension (the personalistic and the naturalistic) is included in the unitary apperception of the human."[13] Husserl's concern in this study is with the phenomenology of the body. *Leib,* the lived body, *is* material spirit for him: its stratum of *hylē* grounds the flow of noesis. ("*The intentional functions,*" he writes, "*are bound to this stratum;* the matter receives a spiritual forming, just as . . . the primary sensations [*hylē*] undergo apprehension, are taken up in perceptions" (160).) More generally, he opposes the naturalist reduction of spirit to nature: the spiritual cannot be fully explained by cause and substance, he maintains. Although Husserl largely puts God out of play in the first book of *Ideas,* and distinguishes soul from spirit in his own way in the second book, he nonetheless seeks to find a phenomenological path to God that does not rely on what the positive religions have said about him.[14] Also, without intending to do so, he gives us clues to how we might rethink the teaching of the spiritual senses today so that we might keep faith as firmly as one can with 1 John 1:1–2.[15]

As is well known, Husserl maintains that by performing the *epochē* and transcendental reduction we may pass from the natural to the transcendental attitude, and we can there examine a phenomenon as it is concretely embedded in our intentional horizons.[16] When I perceive something my intentional ray exceeds itself, involving other intentional relations that are implicit in the act; there is always a "meaning more," he says, and when I examine the phenomenon in its implicit as well as its explicit horizons I may gain a fuller, deeper understanding of my relationship with it.[17] I grasp *how* I am intending, and *how* the phenomenon is giving itself. The phenomenon flashes and fires in ways it would not were it perceived solely in the natural attitude and allowed to remain abstract. "Phenomenological explication makes clear what is included and only non-intuitively co-intended in the sense of the cogitatum," Husserl writes in the *Cartesian Meditations,* and adds that it does so "by making present in phantasy the potential perceptions that would *make the invisible visible*" (48; my emphasis). I shall return to "make present in phantasy" a little later. For now it need only be stressed that the question whether the phenomenon exists inside or outside consciousness has been turned off: for the time being it illuminates nothing at all. We are left to consider how something has given itself, not its pre-given state or the causal structure of its givenness.

We may add to phenomenology another protocol that does not change it but that clarifies its range. For we may observe that for the Christian, there is also a supernatural attitude.[18] Within this attitude, as when devoutly reciting the Nicene-Constantinopolitan Creed at Mass, one has a thetic relation with all manner of presumed realities and real events concerning the nature of God and the activities of Christ. One may say, "I believe *in,*" not "I believe *that,*" but the Creed is either declarative or interrogative in mode. So when saying or singing the Creed one is attesting to revelation as interpreted by the Church, and declaring that this picture of reality is solid and reliable, although not open to verification. When a person of faith performs the *epochē* and reduction, he or she passes from the natural and supernatural attitudes to the transcendental attitude. The truths professed in the Creed are not denied but are allowed to fade as theses, and we gain the opportunity of a pretheoretical experience of what they point to. In perceiving something, a Christian can make explicit other intentional horizons that until then had been implicit, and one of these will be faith. The faith I have in mind is not the belief that is implied in all the positings of anticipations, perceptions, and memories, or the rational faith that Karl Jaspers urges but religious faith, *fides qua.*[19] Dogmatic elaborations of faith—*fides qua iustificat, fides salvifica,* and so on—cannot become issues for the person explicating intentional experience. Similarly, exactly what Christians name by "divine spirit" (the nature of *ipsum esse subsistens,* for example) loses its urgency as a question.

Yet a Christian does not cease being a believer after performing the *epochē* and reduction. The self has been stilled, not changed; the world remains, though no longer as one's goal. Faith too remains; it has been sedimented in the psyche as a number of acts of which one is unconscious, although they can be recovered, sometimes by accident and sometimes by discipline (through "spiritual exercises," for example). In part, faith is passive, a number of associations and habituations, but it is also in part active, for a new association can jog the mind so that sedimented acts return to consciousness with vivacity and power or so that one will make one sort of intentional act rather than another. Reflection can move backward to passive synthesis or forward to the world, or backward in order to go forward. Faith remains, passively and actively (as faith *in,* not faith *that*), since the person of faith continues to be passionately invested in the divine.[20] Now, though, that person's intentional life is open to his or her inspection. So one might see, when looking at a landscape—sunlight on clouds in the sky, blue hills in the distance—that it is charged with unforeseen significance because it is being intended in a manner that until then had not been noticed, let alone explored. One sees that it is beautiful, but that is not all that touches one. Now both the meaning and the construction of it can be considered. Doubtless one has always been oriented to the world as such, but intentionality has put one concretely in relation with the clouds and the landscape in such a way that neither the subject nor the object has priority over the other. Only after the fact has one's thought been founded, and by what it has constituted as meaningful by implicit as well as explicit intentional acts.

Accordingly, a Christian might not just see clouds and mountains but also, on reflection, see them through the eye of faith, perhaps with other common intentional horizons in place: anticipation and hope, desire and imagination, love and memory, for example. One might experience pre-theoretically what the thesis "I believe in one Lord Jesus Christ, the only begotten Son of God" asserts in a creedal mode. One could say, in a manner recalling Saint Gregory of Nyssa (though not Saint John of the Cross), "I can 'see' Christ in the clouds, and the landscape as supported by Christ." It would take a very long time to unfold this judgment with full phenomenological rigor. For tacit support, I turn to Husserl, much as one touches a banister when climbing a steep set of stairs. Reflecting on the exclusion of transcendence, Husserl notes that even so, "there must be, therefore, modes in which transcendencies are made known other than the constituting of physical realities as unities of harmonious appearances; and ultimately there would also have to be intuitional manifestations to which a theoretical thinking might conform, so that, by following them rationally, it might make intelligible the unitary rule of the supposed theological principle."[21] Our lived experience leads us to affirm a divine, transcendent reality, but we do not presuppose that reality in order to explain our lived experience. Husserl inches forward from here in one of his research manuscripts: "God can be no object of experience (as in the sense of a thing or a human)," he writes. "But God would be 'experienced' in each belief that believes originally-teleologically in the perceptual value of that which lies in the direction of each absolute ought and which engages itself for this perpetual meaning."[22] This is the closest that Husserl comes to touching the tradition of the spiritual senses: God would be "experienced" only in the understanding. It is this "would be 'experienced'" that interests me. The scare quotes indicate that God is experienced in a doxic positing of an absolute ought: not directly but only indirectly and vaguely, without profiles.[23]

Some distinctions are in order. Saint Augustine tells us that there are three ways of seeing: the "bodily," the "spiritual" (imagination and memory), and the "intellectual."[24] Husserl shows how the first involves the second and third. When reflecting on acts of perception, one can make other implicit intentional acts—faith, to be sure, but also hope and love—explicit, and in so doing "see" God in the world. Intentional acts may be considered as "spiritual" (*geistige*) senses. I point out that not all senses are spiritual, even in this particular sense: nonintentional sensibility is left aside here. As well, no epistemological claim is being made about an objective "religious experience": that Christ has appeared in the clouds or has revealed himself in a visionary way in the landscape, for example. The intentional experience is noetic, and what it sees (the clouds, the hill) is the noema, with "Christ" inscribed on one or more strata of the noematic structure. Strictly speaking, with intentional acts the existence of God is irrelevant to the experience of God. (This is another reason to read "experience" here as "'experience.'") The second point is the bolder, though, and is drawn from Husserl himself: when reflecting on lived experience one may apprehend a deep pattern that leads one to posit God as real. The transcendent deity is always and already an irreducible trace in consciousness.[25] Here one may "experience" God in the sense of his transcendence being implied by enough lived experience and then posited as real by the subject. Going further, one may contend without leaving phenomenology that there is a region of being in which God may offer himself to be intuited in one way or another, and that this region supplies its own evidence (in the sense of *Evidenz:* made evident), which is unlikely to be indubitable.[26] There are mystics and visionaries, after all, and they brood over what counts as evidence in their experiences.

Let us take a step back from these three points. On my understanding, the person who responds to what has been made manifest to us in Christ not only is converted from death to life but also has converted his or her gaze.[27] To respond to the *kerygma* is to return to listen closely to what Jesus tells us; it is to have these two conversions taking place, the one superimposed on the other. For Jesus's preaching, especially his telling of parables of the kingdom—for which he was ruthlessly punished by crucifixion, and the truth of which was vindicated by his resurrection—prompts a reduction that allows people to shift their gaze from "world" to "kingdom." In parable the kingdom is briefly phenomenalized in and through ordinary words. A parable changes how we see things, regardless of whether we have heard it from Jesus in the flesh or heard it millennia later in scripture and preaching. Jesus is a phenomenon that was made manifest, both in his life and after his resurrection, and the kingdom is a phenomenon that was disclosed not only to his disciples and the others who heard him preach but also to those who stand in the light of God. To be sure, we mostly have empty intuitions of the kingdom, but on occasion they are filled, partly or wholly, in such a way as we can glimpse what its full reality might be. So too we may pass from *olam* and *kosmos, orbis terrarum* and *imperium,* to the possibilities of the *basileia.* The Christian is no longer one of those people who, as Maurice Blondel said, "see too clearly to see properly."[28] Reborn, he or she has a gaze that can see the kingdom breaking into the world (and can see Christ as *autobasileia*), and has a calling to develop that adjusted sight through prayer, reception of the sacraments, and living a life through which goodness shines. He or she does not always find a new range of experiences ("mystical experiences," let us say), and often enough blurs his or her gaze by living bluntly. But a Christian always has the chance to experience "experience" anew.[29] As material spirit, Christians can look at the material world and also "experience" the kingdom. What becomes manifest in the world is the possibility of something other than "world."

I do not propose to reject the spiritual senses as attested over the centuries from Origen to Saint John of the Cross and beyond but only to rethink them on the basis of spirit rather than soul. The spiritual senses are quite real, but they do not constitute an inner life that is independent of the external world. In phenomenology, as we have seen, there are three ways in which we can talk about seeing God: (1) by way of various implicit horizons being made explicit, (2) by discerning a pattern that has a teleological unity, that cannot be regarded as purely immanent in consciousness, and that cannot be reduced, and (3) by intuiting a particular region of being in which God reveals himself with the *Evidenz* appropriate to that region. Now, it may be that (2) and even (3) may cue *epochē* and reduction, but it is what is cued that is primarily of interest here. The spiritual senses of intentional analysis do not point us out of this world to another one above or beyond it, whether through inner sight or through a blinding of that sight; rather, they help us pass from "world" to "kingdom." On making the *epochē* and reduction, we see, first, that things are *with* us, not outside us or within us: they are not there to be mastered, and we are not already masters of them. We abide in a relation of mutual constitution—the phenomenon as meaningful, and I as the subject pole of the relation—that exceeds any asymmetric subject-object relation. Perhaps we can even show "from beneath how God constitutes the world."[30] That much Husserl can teach us, and it is a great deal.

However, a Christian who has reflected on what he or she sees and who has made explicit what was only implicit stands in a world that is no longer just a world. If Husserlian phenomenology seeks absolute lack of presuppositions, Christian phenomenology, taking its lead from Saint Bonaventure's *reductio* as much as Husserl's reduction, acknowledges the absolute presupposition, God: the light of God, the power of God to manifest himself, the fleshly manifestation of God in Christ.[31] The transcendental turn, the "inquiring back into the ultimate source of all the formations of knowledge," is to the unconditioned: not the "I" but the Creator of the "I" and all that it engages.[32] One sees oneself not just constituting events as meaningful but, as created, able to constitute creation as meaningful in one's lived relation with it. We begin to glimpse what Jesus meant by "the kingdom," its presence in the world, and above all its many and terrible absences. Here at least *epochē* and reduction do not disengage one from the world, so that one is free to contemplate the kingdom without commitment to it; they place one in a situation so that one may be claimed by the kingdom, emptied of "the natural man" by that claim and pulled ever more deeply into the mystery of Christ. This is not mysticism; it is everyday Christianity, *lived* Christianity, Christianity as *life.* Unless we are mystics, the phenomenality that presses on us is the manner in which phenomena are given to us in faith as well as perception, anticipation, memory, imagination, and other intentional horizons. Yet the language of fulfilled and unfulfilled intentions breaks down when entering the kingdom; instead, one needs to speak now of being overwhelmed and now of desolation. To enter the kingdom is to risk humiliation and death before being raised again.

Of course, what Saint Ignatius Loyola in the "Spiritual Exercises" calls an "application of the senses" is relevant here, for in any religious education, however basic, the imagination and memory are trained.[33] Yet I am not thinking first of all of the need to impress scriptural scenes on the mind and heart but rather of indicating a way in which lived experience can be implicitly oriented by faith and then made explicit, a way of passing from world to kingdom. The kingdom is not given to us as a system of explanation of what happens in this world ("revelation," "miracles," "visions," and so on) or as so many items of knowledge but rather, as George Herbert so beautifully said, as "the land of spices; something understood."[34]

"I can 'see' Christ in the clouds, and the landscape as supported by Christ."

To continue exploring what is involved in this judgment, and to do so more concretely, I want to stay close to a poem, a Petrarchan sonnet, by Gerard Manley Hopkins, "Hurrahing in Harvest," written in September 1877. It was, as he said to his friend Robert Bridges, "the outcome of half an hour of extreme enthusiasm as I walked home alone one day from fishing in the Elwy."[35] In its singular way it offers clues to developing a theology of the senses and a theology of manifestation. Here is the poem:

Summer énds now; now, bárbarous in béauty, the stóoks rise
  Around; up above, what wind-walks! what lovely behaviour
  Of silk-sack clóuds! has wilder, wilful-wávier
Méal-drift moulded ever and melted acróss skies?

I wálk, I líft up, Í lift úp heart, éyes,
  Down all that glory in the heavens to glean our Saviour;
  And, éyes, heárt, what looks, what lips yet gáve you á
Rápturous love's greeting of realer, of rounder replies?

And the azurous hung hills are his wórld-wíelding shoulder
  Majestic—as a stallion stalwart, very-violet-sweet!—
These things, these things were here and but the beholder
  Wánting; whích two whén they ónce méet,
The héart réars wings bóld and bolder
  And hurls for him, O half hurls earth for him off under his feet.[36]

Two straightforward observations should be made to situate the poem and the reading that I propose, a reading less concerned with literary appreciation or evaluation than with continuing the phenomenological theology already introduced. For this poem, like most others, proceeds phenomenologically; it works within *epochē* and reduction. Yet unlike many poems it also extends our notion of reduction: it leads us from world to kingdom. First, I note that Hopkins tells Bridges that he "walked home *alone*" (my emphasis): there is no question of intuiting the presence of Christ on his return from fishing in the Elwy, a claim that Bridges would have found incredible, though one that Hopkins would not have been afraid to put to him had he reason to do so. The poem has bracketed that sort of miraculous event and makes explicit the meaning of Hopkins's relation in faith with Christ. The entire poem is set in the mode of *how,* not *that* or *what;* it is concerned, as we shall see, with how the kingdom manifests itself to the speaker, Hopkins, and how he lives with respect to it. Second, this *how,* this relation in faith, has been educated, specifically by Hopkins's intense formation as a Jesuit, which meant being immersed in the "Spiritual Exercises" of Saint Ignatius Loyola.

Viewed from far enough away, we can see that "Hurrahing in Harvest" was composed between two "long retreats" of thirty days: the first undertaken in 1868, when Hopkins was a novice, and the second in 1881, when he was a tertian. Over the course of his life as a Jesuit he undertook a further twenty retreats, each of eight days. He commented, quite selectively, on the "Spiritual Exercises" in 1881 and less fully in 1883. Of particular importance to Hopkins's poems is the second week of the long retreat. The exercitant meditating on the incarnation of Jesus Christ is directed by Saint Ignatius to follow a particular sort of mental prayer, one that has grown out of the monastic practice of *meditatio,* "the unraveling of something complicated," as Hugh of Saint Victor says, which for Saint Ignatius involves responding in a highly disciplined manner to specific images.[37] The imagination is to be used in *meditatio,* as Richard of Saint Victor reminds us.[38] Saint Ignatius agrees, and asks those taking the retreat to produce a *compositio loci;* for example, "to see in particular the house and rooms of Our Lady, in the city of Nazareth in the province of Galilee," "to listen to what the angel and Our Lady are saying," and then "to see in imagination the road from Nazareth to Bethlehem." The directions are specific: "Consider its length and breadth, whether it is level or winds through valleys and hills. Similarly, look at the place or cave of the nativity: How big is it, or small? How low or high? And how is it furnished?"[39] This "mental prayer," then, is not strictly mental; it involves all the senses. Nor is it neutral phantasy, as Husserl conceives it, for the exercitant posits the reality of the scene he or she imagines.

Hopkins translates Saint Ignatius's instructions, originally written in Spanish and then twice translated into Latin in 1548, on how to conduct the fifth contemplation of the nativity of Jesus. They are clearly of more than usual significance to him:

> The first point is to see the persons with the eye of the imagination, *meditating and contemplating in particular their circumstances* [meditando et contemplando in particulari circumstantias eorum], and from the seeing of them to get some fruit.
>
> Secondly, to hear with my hearing what they say, or might say, and by reflecting on myself to get some fruit.
>
> Thirdly, *to savour and to taste,* by smell and by taste, the infinite delicacy and sweetness of the divinity, of the soul and of the virtues and of the rest of the things that belong to the person whom I am contemplating, and by reflecting on myself to draw hence some fruit.
>
> Fourthly, *to touch* by touching, that is to say to kiss and to embrace the ground where such persons leave their footprints and the places where they recline, always with a view to the fruit that I may draw from thence.[40]

To which Hopkins adds the following glosses on the Latin version:

> "Meditando . . . circumstantias earum" / inferring what they must have been, "contemplando" / observing what they are. . . .
>
> "Odorari" etc—Here he speaks of metaphorical taste and smell. You may suppose each virtue to have its own sweetness—one rich,

> another fresh, a third cordial, like incense, violets, or sweet herbs, or, for taste, like honey, fruit, or wine.
>
> "Tangere" etc—I suppose that St Ignatius means us to do what we might have done if present and not to do what we should not have ventured to have done, and this also shows how strongly he means us to realize the scene. (175–76)

Hopkins is impressed by how strongly Saint Ignatius wants those on retreat "to realize the scene": it is a matter of imagining oneself in the particular material circumstances of the Holy Family. Yet Hopkins distinguishes, perhaps more firmly than Saint Ignatius intended and other than how the medieval tradition usually specifies, between meditation and contemplation.[41] When meditating he takes himself to be instructed to impress the scriptural scene upon his heart and mind, and when contemplating he believes himself to be called to observe what the same people are in themselves. They are to be detached to some degree from the particular scene, which means that they can be reconceived and attached elsewhere: in the clouds, in the hills, anywhere.

Contemplation, as Hopkins conceives it here, is not quite what the monastic tradition has deemed it to be, a loving gaze directed toward the changeless God rather than toward the world, in part because Saint Ignatius has reset the distinction between *meditatio* and *contemplatio* and hence redirected the meaning of "contemplation."[42] No distinction is drawn between active and passive contemplation, for example, as has been standard practice since Denys the Carthusian in the fifteenth century. Contemplation is entirely active, consisting of observation of *what* things are, their quiddity, not of passing beyond the spiritual senses. It is done, as Saint Augustine observes, in faith for the most part, not through a vision.[43] Also, knowingly or unknowingly, Hopkins remains close to Richard of Saint Victor's understanding of the third species of contemplation in *The Mystical Ark:* the grasping of the "quality of invisible things by means of the similitude of visible things" and the knowing of "the invisible things of God by means of visible things of the world."[44] A contemplative may rise higher than this level, although a contemplative *as poet* must always write at this level. Even "Oscura Noche" is pitched, as poem, at the lower level, although it speaks of a higher level of spiritual attainment, passive contemplation.

Some years before writing his commentary on the "Spiritual Exercises," while still at Oxford, Hopkins addressed the theme of contemplation. There are "two kinds of energy" in the mind, he wrote, one concerning the transitional and the other the abiding. Contemplation absorbs the mind, "for contemplation in its absoluteness is impossible unless in a trance and it is enough for the mind to repeat the same energy on the same matter."[45] He then notes that the prayerful gaze in its highest moments is close to the aesthetic gaze, though the latter adds something to it: "Art exacts this energy of contemplation but also the other one, and in fact they are not incompatible" (307). He goes on to talk about the complex relation between form and matter in art, and then steps back and distances himself from transitional energy: "The saner moreover is the act of contemplation as contemplating that wh. really is expressed in the object" (308).

Saint Ignatius seeks to immerse the exercitant in the materiality of a scriptural scene, and Hopkins seems temperamentally inclined to follow him. It is not a question of perceiving, through the spiritual senses (as conceived by Origen and others), the odor of sweetness in divine things, although one may "*suppose* each virtue to have its own sweetness [my emphasis]"; it is an activity of the imagination (rather than, say, the stirring of associations). At the same time, Hopkins also contemplates what is expressed by what he observes. To contemplate is to see properly: the *what* is preceded and carried by the *how.* The best vehicle for this *how,* the young Hopkins says (and it is hard to imagine the older Hopkins entirely disagreeing with him), is art. "Hurrahing in Harvest" certainly keeps an eye on the transitional, while also revolving the essence of what grips his attention. It is contemplative in that Hopkins detaches a biblical person, Christ, from particular scriptural scenes in order to see what "really is expressed" by him.

The poem begins with a strong opening statement, much like some of Horace's odes, yet immediately distances itself from canons of classical elegance: the stooks, bound sheaves of barley, are "barbarous in beauty."[46] They are not Greek, Roman, or Christian but utterly savage in their appearance, as though they have unkempt beards. We are in the midst of an event, or rather two events that come at the same time: "Summer ends now," we are told, and "now, barbarous in beauty, the stooks rise / Around" as Hopkins walks past them. He sharply registers the phenomenality of each: the end of summer in the presence of the stooks, and (in a violent enjambment) how the stooks are giving themselves to him, rising together as one, pointing to the sky, even though they are purely natural and their arrangement suggests a pagan ritual. The sheer beauty of the stooks in the fields around him also encourages the mind to ponder higher things. So Hopkins looks "up above," detaches himself from the world before him. Unlike pagans, he cannot view the harvest without also experiencing how the Bible has used the metaphor, as a figure of impenitence (Jeremiah 8:20) and the end of the world (Matthew 13:39). The eschaton is taken wholly positively here with no fear of judgment or damnation, as there is in "The Wreck of the Deutschland" and some of the terrible sonnets.[47] He sees, first, large clouds with the roughness and bulk of sacks and the smoothness of silk. Like him, they are walking: as below, so above. The clouds pass in a dignified manner along "wind-walks," moving not stiffly but gracefully, calling forth our admiration and even affection ("lovely behaviour," he writes). At least that is what we are likely to think at first. On reflection, it may be that the clouds are wearing sackcloth, and that because of their perfect penitence they are now as smooth as silk. Or again, it may be that the clouds are wearing sacks (from the French *saques*), silk gowns that hang loosely from the shoulders of ladies and flare out a little as they promenade.

The clouds are like the blessèd walking through the heavens in the fullness of the kingdom. Looking higher, Hopkins sees cirrus clouds, wild and wavy, also barbarous in beauty; and we remember that in "Pied Beauty" he praises "All things counter, original, spáre, strange." If he sees as Ruskin does, it is not entirely so, and decidedly not to Ruskin's ends.[48] For he sees with the eye of faith, even when it is not made immediately apparent. Already, in a single glance, the stooks have imaginatively been transformed into "meal-drift," for the high small clouds resemble coarsely ground grain. Hopkins anticipates the separation of the wheat and the chaff in the great judgment (Matthew 3:12) and sees it concretely prefigured now in actual cirrus clouds. Has there been anything more beautiful in this way? Perhaps not, but there surely will be—so the implied answer runs—when we come to speak of the end of time, which will be not in terms of wind but of what the wind stands for, the Holy Spirit. The more we interpret the poem, the more we nudge it closer to the supernatural attitude. To avoid passing wholly over into the supernatural attitude, we must perform the reduction ourselves. "Poetry is in fact speech only employed to carry the inscape of speech for the inscape's sake," Hopkins says, and we need to be able to pass from speech as thetic to speech as inscape, "that is species of individually-distinctive beauty of style."[49] To interpret a poem is always to risk losing the poem as poem.

It is with high anticipation, as well as with memory and faith, that Hopkins begins the second quatrain. Already implicit horizons are beginning to become explicit. "I wálk, I líft up, Í lift úp heart, éyes, / Down all that glory in the heavens to glean our Saviour," he writes. The buoyant first line is saturated with his experience of literature and the Bible, especially the Authorized Version of his Protestant days. As Hopkins walks along the road back to Saint Beuno's College, he follows the hint of the stooks ("rise"), though in his own way. We are likely to think first of Milton's Adam raising his head to the heavens on waking:

> Straight toward heaven my wondering eyes I turned,
> And gazed a while the ample sky, till raised
> By quick instinctive motion up I sprung,
> As thitherward endeavouring, and upright
> Stood on my feet.[50]

Also, though, it is likely that we shall recall the situation of Joseph in prison ("Yet within three days shall Pharaoh *lift up thine head,* and restore three unto thy place" [Genesis 40:13; my emphasis]). Hopkins looks to the heavens in hope of the fullness of the kingdom; it is a release, though, that will come only with the parousia. In the meantime he knows full well the injunction, "*Lift up your eyes,* and look on the fields; for they are white already to harvest" (John 4:35; my emphasis). He does not mechanically repeat scripture but, as the marking of the rhythm makes plain, fully appropriates in his lived body what is said there: "I *líft* up, *Í* lift *úp*" (my emphasis).[51]

Hopkins raises his heart first, and then his eyes: his perception is informed by his heart, which is prior to cognition and is suffused by his attachment to Christ. The poem's focus is Christological; more particularly, it is soteriological and eschatological. The "skies" are now "heavens," and their glory is more than sunlight shining through the clouds; it has become divine majesty. It is there that one can "glean our Saviour," the allusion being to Ruth 2:3, though doubtless mediated by Keats's "To Autumn," now bespeaking the marriage of the soul to Christ, and pointed to indicate that in natural beauty one can find vestiges of Christ. The allusion is not accidental. Matthew tells us that "Booz begat Obed of Ruth" (Matthew 1:5) in the royal line that extends all the way to Joseph, the husband of Mary. Because perception when properly informed can find Christ manifest in the world, Hopkins now addresses his eyes first and then his heart: "And, éyes, héart, what looks, what lips yet gave you a / Rapturous love's greeting of realer, of rounder replies?" Things have changed since "Nondum" (1866) when he wrote, "God, though to Thee our psalm we raise / No answering voice comes from the skies." Now he has an answer. And we also see things differently from "The Wreck of the Deutschland" (1875): there we heard in stanza 5, "For I greet him the days I meet him, and bless when I understand," and now it is Christ who greets Hopkins. Yet in "Hurrahing in Harvest" Hopkins figures this greeting by way of an address to himself—himself as material spirit (physical eyes and spiritual heart)—because he has become the object of a vivid counterintentionality, Christ's. "What you look hard at seems to look hard at you," Hopkins sharply observes in his journal in 1871.[52] More specifically, what at first was the gathering of the *vestigia dei* has suddenly become something more whole and more real than could ever be anticipated. The gleaning has resulting in a rich harvest: Christ greets Hopkins in a manner that could not be "realer" or "rounder." In the "Spiritual Exercises" the contemplation ends with a colloquy that realizes the encounter with Christ; here a colloquy takes place in the middle of the poem, and adumbrates the possibility of other colloquies for other people ("whích two whén they ónce méet").

No poet, unless it was Blake, would say that Jesus Christ has actually appeared in the clouds. To talk of supernatural vision here would be to go badly wrong in reading this poem (but not of course when reading "Jerusalem" by Blake or "Noche Oscura" by Saint John of the Cross). There is no special revelation, only a conversion of the gaze that intensifies the meaning of general, public revelation for the poet. When Hopkins looks at the clouds he passes from speaking simply of himself ("*I* wálk, *I* líft up . . .;" my emphasis) to recognizing "*our* Saviour" (my emphasis). We glide from the self and its world to the possibility of the kingdom, and Hopkins, for whom, like all the living, the kingdom is not yet fully present, can only *glean* Christ in natural beauty, cannot see him whole, and certainly not in his glory. Looking at the clouds, and making implicit intentional horizons explicit, allows Hopkins to say that he "sees" Christ in natural beauty, understands him to be there, finds "that wh. *really* is expressed" by the clouds (my emphasis). He grasps the *morphē* of Christ, not the *hylē* of a resurrected body or tiny droplets of water; there is no intuition of another "phenomenological I," no question of empathy, only an inscape that attracts him, that is part of the "constitutive duet," and that is perhaps aroused by the sort of teleology that Husserl evokes when thinking of the "experience" of God.[53] It is not even a phantasm that he beholds. Husserl tells us that "In lively intuition we 'behold' centaurs, water nymphs, etc.; they stand before us, depart, present themselves from this side and that, sing and dance, and so on. All, however, in the mode of the 'as if.'"[54] There is no "as if" in Hopkins's perception, though: he directly sees an inscape in the clouds that bespeaks a transcendent ordering of the matter of the clouds that he identifies with Christ. "All the world is full of inscape," he writes, "and chance left free to act falls into an order as well as purpose."[55] But perception tires; one must continually refresh one's mind to perceive inscape.[56] Husserl would add that one must repeatedly perform the reduction. It too is a "spiritual exercise."

Instead of speaking of Christ as a fantasy we should speak, rather, of an intentional correlative that has been long since formed in the tradition and is inscribed on the noematic strata of the poet's experience. Christ is made "present in phantasy," to use Husserl's expression, not in the sense of being merely imagined but in the sense of being posited as real from within presentification rather than presentiation, *Vergegenwärtigung* rather than *Gegenwärtigung.*[57] Not that this is merely a subjective projection, for any Catholic with a decent awareness of the iconographic tradition and sufficient piety and imagination would be inclined to "see" the same thing. Not every Catholic sees inscape, however. Hopkins grasps things in his own way and only, it seems, if there is a peculiar and rich beauty that calls to be registered. Let us consider a passage from his journal of 1871. "What is this running instress, so independent of at least the immediate scape of the thing, which unmistakably distinguishes and individualizes things?," he asks himself (215). It is not something purely subjective. "Not imposed outwards from the mind as for instance by melancholy or strong feeling: I easily distinguish that instress" (215). He had known how to do so since he was an undergraduate at Oxford when he was struck by Parmenides' insight that being is and nonbeing is not. "I have often felt when I have been in this mood and felt the depth of an instress or how fast the inscape holds a thing that nothing is so pregnant and straightforward to the truth as simple *yes* and *is.*"[58]

At risk for him now, though, is something that exceeds mood as an opening onto being, though in speaking of mood in this way he anticipates Heidegger on mood, *Stimmung,* or attunement, *Befindlichkeit,* and indeed attunements as triggers to reduction.[59] The instress in question is the power of the divine to hold nature and arrange it in unique and usually hidden patterns, which are nonetheless manifestations of divine transcendence for those who have eyes to see. One might say that when these patterns are experienced through *epochē* and reduction they may be called "inscape." To find inscape in nature is to find spirit in matter; it is the manifestation of God in and through nature, not by way of mystical experience but by way of the spiritual senses as conceived by way of spirit rather than soul. Often inscape is descried in clouds, as Hopkins's journal testifies time and again, although a particularly suggestive passage has him studying it not in the clouds but in trees in early spring, "for the swelling buds carry them to a pitch which the eye could not else *gather*—for out of much much more, out of little not much, out of nothing nothing: in these sprays at all events there is a new world of inscape" (205; my emphasis). There is a sense that at sundry times nature reaches a pitch, there is a ripening of something so that its individuality is distinctly felt; then there is permitted the gleaning of a unique material pattern that has intense religious significance.

I return to the poem. Having raised his eyes in the context of his heart, Hopkins now addresses his eyes first and then his heart: his perception has already been oriented to see not material nature but rather material spirit, Christ in the natural beauty of the clouds. A limit to experience, having to *glean* the Saviour in the clouds, is now overcome by Hopkins passing from being the subject of perception to being the object. The focus is less on a being than on a relationship, one that is concretely experienced in faith. No one has ever given him "rounder" replies because the relationship is of sinner and Saviour, and no one has ever given him "realer" replies because Christ is himself that which is most real. Needless to say, these replies are not audible sounds. With the exception of mystical auditions, such as the one that Margery Kempe claims to have heard, only human beings, who characteristically reply to greetings with far less honesty and less weight in their words, talk to one another in words.[60] God speaks "in the voice of an inward essence through the mind," as Saint Gregory the Great says.[61] Or, in the terms I have been developing, Christ replies fully to Hopkins's greeting by way of his intentional horizons: scripture that he remembers, the kingdom that he anticipates, and the beauty that he perceives. The "replies" exceed any temporal organization of question and response. And even this experience of fullness is linked to a nonexperience: the promise of fulfilled life with Christ in the kingdom. All the same, one material spirit, Hopkins, finds Christ by way of quite another sort of material spirit, inscape.[62]

Lowering his gaze a little, Hopkins sees the mountains, now blue in the distance, and sees them with eyes educated by Ruskin ("azure" being one of the sage's favorite adjectives). Yet he looks with a doubled gaze, at once theological and aesthetic. The hills are described as "azurous," Hopkins's version of "azureous," coming presumably from the Late Latin masculine adjective *azureus.* These hills are "hung," supported from above. Earlier the stooks seemed to "rise," and so directed his gaze to the heavens, and now that Hopkins's heart has informed his perception he realizes that when seen properly, the hills are suspended from the heavens by the will and power of God, who has also decorated them with the blue haze of a late summer afternoon. Held from above, these hills are also a sign of the earth being supported from beneath; they are Christ's "world-wielding shoulder." The one majestic shoulder looks like two hills, one at the top of the arm and the other sloping up toward the neck. This is Christ as the true Atlas, supporting the whole world, and we recall the description of him in stanza 33 of "The Wreck of the Deutschland" as "Our passion-plungèd giant risen." Christ is not phenomenalized here: we do not see him with our physical eyes or with one of the spiritual senses in the older understanding of the expression. Hopkins "sees" Christ on the noematic structure of the phenomenon "Christ as value." How is Christ given to him? In a contradictory manner, it seems, in two profiles at once: "as a stallion stalwart, very-violet-sweet!" What Hopkins sees with his bodily eyes is the saddle of the hills, which suggests the stallion, and he sees it at the coming of evening when the color of the hills changes from azure to violet. This avowal of sweetness is the closest that Hopkins gets in "Hurrahing in Harvest" to the spiritual senses as classically conceived. Christ is "very-violet-sweet," yet we remember the poet's gloss on Saint Ignatius's "Spiritual Exercises": "You may *suppose,*" he tells himself, "each virtue to have its own sweetness—one rich, another fresh, a third cordial, like incense, *violets,* or sweet herbs" (my emphasis).

We have passed from a glimpse of the kingdom to Christ as himself the kingdom, and now the lyric ends with the possibility of anyone, not just Hopkins, recognizing the singular relation that one may have with Christ, of passing from "world" to "kingdom." The next lines show us how this happens. "These things, these things were here and but the beholder / Wánting." The repetition suggests the excitement of what Hopkins calls "pitch" and what, in a quite different register, Husserl calls the conversion of the gaze.[63] But what are "these things"? They are the stooks, the clouds and the hills: reduction does not change what is there to see only how it is seen. ("The question is not what you look at—but how you look & whether you see," as Thoreau said so well.[64]) They were *here,* had been created, and the manifestation of Christ was indicated by the stooks and given through the clouds and hill; only the dative moment of the manifestation, a particular person, was needed for the manifestation to be received. It was always possible not to see these things as "world," as so many representations, but as "kingdom," as a life lived in the emptiness and fullness of a relation with divine love itself. The surprise is that the *kingdom* was here too, not just the natural world, and only someone properly attuned to it was lacking to see it. Once attuned, Hopkins responds to the phenomenality of the kingdom as it breaks into the world.

Something in the stooks, their beauty, and the Greek-Christian association of beauty and elevation urges Hopkins to make the reduction and so "see" the kingdom, and turn him from being merely a viewer, someone who lifts up his eyes, to becoming a "beholder," someone who sees the true significance in what is shown, who contemplates, and is beholden, tied to what he sees. Earthly beauty leads to heavenly Beauty: "I do not think I have ever seen anything more beautiful than the bluebell I have been looking at," Hopkins writes in his journal, "I know the beauty of our

Lord by it."[65] To return to the less elegant language of Husserl, the movement here is from "presentiation" (*Gegenwärtigung*) to "presentification" (*Vergegenwärtigung*). Hopkins has clear, vivid intuition of the landscape's beauty that also gives rise, by way of a highly trained memory for scripture and images, to an anticipation of a higher Beauty that is posited as real. In this poem, however, the movement from beauty to Beauty does not have the structure of a Platonic ascent but rather of a Basilaic temporal paradox: the kingdom is already here but not yet fully here. We can glean Beauty by way of the beauty of the stooks and the clouds, yet once gleaned that Beauty will also be found embodied in the beauty of the hills. The "spiritual senses" as rethought by phenomenology are in constant movement between *Gegenwärtigung* and *Vergegenwärtigung,* between positing the beauty of nature (gleaning what is here) to positing the reality of Christ in Beauty (not yet here). We contemplate that movement, and in doing so we contemplate the kingdom. It happens not in the neutral mode of fantasy but in the shuttling back and forth of presentiation and presentification and, within the latter, from memory to anticipation.

Now, contemplation is not without outcome, as Blondel reminds us: "even in the most 'contemplative' form of activity, *theorein* (contemplating), there is a material fashioned: and this material we sculpt in thinking and willing, is our members and, through them, the milieu where they make their impression."[66] Contemplation changes us, and we change the world. Here the beholder enters the kingdom, to the extent that he can, in joy, and celebrates the moment in making a sonnet, following the tradition of George Herbert, who in *The Temple* (1633) effected the change in sonnets from being secular love poems to religious love poems. In that very moment of entering the kingdom, though, Hopkins realizes that the kingdom has not yet fully come, that there are beholders "Wanting." The Welsh, in fact so many of the British, are not yet in the kingdom or even close to it, though perhaps they are wanting to enter it in an inchoate way. It is not irrelevant that Hopkins, now walking back to the seminary, has been fishing. His background thought is of being a fisher of men ("Come ye after me, and I will make you to become fishers of men" [Mark 1:17]).

In the final three lines we slide from the first to the third person. When someone, anyone, "meets" Christ, it is through the realization that he is already there, invisible, behind the play of representations that make up "the world." The meeting presumes eyes, but the focus is solely on the heart: it "réars wings bóld and bolder." The heart does not *grow* wings; it *rears* them, like a loving parent, and it can do so because it is has been affected and is now affecting. Also, there is a suggestion of a stallion rearing on its back legs, shaking off a burden. Hopkins fully appropriates *Phaedrus* 249d, of course, but also Psalm 55:6 ("Oh that I had wings like a dove! *for then* I would fly away, and be at rest") and perhaps also Isaiah 40:31 ("But they that wait upon the LORD shall renew *their* strength; they shall mount up with wings as eagles"). It is what Richard of Saint Victor calls *sublevatio,* the raising of the mind, except that it is also a raising of the body.[67] The new wings "hurl for him," we are told at first; they throw the earth down with impetuous force, finely captured in the sprung rhythm. Then we hear a modified claim, "O *half* hurl earth for him" (my emphasis). First we experience the feeling of hurling without limit, of pushing down and rising, and only then the realization that even an ecstatic leap can be at best a half measure: we leap to some degree, but not wholly into the clouds to enjoy the fullness of the kingdom. Richard of Saint Victor would say that contemplation through the imagination is insufficient to stay in heaven, that only the highest contemplative "begins to dance and to make gestures in a certain way because of its excess of joy, to make some unique spiritual leaps, to suspend itself above the earth and all earthly things."[68] For Hopkins, though, things are different. It is enough, more than enough, to half hurl oneself, for Christ is also *here,* in the landscape, and is supporting it from beneath. Hopkins hurrahs not only in the time of harvest but also in the act of harvesting Christ and finding him not only above but also below. The kingdom has given itself in anticipation, as much as in other ways. For the kingdom into which he has surely come, indicated by the Society of Jesus and indeed the seminary to which he is walking home after fishing, is not yet fully the kingdom of heaven. Material spirit, a human being, Hopkins must wait until he can become a spirit, though of an infinitely different sort from Christ, who can support the world with instress and appear as inscape: material spirit of quite another kind.

"Hurrahing in Harvest" begins with an ending, and meditates on another ending that has not yet come. It marks the presence of nature and even the glory that is beyond nature, while responding with joy to a presence that has not yet come. It is a lyric of multiple phenomenalities received in different ways: the beauty of nature, the surprise of the kingdom breaking into the world, and the "not yet" of the kingdom and of Christ as kingdom.[69] Hopkins does not subscribe to Tatian's notion of the soul as "material spirit," yet if we talk of "material spirit" to evoke human beings in their intentional life, the expression tells us something about this poem. The different ways in which Hopkins can respond to Christ, the limitations of that response, and that our existence on earth, in the world and in the kingdom, is a middle stage of "already-not yet": our spirit, or rather our soul, is still weighed down. Yet it is still in contact with inscape that gives us glimpses of the kingdom. Divine spirit does not disdain the material: the incarnation bespeaks that its beauty is good and, if looked for properly, the spiritual may be found in what has been created. Indeed, it offers itself here and now to be seen, heard, and touched in anticipation of greater phenomenalities. The theology of manifestation and the theology of the senses, Hopkins teaches us in fourteen lines, are to be found in a theology of the kingdom.

Augustine, Rosenzweig, and the Possibility of Experiencing Miracle

VIRGINIA BURRUS

> And whatever miracle happens in this world, it is certainly a lesser marvel than the whole world, that is to say, the heavens and the earth and all that is in them, which God undoubtedly made. But the manner of its making is as hidden from humanity and as incomprehensible to humanity as is the one who made it. And so although the miracles of the visible world of nature have lost their value for us because we see them continually, still, if we observe them wisely they will be found to be greater miracles than the most extraordinary and unusual events.
>
> **—Augustine, *City of God*** [1]

> How can the possibility of experiencing miracle that arose for us with Creation be recognized within Creation itself? Or, to ask more materially—apparently more materially—where within Creation is the "creature"? . . . Where is the mystery unveiled as miracle?
>
> **—Franz Rosenzweig, *The Star of Redemption*** [2]

At a crucial turning point in his *Star of Redemption,* Franz Rosenzweig raises the question of "the possibility of experiencing miracle." In so doing, he draws inspiration from Augustine's *City of God.* The pursuit of the "trace of Augustine" in Rosenzweig's magnum opus is no easy task, however, as Francesco Paolo Ciglia's recent research in this area has shown.[3] According to Rosenzweig's own framing, *Star* is a work initially conceived "in the form of a biblical commentary" but finally written "under erasure of the text [*unter Weglassung des Texts*]."[4] Editing out his sources, biblical or otherwise, the German-Jewish philosopher hopes to renew them as living speech. Interpretation thus becomes, for him, a (re)voicing of what is latent in writing's silent repose, paralleling the ongoing revelation of creation in time: "What was mute becomes audible, the secret manifest, what was closed opens up, that which as thought had been complete inverts as word into a new beginning" (*SR,* 119). Yet to make manifest is also to put the seal on secrecy; as Elliot Wolfson observes, with respect to Rosenzweig's thought: "the way of speech . . . is to reveal and to conceal, to uncover and to re-cover, not successively, but concurrently."[5] Thus, by rendering Augustine "a living conversation partner," as Ciglia puts it, Rosenzweig simultaneously obscures the textual site of the dialogic encounter.[6] However much obscured, the Augustinian text is no less generative. Elsewhere Rosenzweig adduces the church father as an example of the characteristically Christian tendency to view the text as a mere container of truth, whereas "with us the text is the perpetual site of truth."[7] He arguably reads Augustine least well when he is distancing himself from him: one thing among many that these two writers clearly share is an intense attunement to the performativity of language and a strong linking of linguistic performance with textual interpretation.[8]

The meditation on miracle contains two of the very few explicit references to Augustine in the entire *Star.* Neither constitutes an actual citation or even mentions the title of a work. Nonetheless, these two references carry the weight of testimony in Rosenzweig's incipiently postmodern retrieval of a premodern theory of miracle[9]—a theory that will ground his understanding not only of revelation as such but also of the irreducible relationality, and thus temporality, of divinity, cosmos, and humanity. Other sources for his understanding of miracle might have been named—notably, the medieval Jewish philosopher and poet Yehuda Halevi[10]—but it suits Rosenzweig's broader scheme that it should be a patristic figure who aids in "the transition from the mystery to the miracle" (*SR,* 100), that is, from paganism to revelation. The Christian is, by origin, a converted pagan (*SR,* 419), and the Christian of antiquity still manifests a convert's zeal, he suggests: "no scholastic of the Middle Ages dares to treat the wisdom of the Greeks with such triumphant audacity as does Augustine" (*SR,* 298). For Augustine, who likewise introduces miracle into his *City of God* to mark a transition from paganism to revelation, it is the Hebrews of scripture—Abraham, Moses—who facilitate the shift (*CG* 10.8). Augustinian supersessionism is, then, not only mirrored but deliberately inverted in Rosenzweig's thought.[11]

The question of the influence of Augustine's *City of God* on Rosenzweig's *Star of Redemption* is my necessary (and recurring) starting point; it is not, however, my central concern. Rather, I am drawn by a series of insights regarding temporality, testimony, and materiality that converge on the topic of miracle in and across the thought of Augustine and Rosenzweig. These insights are often missed by interpreters of Augustine's work in particular, many of whom appear to find his enthusiasm for the miraculous an embarrassment at best, and at worst, an infelicitous balance of scientific skepticism and willful credulity ominously resonant with current fundamentalisms.[12] Placing Augustine's "new theology" (as Rowan Greer names it)[13] into renewed conversation with Rosenzweig's "new thinking" (as Rosenzweig himself proclaims it),[14] we may discover something considerably more promising—a breaking open, via the inbreaking of the flesh, of understandings of history, truth, and transcendence. Admittedly, the temporal presumption of this promise may seem a bit shaky: surely any possible Augustinian, if not also Rosenzweigian, transformation of thought—"post-Platonic," "post-Hegelian"—has long since taken place, or it never will. But what interests me is not the progression of thought across time so much as the return of a moment in which thought strains to pitch itself beyond its own limits, a moment of excess and possibility.

It's About Time

Rosenzweig's central placement of the essay on miracle in his *Star of Redemption* may already be read as a dialogic engagement of book 10 of Augustine's twenty-two-book *City of God.* There the discourse of the miraculous is positioned near the close of what Mark Vessey aptly describes as "a laborious critique and overwriting of the cultural encyclopaedia of the Greeks and Romans."[15] Liberally spiked with scriptural allusions, Augustine's discussion of miracles mediates a transition toward what is, if not exactly a "biblical commentary written under erasure of the text" (to borrow Rosenzweig's language), something nonetheless rather similar: in the second half of the work, scriptural citation carries and is carried by a sweeping narration of salvation history that both issues from and returns to "the text as the perpetual site of truth."[16] As Augustine explains elsewhere, the *City of God* can be packaged as either a two- or a five-volume work.[17] What is part 2 on one count (books 11–22) is on the second count subdivided into three volumes in such a way that "four [books] should describe the origin of that City, four its progress, or rather its development, and the four last the ends in store for it."[18] When the topic of miracle arises again—and it does, with irruptive force, in books 21 and 22—it is at the close of the last of the "volumes," at the point where anticipation finally prevails over recollection, and a text increasingly at odds with its own linearity begins to bend time toward eternity.

Whereas Augustine first engages in apologetics and only subsequently unfolds a tripartite account of origins, history, and ends, Rosenzweig has, as it were, subsumed the initial *apologia contra paganos* under an account of pretemporal potentialities in his own more tightly triadic and notably less linear work. The six-pointed "star"—its doubled (and further multiplying) triangulations inscribed with demanding precision—is no mere nickname for the text, nor is it simply an illustrative metaphor. It is, rather, a complex literary incarnation—an incarnation of no less than *all*—and yet not "*the* all" of a philosophy that stretches "from Ionia to Jena," as he puts it (*SR,* 18). Dramatically shifting away from such a long-standing tradition of thought by invoking a renewed exchange of philosophy with theology, Rosenzweig insists on the irreducibility of the triad of God, human, and world, related through the equally irreducible processes of creation, revelation, and redemption. While the success of his intellectual venture may be debated, it is difficult to resist the lure of the attempt to reconfigure totality as a relational multiplicity, temporality as a spiraling dance with eternity. The discussion of miracle lies close to the heart of the literary *Gestalt,* not concluding part 1 (as in Augustine's *City of God*) but introducing—or, rather, initiating—part 2 of the three-part text. Initiating part 2, it opens out onto the entire work. It is with part 2 that "the new thinking's temporality gives rise to its new method,"[19] as Rosenzweig elsewhere observes, and in some sense—in some very important sense—the timeliness of time therein engaged subsumes and transforms the everlasting and the eternal, the protocosmic and the hypercosmic dimensions explored in parts 1 and 3.[20] Miracle is thus positioned not only as the bridge between paganism and revelation, as with Augustine, but also, and more explicitly and emphatically than in Augustine's work, as the point where "time itself happens."[21] Yet perhaps the very differences introduced by Rosenzweig, structural and otherwise, may also be imagined to have taken their cues from Augustine.

Rosenzweig's initial mention of the ancient theologian is brief and almost breezy: "When Augustine, or some other Church Father, had to defend the divinity and truth of revealed religion against pagan attacks and doubts, he rarely neglected to point to miracles" (*SR,* 104). Though at pains to avoid direct citation, even seeming to simulate forgetfulness (was it Augustine or someone else?), Rosenzweig is nonetheless in close conversation with the author of the *City of God* at this point. He doesn't quote chapter and verse, but we can: book 10, chapter 8, provides a plausible starting point. There, as witness against those Platonists who promote the worship of "false gods," Augustine recalls "the miracles done as attestation to God's promises, by which he predicted to Abraham thousands of years ago that all peoples would receive a blessing in his seed." Such a millenia-spanning and seductively open-ended marvel of foretelling seems to lend ready support to Rosenzweig's central proposal that "miracle stands out because it is predicted" (*SR,* 104). Augustine's account of how God allowed Pharaoh's magicians "to perform some miracles so that they might be overcome even more miraculously" (10.8) is, moreover, echoed closely by Rosenzweig's assertion that "Moses' miracles were even more miraculous than the miracles of the adversary"—namely, Pharaoh. Miracles overcome miracles: scriptural wonders not only exceed pagan ones but are also ever exceeding themselves. "It would take too long to mention them all," Augustine protests, having just recited an impressive list (*CG* 10.9). Rosenzweig abbreviates the list but elaborates the point.

As he observes, the logic of intensification that dictates that "the more miraculous it is, the truer it is" runs contrary to modernity's preference for the lesser miracle (*SR,* 104).[22] Such discrepancy rests on another, he argues, namely, the ancient identification of miracle by its signifying power rather than its defiance of natural law. The miracle captures attention not because it disrupts ordinary causality but because it reveals the divine purposefulness that permeates a cosmos that is ever unfolding in time. Rosenzweig admits that "the singular miracle, in a totally miraculous world, totally devoid of laws, and enchanted as it were, could not stand out as miracle" (*SR,* 104). Yet he seems drawn to the view, also endorsed by Augustine, that "the whole world" is a miracle, emerging from beginnings "as hidden from humanity and as incomprehensible to humanity as the one who made it" (*CG* 10.12). Any strangeness or improbability that may attend the miracle is merely "make-up" or "decorative," and thus dispensable (*SR,* 104, 107), insists Rosenzweig. What defines the miracle is its distinctive relation to temporality. "Miracle is essentially 'sign.' . . . Miracle and prophecy go together," he notes succinctly (*SR,* 104–5). Prophecy awaits its fulfillment in miracle, and miracle recalls its origin in prophecy. Miracle thus reveals, through hindsight rebounding as foresight, the inherently providential character of life experienced in time. "Hence the joy in miracle," writes Rosenzweig. "The more miracles there are, the more providence there is" (*SR,* 105).

Although positioned as an end in relation to prophecy's beginning, for Rosenzweig miracle does not inscribe closure but rather marks the openness of time's flow—in which events are predicted only after the fact and thus are never really predictable. In Wolfson's striking phrasing of a similar thought, "the trajectory of time at once circular and linear . . . seems always to lead one back to where one has not been, retracing steps yet to be imprinted."[23] The openness of time in miracle is assured not only by the infinite semiotic potentiality secreted in the abyss of "creation before creation" (*SR,* 119)—the fact that the possibilities for a prophetic fulfillment are limitless—but also by the infinite inpouring of love that saturates the moment, rendering the cosmos radically and inescapably relational. As Rosenzweig puts it, "And precisely unlimited providence—this, the fact that really, without God's will, not a hair falls from a person's head—is the new concept of God that revelation brings; the concept establishes God's relationship to world and humanity with an unequivocalness and unconditionality" (*SR,* 105).[24] This "unequivocal and unconditional" relationality would seem to dictate that not only the future but also the past is indeterminate—that the complexity of causality, arising from the complexity of relationality, is such that there are limitless possible prophecies leading to a particular fulfillment, as it were. Miracle, in Rosenzweig's thought, thus emerges as a figure—one might also say an intensification—of time's redemption, in which "every moment must be ready to receive the plenitude of eternity" (*SR,* 245). Yet it is initially with the bridging of *creation and revelation* and only subsequently with that of *revelation and redemption* that miracle is identified—with the relationship of time to its own elemental primordiality first, and to its transcending eternity second, in other words (*SR,* 117). As Eric Santner observes, Rosenzweig intends that the tilt toward creation will provide the philosophical securing of "the 'materialist' dimension" within the theological understanding of revelation as novel event.[25]

Turning back to the dialogue between Rosenzweig and Augustine, we might now ask how far their agreement can be stretched. Rosenzweig seems to have engaged book 10 of the *City of God* at key points—the link between (and among) prediction, signification, and miracle; the correlation of miracle's intensity with its claim to truth; and the embedding of miracle within creation. At the same time, he has arguably placed more stress, and a different kind of stress, on all of these points by decisively shifting the context of thought. A loosely woven apologetic discourse turned against Platonist theurgy has been dropped into a meticulously crafted theological-philosophical confabulation, where it serves less to refute than to convert the "paganism" of philosophical idealism, while at the same time directly challenging the ongoing reign of nineteenth-century historicism. Clearly, Rosenzweig has taken Augustine's theory of miracle to new places. Might they be places Augustine himself would have been happy to go?

The relation of miracle to creation has often been considered a point of unclarity or inconsistency in Augustine's thought. To some, he seems to conflate the natural and the miraculous in such a way as to render one or both concepts meaningless; to others, he seems to confuse the subjective miracle (that which evokes wonder) with the objective miracle (that to which extraordinary or supernatural causation must be assigned).[26] Without denying either Augustine's inconsistency or his failure to work out a fully satisfying account of the miraculous, I would nonetheless suggest that Rosenzweig's own thought on miracle puts us on the path of "what he [Augustine] was trying to say, what he might have said, or even . . . what he ought to have said," as James Wetzel so nicely limns the productively ambiguous interpretive slide from history of philosophy to philosophy itself.[27] It does so in part because Rosenzweig has already been following Augustine's lead in his theorizing of time: here he is a careful reader of *Confessions* as well as of the *City of God,* as Ciglia has argued.[28] In an early notation, Rosenzweig explicitly credits Augustine with a concept of time that gives weight to the present as prior thought had not, combining aspects of pagan and apocalyptic temporalities so as to situate the present as "the principle of 'past' and 'future.'"[29] The *Star* appears to extend this fundamental Augustinian insight.[30] There, as we have seen, miracle discloses the present moment as the future of a particular past previously unknowable at such. Is it not also the past of a yet unknown future? Spanning the gap by perching at the reversible pivot point of temporality, miracle is the call that responds and the response that calls from within the rupture of time—time gathering time to itself, and thereby spilling beyond itself. As such, miracle is both natural and exceeds nature: it is nature in the self-exceeding of its becoming.

But where, finally, does all of this leave one of Augustine's most famous and most controversial theological innovations, namely, his doctrine of predestination? How can time be open if all that ever was or will be is foreordained? My Rosenzweigian reading of Augustine's theory of time (which is also, of course, an Augustinian reading of Rosenzweig's theory) might seem to falter in the face of such a flat contradiction. Alternatively, it might contribute to opening Augustine's doctrine to new possibilities. Rosenzweig himself acknowledges that miracle so abounds with "unlimited Providence" that it seems thereby to inscribe "the predetermined constraint of the laws of the world" (*SR,* 105). He playfully likens creation to an already packed suitcase that merely awaits unpacking (*SR,* 124). Yet creation *takes time,* he also thereby intimates, and its time—the time of divine self-revelation—runs backward to move forward, redeeming promises shrouded in the mystery of beginnings, plucking life from the overflowing depths of possibility. Although *all may be foreknown*—indeed, all may be both decided and provided for in advance—each moment, unpacked, arrives nonetheless as a gift that both shatters and restores time's certitude. The gift is divine love, both Augustine and Rosenzweig assert, granted and received freely and yet inexorably, and simultaneously free and inexorable precisely because it demands *presence*—because it is "always in the today and entirely in the today." "God always loves only whom and what he loves," writes Rosenzweig, "but what separates his love from an 'all love' is only a 'not-yet'; it is only 'not yet' that God loves everything besides what he already loves" (*SR,* 178). Correspondingly, as the Augustine of both the *Confessions* and the *City of God* might have it, it is only "not yet" that humans submit utterly to God's love by responding fully to "the call to love whole-heartedly in the midst of mortality."[31] Although we know in advance how the story must end (it *is* a romantic comedy, isn't it?), it is precisely the bittersweet suspense of the "not yet" of that end that makes the story uniquely appropriable as *ours.* As Wetzel puts it, "I can confess to my own redemption but not to yours. . . . Confession is always in the first person, always addressed to God, and always a mix of joy and sorrow." Wetzel adds, "In the end, grace may prove irresistible, but love can never be forced. Augustine knew this."[32]

Rosenzweig knew it, too. Poured into time, eternal love overflows the human soul, opening it to "the infinite chaos of the world," so that the "I and thou" of the divine-human love affair triangulates and multiplies into a collective "we" (*SR,* 257). *It is only "not yet."* Such is the stretch of expectation by which eternity continues to seduce time, exposing human hearts, and the cosmos itself, to ever-renewed possibility. It does so against all odds, one might say. It is a miracle that we remember, and still we hope.

In/Credible Witnesses

The miraculous is necessarily singular, so much so that singularity itself may be deemed miraculous. Augustine marvels that, despite the great number of humans and all that they share in common, no two are exactly alike: "each individual has his or her unique individual appearance" (*CG* 21.8). So it is that every miracle must receive unique validation: each requires its own proof, as Rosenzweig notes. The burden of proof falls on the personal testimony of an eyewitness, and preferably more than one eyewitness. Even circumstantial evidence—evidence of the "success" of the miracle—requires the supplement of testimony to its actual miraculousness, that is, to its occurrence as the fulfillment of prediction, in Rosenzweig's terms. To witness is to believe, and to believe is to give witness, demanding belief from others in turn. There is, then, a multiplication of the testimonial in miracle (one could equally say, of the miraculous in testimony): paradoxically, singularity not only creates a multitude—"each individual"—but also amplifies itself through iterative attestation. It draws intensity as well: strong testimony calls for strong belief, and the strongest belief is the belief that has overcome the strongest disbelief. It's a miracle!, we are assured.

But where is the proof of this miracle?, we ask. We *must* ask. (We must not hold credence cheap.) What might best persuade skepticism? In antiquity, witness under oath and witness under torture constitute the strongest forms of testimony, Rosenzweig asserts, with the latter trumping and eventually displacing the former. The higher the price paid to defend belief, the more believable is the witness. The highest price of all: to give one's very life. The excessiveness of such self-expenditure matches that of the miracle to which it gives witness: for the martyr, *imitatio Christi* is more than mere mimesis. It is the strongest testimony matching the strongest miracle and demanding the strongest belief.

When Rosenzweig invokes Augustine directly for the second (and final) time in the essay on miracle, it is in the context of his discussion of the significance of testimony. "So the two proofs, testimony by oath and testimony by blood, blend and, after several centuries, finally became a single proof in Augustine's famous appeal from all single reasons based on the present, historical phenomenon, the *auctoritas ecclesiae,* without which he would accord no credence to scriptural authority" (*SR,* 107). The passage to which he here alludes comes not from the *City of God* but from a treatise entitled *Against the Letter of Manichaeus Called Fundamental,* where Augustine asserts, "For my part, I should not believe the gospel except as moved by the authority of the whole church [*catolicae ecclesiae . . . auctoritas*]" (5). There is no direct mention, we note, of miracle in the original text. Rosenzweig appears to have woven a "famous" line about the credibility of scripture into his continuing dialogue with book 10 of the *City of God,* on the topic of the credibility of (scriptural) miracle. There, Augustine has set up a perplexingly circular argument: miracles attest to the authority of scripture, which commands the worship of the one God alone (*CG* 10.7), yet it is scripture that testifies to miracles—so many they cannot all be recounted (*CG* 10.9; see also 10.8, 13, 17). "Will someone say that these miracles are false and did not take place, but were written as lies?," he asks (*CG* 10.18), apparently intending this as a rhetorical question. All sacrifices to false gods have been put to an end by the sacrifice of the one God who became incarnate, a sacrifice ritually enacted in the sacrament of the Eucharist, he continues. Demonic attempts to force Christians to make sacrifices to false gods have had the happy result of producing martyrs: "the city of God holds such citizens so much the more famous and honorable the more bravely they struggled against the sin of impiety, to the point of shedding their own blood" (*CG* 10.21).

By the time he reaches the topic of martyrdom, Augustine may seem to have drifted away from that of miracle, as it is the problem of false worship on which his own discussion turns. In Rosenzweig's compact rendering, however, the martyrs are made the ultimate witnesses of miracle—first to "the miracle of the empty tomb" and later to "the credibility of those who transmitted the miracle to them" (*SR,* 106–7). By Augustine's day, he suggests, it is possible to point to "the church" as the authoritative embodiment of the testimony of the martyrs. The authority of the church moves Augustine to believe scripture, yet scripture—more specifically, scriptural prophecy (*SR,* 106)—predicts the miracle in which the authority of the church is grounded. If anything, Rosenzweig has accentuated the circularity already present in Augustine's text, thereby refusing a sequential account. The miracle of belief, like the miracle of revelation to which it always already responds, is entirely in the present.

Augustine engages the issue of testimony and credibility more directly and at greater length in book 21 of the *City of God,* where he takes up the perhaps surprising challenge of demonstrating the miracles of hell. His argument—namely, that the damned are punished with eternal bodily suffering—will evoke incredulity, he acknowledges. And indeed, his logic is not particularly convincing. People experience or hear about all kinds of strange and incomprehensible things every day and believe them, so why could they not believe in eternal bodily punishment?, he asks. Moreover, God has created all the miracles of the world (above all, the miracle of creation itself), so why could God not bring about eternal bodily punishment? His appeal to scripture is no more compelling than is the logic of such rhetorical questions: he initially cites the gospels not as testimony to his particular claims about hell but rather as support for his choice to speak of hell before heaven (*CG* 21.2). Ultimately, however, as Thomas Smith argues, "he invites the reader . . . to consider the prospect of a person burning everlastingly not as a horror, nor as an affront to justice, but as a *miraculum,* a wonder wrought by God, akin to but far greater and more significant than those marvels catalogued" in book 21 in an attempt to render hell believable—that is, worms that live in hot springs, salamanders that live in fire, peacocks with nonrotting flesh, fire itself, lime, diamonds, lodestones, and so on (see *CG* 21.2, 4).[33] Under the sheer force of Augustine's insistent marveling, the prospect of unending bodily pain comes to arouse a pleasure neither voyeuristic nor vengeful but rather more purely aesthetic, constituting "the perfect erotic counterweight to that upward-soaring desire that lifts the saints to eternal beatitude." Smith concludes, "Hell is no longer a *res horribilis,* but a *res mirabilis.*"[34] We believe it *because* it seems miraculous, then.

The intensification of pain (as well as of pleasure) fuses body to soul while drawing time to a standstill: this is an enormously significant claim in the theological context of Augustine's work. The divine comedy is doubled and shadowed by tragedy, in other words. Paradoxically, it is that which lies outside time that seems to be fractured, the flow of time that holds us together. Despair and hope split from one another in the lure of time's beyond, a lure and a beyond that are woven into the fabric of temporality itself. And yet despair and hope do not lure in identical ways, and hell and heaven are not simply separate residences in the same eternity. Put differently, not every marvel is a miracle, and this is so not because some events turn out badly but because some events—no matter how much they may amaze—do not open time but close it. Some moments, some lives, are never fulfilled, never so filled with time that they overflow—never fully momentous. That is hell, and hell is real: this Augustine believes. But he cannot prove it. He cannot even offer strong testimony.[35] The arguments of book 21 supporting eternal punishment are predominately refutations, or negations, of opposing viewpoints. However, the *via negativa* is preceded by a road to nowhere, and the aimlessness of the initial chapters of book 21 pulls against the sense of purpose subsequently injected by refutation. It is as if Augustine has deliberately strewn his readers' path with random objects that catch the eye because of their apparent anomaly; in the end, however, they pose no gripping challenge for *belief*, precisely because they are not endowed with meaning. As signifiers, they are empty, lacking a past and thus a future.

They *could* have significance, of course. *All* phenomena within creation "would be a source of astonishment to all who observe them if it were not human habit to restrict wonder at miracles to the rarities," he does not tire of repeating (*CG* 21.8). Even rarities can function both to remind us of all that we will never understand about our world and to open up new insight—as has recently been the case, for example, with the discovery (or perhaps, given Augustine's own testimony, *re*discovery!) of worms living in oceanic hot springs who not only survive extreme heat but also "photosynthesize" without light, something previously believed impossible.[36] However, Augustine's own worms take us nowhere, nor are they meant to: neither he nor his supposedly incredulous interlocutors seriously doubt that they exist or that they are in some unknown but potentially knowable way well adapted to their hot bath; they are merely odd, not incredible, thus placing no serious tax on belief (*CG* 21.2). Tellingly, a brief imaginative experiment with placing the odd worms in hell itself via invocation of Mark 9:42 ("their worm never dies and their fire does not go out") fizzles when Augustine refuses to press the issue: "Then let each one choose the alternative he prefers; he may think either that the worm, along with the fire, refers, in the literal sense, to the bodily punishment, or that it refers to the punishment of the soul, the word being used by a transference of the sense from the material to the immaterial" (*CG* 21.9). By this point, he has apparently grown weary of tallying the inexplicable oddities that he claims either to have witnessed himself, to have heard attested by a reliable source or a less reliable one, or to have merely read about in texts of varying authority. He may seem to be assessing the relative degrees of credibility claimed by the various sorts of testimony he has collected, but he does so only in order to profess ultimate indifference. The longer his list of marvels grows, the less it draws his interest: his readers may believe these things or not, he says, adding that he himself does not believe all of them (*CG* 21.7). The rhetorical force of his discussion of miracles in book 21, undertaken to evoke belief in hell, is thus that of *strategically failed testimony,* I would suggest.

Augustine has worn down incredulity, but he has equally worn down credulity. To the extent that we believe in hell, we do so not because of the effective witness of Augustine's own belief but because we are too tired to care anymore—or perhaps because it is simply a relief to believe *something.* Either way, belief in hell is a weak belief, responding to a text that has drained itself of testimonial power. If hell is a miracle, this is, paradoxically, because it is a world without miracle—impossible impossibility. So it is that hell must come first, as Augustine insists: possibility must arise from impossibility, belief from unbelief, creation from nothing. Hell must also come at the end of time, for it *is* the very ending of time.

Yet Augustine is not, of course, finished. After the ending of time comes the end of ends, after the pain of hell the pleasures of the heavenly city—after book 21, book 22. Turning to a topic of such infinite promise (where, indeed, God's promises and his own converge [*CG* 22.1]), he begins finally to tell of miracles satisfyingly incredible—thus, worth believing. Rather than wearying their narrator, they intensify his excitement: he can't get enough, it seems. Indeed, the miracles that pave the imaginative path to heaven multiply at a dizzying rate. The sense of immediacy is striking, and to many modern readers off-putting. Whereas the account of miracles in book 10 weaves time on the sturdy loom of scriptural memory, and that of book 21 threatens to shut time down with merely "natural" anomalies, book 22 attempts, audaciously, to give testimony to *present* miracles in such a way as to draw eternity deep into time's materiality—sometimes to grotesque effect, as we shall see.

In chapter 8, a veritable *libellus miraculorum,* Augustine begins by explicitly addressing the question of the relation of scriptural miracles to others. The scriptures enact a perfect testimony, he affirms, at once predicting and fulfilling the central miracle of faith and disseminating that witness throughout the world; but that does not mean that miracles have ceased. Revelation continues, yet the ongoing irruption of marvelous events is typically overlooked even by the people in the very communities where the events occur. Relatively well known, he avers, is the case of the blind man of Milan whose sight was restored when the bodies of the martyrs Protasius and Gervasius were discovered by Bishop Ambrose. Less well known, however, is the astonishing cure of a deeply buried rectal fistula that Augustine himself has, astonishingly, witnessed personally—and now narrates at surprising length. By the time he has finished, a man's very rectum has born witness to a multitude, its scars offering testimony to the mysterious depths of pain, disclosing the limits of human arts of healing and the possibilities that exceed those limits: "The bandages were untied; the place was bared. The surgeon examined it, and knife in hand ready for the incision, he searched for the fistula that was to be cut. He inspected it closely; felt it with his fingers; then he examined it in every way—he found it to be firmly cicatrized. The rejoicing that followed, the thanksgiving to God . . . —all this I have not the words to express." This strange story swiftly gives rise to other tales of healing: breast cancer, gout, hernias, demonic infestations, paralysis, coma, and a dislodged eyeball are all among the ills miraculously cured yet too little talked about, Augustine feels. An underdressed man is unexpectedly granted money for a coat. Children's corpses are revived, and this happens more than once. In the face of such excess, Augustine is beside himself: "Now what am I to do? . . . I cannot relate all the stories of miracles that I know." Yet he also cannot resist sharing a few more. Indeed, he seems quite overwhelmed by the impossibility of his self-appointed task of making *all* miracles known to *all:* God knows he has tried, but it is simply not feasible for any bishop, however diligent, to impress these tales on the memories of the entirety of God's people. Even those who have heard the stories "do not keep in their minds what they have heard" (*GC* 22.8).

At the end of the end of an already overlong work, Augustine thus pulls out all the stops in giving witness to his credulity and attempting to evoke our own. Many of the miracles he here attests may be less astonishing than the existence of worms in hot springs, for example, but they offer something that the worms of book 21 do not—*stories* that lend temporal depth to an event. These stories testify to the possibility that pain might *not* be everlasting: they push back against incredulity, demanding belief; they push back against despair, seducing hope; they push back against divine indifference, provoking love. Such strong, insistent testimony draws belief toward its outermost limit—eternal joy.

Believing Is Seeing

Both the *City of God* and the *Star of Redemption* end with visions of what might be described as "a totally miraculous world" (*SR,* 104), in which the miraculous is nonetheless perceptible as such. Rosenzweig brings us to the "gateway of eternal life," as he names it. Here the articulated temporality of speech gives way to the timelessness of visual communion occurring at "that border of life" where eternity impinges on time—where God can be glimpsed. And what does God look like? Like light, like a face: a shining face peering out from an overwrought astral symbol, at once mirror and metaphor for the human—blatantly and almost parodically so, as Rosenzweig composes the scene. To meet God face-to-face, then, is to encounter the naked truth that God can only be revealed in and as the masking of becoming, through the poetics of figuration, argues Wolfson.[37] Indeed, the star is not a symbol of God per se but rather presents the all of existence in its mobile and enmeshed relatedness—"countenance that looks upon me and from out of which I look." At the end of time we are also still in its middle, then. Rosenzweig continues: "But what he gave me to see in this beyond of life is—nothing different than what I was permitted to perceive already in the center of life; the difference is only that I see it, no longer merely hear." At the end of time, we are also back at the silent beginning, as Rosenzweig reminds us as well: "And this last is not the last, but that which is always near, the nearest; not the last then, but the first. How difficult is such a first! How difficult is every beginning!" (*SR,* 446–47).

Whereas Rosenzweig offers a meticulously drawn *Gestalt* of the abundance of life lived outside time (which is also to say in its center), Augustine, perhaps foolishly, attempts a more literal rendering—depicted in the realest of real times, as it were[38]—in which horror and wonder, beauty and the grotesque become very nearly indistinguishable. The prematurely born, the cannibalistically ingested, the gapingly wounded, the fat and the thin, short and tall—all of these challenges (and more) he considers as he grapples with the concept of bodily resurrection (*CG* 22.13–20); he considers too the fundamental problem of the apparent too-muchness resulting from eternity's all-at-onceness: just imagine the pile-up of hair and fingernails!, he urges (*CG* 22.19). Yet Augustine is convinced that the resurrected saints will rejoice in gazing on one another and that they will see not excess flesh but exceeding beauty—divine beauty. Indeed, the saints will see God "*in* the body itself [*in ipso corpore*]." Will they also see God "*by means of* the body [*per corpus*]"?, he wonders (my emphasis). If so, will their eternal eyelids never close? Alternatively, if they look with spiritual sight, what *is* this, and how does it relate to bodily seeing? While professing uncertainty, he is inclined to imagine that spiritual sight is something akin to the ability to sense the life force (*vita*) invisibly animating visible bodies: "Perhaps God will be known and visible to us in such a way as to be spiritually seen by each one of us in each one of us, seen by the one in the other, seen in him or herself, seen in the new heaven and the new earth, seen in the whole creation as it will be, seen also through bodies in every body, wherever the eyes of the spiritual body are directed with their penetrating gaze" (*CG* 22.29). Like Rosenzweig, Augustine here seems to embrace, through the medium of vision, a thoroughgoing panentheism that approaches a mystical atheism[39] while turning aside from it at the same time—with the full ambivalence of a love that both does and does not desire to reach its end in absolute dissolution.[40] To meet the divine "face-to-face," to see through the eyes of love, is to perceive God *fully embodied in creation,* and to do so from the vantage point that is no vantage point, namely, from the vantage point of one's own embeddedness in creation.[41] To perceive bodies in their—no, in *our*—plenitudinous excess and poignant finitude—to live fully in the eternity of *this* day—is already to see God. Is it then also to *be* God, however partially and imperfectly—*however in need of all of the rest*?

Excess and Possibility; or, The Scar of Redemption

Augustine's critics pronounce him lamentably credulous with regard to miracle. They worry that his views not only reflect but also hasten the demise of science and rationality, surrendering nature to the arbitrary tyranny of the supernatural. Reading him in renewed conversation with Rosenzweig, I am suggesting something different, namely, that Augustine's doctrine of miracle seeks "to ask more materially—apparently more materially—where within Creation is the 'creature'" (*SR,* 118). As Greer phrases it, "Augustine can distinguish between two modes of God's creative power, the natural and the miraculous"; however, "the two modes tend to fuse together."[42] The reason is not only, I think, that Augustine often deploys a definition of miracle as largely subjective, a measure as much of the human capacity for submitting to wonder as of the wondrousness of creation. It is also because his objective understanding of creativity and creatureliness requires that these modes "tend to fuse together" and also that they never quite do so: nature, in this view, is ever exceeding itself. The distinctions between the subjective and the objective collapse, moreover: we cannot remain outside the frame of creation, as if disinterested observers. If miracle happens, it happens in the present, and it demands our presence.

Rosenzweig initially dismisses the merely "decorative" miracle, yet he pursues the beauty of life apprehended through belief. *Vertrauen*—belief, faith, trust—"is the easiest of all, and just for that reason the hardest," he writes on the last page of the *Star.* "It dares at every moment to say Truly to Truth" (*SR,* 447). For Augustine, there arguably remains nothing but *decor,* or beauty, when belief in the miracle of divine creativity finally overcomes resistant skepticism—when it finally says "Truly to Truth." So it is that the goods of creation are not to be exploited for other ends but enjoyed solely for their inherent loveliness: "necessity must surely pass away and the time will come when we shall enjoy each other's beauty alone, without any lust" (*CG* 22.24). Exemplary in this respect are female genitalia (most commodified of body parts!), which will ultimately exchange procreative functionality for a renewed beauty *(adcommodata . . . decori novo* [*CG* 22.17]), becoming as sheerly and delightfully decorative as male nipples currently are (*CG* 22.24), he asserts. Even outright insults to beauty will become pleasurable to viewers: because of the intensity of love directed toward the blessed martyrs, "we will want to see the scars [*cicatrices*] of the wounds on their bodies," Augustine insists, adding that "the signs [*indicia*] of their glorious wounds will be perceived in that immortal flesh." The very histories of suffering inscribed on beloved bodies will be rendered beautiful, then—and all bodies will be beloved, in the end of ends. (It is at this point that pain acquires the significance that it lacks in Augustine's "hell.") Citing the gospel passage to which Rosenzweig also alludes in his testimony to the providential character of miracle (*SR,* 105), Augustine acknowledges that God has promised that "the hair of your head will not perish" (see Luke 21:18). Loving each particle of creation, God will preserve all—including what might have appeared to be defects but are now revealed as "signs [*indicia*] of virtue" (*CG* 22.19).

Here we double back on Rosenzweig's definition: "Miracle is essentially 'sign' [*Zeichen*]." A thickening within time, its density draws our attention like a scar. Like a scar, it has a story to tell—a story like no other, because written in flesh. Witnessing to the promise of the past, miracle, like a scar, carries memory into the future of an ever-emerging present; "hyperbolically, it both conjures and reveals," as Karmen MacKendrick phrases it.[43] Miracle conjures and reveals, uncovers and re-covers, "the 'creature' within Creation" precisely by manifesting the extraordinary harbored within the ordinary, the novelty emerging from the already ongoing, the self-exceeding capacity of nature's relationality—and the pain that *may* give rise to joy. If miracle calls for belief in unbelievable possibility, it does so not by transcending the material but by turning back toward it. "And whatever miracle happens in this world, it is certainly a lesser marvel than the whole world, that is to say, the heavens and the earth and all that is in them" (*CG* 10.12).

Here at the end (and without making a new beginning), I must acknowledge the possibility that I have finally floated dangerously free of the material histories of Christianity and Judaism, precisely by performing a reading of Rosenzweig reading Augustine that is *also* a reading of Augustine reading Rosenzweig. The danger, as I perceive it, lies not with the implication that time is reversible—for is the past not "as much determined by the present as the present by the past," as Wolfson puts it?[44]—but rather with the implication that Augustine's and Rosenzweig's mutually resistant supersessionisms are symmetric and can thus be innocently nudged into renewed (and perhaps suspiciously optimistic) conversation. Should not Rosenzweig's resistance to any Christianizing appropriation in particular be respected? If I have taken the risk of such possibly inappropriate appropriation, it is not only because I am lured by the ambition of Rosenzweig's own performative dialogism—"continuous translations, a constant shift of points of view," in Amos Funkenstein's words[45]—but also, and more specifically, because I understand myself to have undertaken less a Christianizing of Rosenzweig than a Judaizing of Augustine,[46] crossing back across a hermeneutical path opened by Rosenzweig himself. Interpretive possibilities arise not when these two thinkers simply converge and confirm one another—it is not a matter of "identification"—but when they can be imagined to engage and exceed one another. As I have tried to suggest, the theory of miracle is one such point: if we can "hear" the account of miracle dialogically, reading across *and thus also beyond* Augustine's and Rosenzweig's texts, we may be drawn to a more profound insight into the materiality of transcendence and the transcendence of materiality.

"Come forth into the light of things"

Material Spirit as Negative Ecopoetics

KATE RIGBY

The figure of light, along with the darkness that is implicitly or explicitly always summoned as its opposite, has played a central and hitherto under-researched role in the history of Euro-Western dualism, the discursive structures and social ramifications of which have been the target of numerous cultural critiques (variously, and in various conjunctions, deconstructive, feminist, postcolonial, antiracist, queer, ecophilosophical, and zoocritical) since the 1970s.[1] Emerging from its mythic association with a series of solar deities and their kingly representatives on earth in the ancient agrarian civilizations of the Mediterranean region, and set to work metaphysically within classical Greek and patristic thought, light came to lord it over the darkness of error, ignorance, flesh, matter, and death as a key trope of truth, knowledge, mind, spirit, and life eternal—a symbolic supremacy that has not gone unchallenged, however, most notably perhaps by the discourse of divine darkness within Christian mysticism of the *via negativa* (a path to which I too will return toward the end of this discussion). The modest contribution to the tropology of light that I wish to make here emerges from my engagement with ecocritical theory at the intersection of literary and religious studies. Taking my cue from the speaker in William Wordsworth's poem "The Tables Turned," who exhorts his bookish friend to "come forth into the light of things," this essay elaborates the theory of "negative ecopoetics"[2] in the direction of a neomaterialist ethics of things that unsettles conventional spirit-matter dualism. The path I take back to Romanticism is nonetheless a circuitous one, progressing by way of an earlier kind of materialism, namely, the historical materialism first articulated on a large scale by Karl Marx, in the light of which the poetics of nature has often been viewed with grave suspicion. Because I remain hopeful of eventually reconciling these two materialisms—the ecopoetic and the sociohistorical—it is with such suspicions that I want to begin.

The most obvious, long-standing, and still politically salient Marxist objection to ecopoetics is stated in a typically punchy manner in Bertolt Brecht's influential poem, "An die Nachgebornen" ("To those born later"):

> Truly, I live in dark [*finstere*] times!
> An artless word is foolish. An unlined brow
> Signals insouciance. He who laughs
> Has not yet received
> The terrible news.
>
> What times are these, in which
> A conversation about trees is almost a crime
> For it entails a silence about so much wrongdoing![3]

Penned in 1937 in Denmark, where Brecht had sought refuge from Nazi persecution, this text poses the crucial question, one with which we too must grapple in our own dark times, of what manner of being and speaking is called for in response to the dire exigencies of the historical hour. For Brecht, that hour, which was not merely *dunkel* but *finster,* "deeply dark," or "pitch black," as we say in English, was defined by the rise of fascism, bringing to a head, as he fondly believed, the conflict between capitalist exploitation and communist confraternity, in which the latter would ultimately be victorious. It is to the imagined beneficiaries of this revolutionary reordering of society, who would, he hoped, once again be able to talk of trees with a clear conscience, that the poem is addressed. The coming crisis is imaged here on the biblical model of redemptive violence as a deluge, and the speaker appeals to those whom he imagines resurfacing from this flood not to judge too harshly those who will have gone down in it. For he recognizes with anguish, but also, it seems, in the spirit of quasi-Leninist apologia, how

> Even the hatred of meanness
> Distorts ones features
> Even anger against injustice
> Makes the voice hoarse. Oh,
> We who sought to prepare the ground for friendliness
> Could not ourselves be friendly.

For the communist writer in exile, one of the things that had to be forfeited was that mode of lyrical poetry that sang the praises of the natural, or at any rate more-than-human, world: *Naturlyrik,* in German. If this was, as he put it in another poem penned on the eve of World War II, a "bad time for poetry" (*schlechte Zeit für Lyrik*), it was, in his assessment, absolutely no time for *Naturlyrik.* While the speaker here acknowledges an inner conflict between "delight at the apple tree in blossom / And horror at the speeches of the house-painter" (that is, Hitler), he concludes that it was only the latter that propelled him to his desk.

In our own day, there are still some who take all talk of trees to imply a virtually criminal silence regarding "so much wrongdoing," whether in the guise of social inequity, economic exploitation, political repression, military conflict, or all of these and others besides. Indeed, there are even some ecocritics who, in their well-warranted concern for environmental justice, are wary of those who persist in singing the praises of earth and sky.[4] I agree that some modes of so-called nature writing certainly do tend to ideologically screen out the sociopolitical and economic dimensions of the current planetary emergency. Moreover, as Val Plumwood argues, under the conditions of capitalist globalization, nature writers in affluent societies whose work celebrates their own special "home" places while disregarding the many, frequently far distant "shadow" places that provide for them materially, risk perpetuating an insidious mind-body dualism.[5] I would nonetheless contend that the opposition assumed by Brecht, namely, between delighting in the more-than-human world and addressing the pressing sociopolitical ills of the day, was and remains a false one. Moreover, at a time of growing ecosocial imperilment, to fall silent about trees altogether would surely be the greater crime, since in our day "so much wrongdoing" afflicts most grievously other-than-human life, and in doing so blights also the existence of many humans, especially those who are already socially disadvantaged, not to mention those yet to be born.[6]

This is hardly a new insight. Hans Magnus Enzensberger, in a bitter reprise of Brecht's address "To those born later" from 1964, refigures the flood in terms of the tide of technological "progress," which, above all in the guise of nuclear weapons of mass destruction, now threatened the very possibility of future generations: "just who is going to resurface from this flood," the speaker of Enzensberger's "Weiterung" ("Consequence") wonders, "if we go down in it?"[7] In another, less well-known poem from this time, "Zwei Fehler" ("Two Errors"), Enzensberger acknowledges the inefficacy of "shooting at canons with sparrows," while nonetheless insisting that to shoot canons at sparrows was simply to fall into the reverse error.[8] In fact, in view of the interconnections between the technoscientific domination of nature and the socioeconomic exploitation of subordinate humans disclosed by Brecht's fellow exiles, Theodor Adorno and Max Horkheimer, in *The Dialectic of Enlightenment,* the error was precisely to imagine that it was necessary to choose between the poetics of nature and the politics of human emancipation in the first place. The burden of Adorno's and Horkheimer's critique, as I read it (as of Ernst Bloch's considerably more upbeat "principle of hope"[9]), is that human freedom, equality, and solidarity cannot be achieved without simultaneously liberating nature, both "inner" and "outer," as they put it, from the tyranny of a narrowly instrumental rationality. From this perspective, even in the face of fascism, Brecht should never have disavowed that conversation about trees: in doing so, he abandoned the song of the earth, "the song of delight in the many forms of life with which we all share our physical world," as Raymond Williams puts it in *The Country and the City,* "to the confident enemies of all significant and actual independence and renewal."[10] This was a symptomatic abandonment, moreover, and one that contributed to the ecological blindness of the "real existing socialist" state where Brecht made his home after the war (and where, incidentally, he returned to writing *Naturlyrik,* whether because he thought the time had come when he could do so with a clear conscience or as a subtle mode of resistance to the instrumental rationality of the ruling regime I leave to Brecht scholars to debate.)

Today, as forests fall to bulldozers and go up in flames at an unprecedented rate globally, and as we hear with dismay of the threat posed by global warming to the great tropical rain forests that ecologists tells us are crucial climatic regulators of the earth as well as treasure troves of biodiversity, the conversation about trees that Brecht understandably but shortsightedly wished to postpone is more pressing than ever. But for that very reason it has also never been as problematic. In the midst of this unfolding ecocide, I am powerfully reminded of Adorno's words on the crisis of art in the wake of the Shoah:

> The more total society becomes, the greater the reification of the mind and the more paradoxical its attempt to escape reification on its own. Even the most extreme consciousness of doom threatens to degenerate into idle chatter. Cultural criticism finds itself faced with the final stage of the dialectic of culture and barbarism. To write poetry after Auschwitz is barbaric. And this corrodes even the knowledge of why it has become impossible to write poetry today.[11]

Read in its wider argumentative context, Adorno is not necessarily announcing the end of poetry per se here. Rather, he is insisting that if it is not to "degenerate into idle chatter," literature, along with other forms of art, needs to acknowledge its own failure, both to prevent a repeat of the unspeakable horror of the Nazi extermination camps and to adequately respond to it in an aesthetic medium. As Elaine Martin has recently argued, Adorno

> calls for a form of art, which bears witness to its predestined failure, artworks which present the fact that the "unrepresentable" exists. Adorno's dialectic emphasizes the indispensability of that which it simultaneously deems impossible, it demands the pursuit of that which it deems futile.[12]

If, in George Steiner's words, the Shoah confronted humanists with the devastating realization that "a man can read Goethe or Rilke in the evening . . . and go to his day's work at Auschwitz in the morning,"[13] so too ecocritics must acknowledge that a woman might well read Wordsworth or Thoreau in the evening (in the somewhat unlikely event that she has any time for reading at all) and go to her day's work for Exxon-Mobil in the morning—and, for that matter, I would not be at all surprised to encounter a Japanese whaling executive with a taste for Basho. And yet, for all that, as I began by arguing, this of all times is no time to abandon the song of the earth. We might have grown wary of that hoary old metaphysical abstraction, "nature," an invention of settler civilizations unknown to hunter-gatherer societies, which, as Plumwood suggested some years ago, we would be able to dispense with altogether in a fully ecological culture,[14] but the plight of the earth's waters, forests, soils, and atmosphere, and of those myriad creatures, human and otherwise, whose life depends on them, obliges us to utterance, even though we know that our words, no matter how artfully wrought, are bound to be insufficient either to prevent or to bespeak the unprecedented horror of the ecocide of which we ourselves are both victims and perpetrators.[15]

In their ardent desire to make the conditions under which a diversity of other-than-human beings could still flourish a matter of concern in the humanities, many prominent early ecocritics, above all in the United States, turned to the genre of nonfiction "nature writing," as it became known, as a privileged modality of environmental literature.[16] Now, there is much to be said in favor of this ecocritical countercanon, as Marxist ecocritic Lance Newman, for example, has shown with regard to Thoreau, widely regarded as the founding father of the genre.[17] What was generally said, however, was that this kind of writing was to be valued above all for its mimetic qualities, its ability to reconnect us with nature by rendering a faithful account of personal encounters with nonhuman others, preferably in nonindustrialized places. This resurgent literalism gave ecocriticism a bad name among those with a taste for modernist art and a commitment to poststructuralist theory, for whom the opacity of the text was a core tenet of belief.[18] Meanwhile, the tendency among some first-wave ecocritics to privilege wilderness and rurality was rightly viewed with suspicion on both postcolonial and ecopolitical grounds.[19] From my perspective, though, the primary problem with what Timothy Morton in *Ecology without Nature* derisively terms "ecomimesis" is the disrespect it pays to the materiality of the more-than-human that is implicit in the premise that merely human words can adequately mediate or correspond to it. Like Morton, I think that ecocritics could do with a good dose of Derrida on language as a locus of absence, slippage, and *différance.*[20] But we might also do well to listen more closely to Adorno, notably when he declares in his *Aesthetic Theory* that "words tend to bounce off nature as they try to deliver nature's language into the hands of another language foreign to it."[21] "Naturalistic art," in Adorno's harsh judgment, "attains only a specious affinity with nature because, like industrial production, it reduces nature to raw material."[22] In a world of ever-increasing hyperreality, in which the other-than-human is at risk of being utterly obliterated by things of human construction (at least at the level of human regard), the recognition of the incommensurability of the written text with that to which it responds is crucial if we are to guard against the toxic logic of substitution. The ecomimetic insistence on the capacity of really good writing to truly render the embodied experience of nature, far from bringing us any closer to the other-than-human, simply seduces us into an idolatry of the text: while claiming to celebrate nature, ecomimesis actually celebrates the human capacity to capture the other-than-human in writing. The logical conclusion of such ecomimetic idolatry would be virtual reality, in which the experience of anything outside your own head is made redundant by means of a perfect simulation. From this perspective, it is the very inadequacy of literature as a vehicle of representation or mode or response and, more specifically, the capacity of the literary text to foreground that inadequacy that is its saving grace.

This, then, is the necessary, or structural, negativity that is proper to ecopoetics. Mary Oliver puts it rather well, and with admirable simplicity. "Writing," in her assessment, "is neither vibrant life nor docile artifact but a text that would put all its money on the hope of suggestion. Come with me into the field of sunflowers is a better line than anything you will find here, and the sunflowers themselves are more wonderful than any words about them."[23] Coming from a poet, this statement might sound like an admission of defeat. But Mary Oliver is clearly not about to lay down her pen, nor should she. As I read it, much of her poetry does in fact say in a host of different ways precisely what she says it cannot say: her writing invites the reader, again and again, to come with her "into the field of sunflowers," as indeed the speaker does in "The Sunflowers,"[24] or into the woods or down to the swamp. At the same time, her writing reminds us that we can't take up that invitation literally: writing is "not vibrant life," and the very fact that we are reading it implies that the author is not with us in person to take us for a stroll. But her writing might incite us to pay greater attention in whatever ways we can to where and how and with whom we currently find ourselves emplaced and enmeshed, and it is on a response such as this that the work of negative ecopoetics would put all its money.

Let me be clear: when I talk about ecopoetic "negativity," or, in Jean-Louis Chrétien's terms, of literature's "falling short," I want these words to be understood in a positive sense. I am not saying that we should all be doing something else (although, as it happens, I don't think that writing and reading literature is all that we should be doing). What I am saying, though, is that it is only to the extent that the text does not deliver what it promises, if that promise is an embodied experience of the more-than-human world, that it might incline us to do something other than simply read, prompting us, as Yves Bonnefoy puts it, to "lift our eyes from the page."[25] Does this mean that I agree with Adorno that only avant-garde abstract art, in its radical negation of representation, will do? Well, no. Because this is not so much a question of form as of positioning: how the text situates itself, or is situated by readers, vis-à-vis the more-than-human world. In fact, I don't see how any text is going to be able to chip a hole in the wall of human self-enclosure behind which we—and here I am referring also, and pointedly, to "we" literary critics and cultural theorists—have for too long been huddling if it does not engage our interest in the other-than-human by naming it in some way. In other words, ecopoetic writing is obliged to both deploy and destroy ecomimesis, crossing out, as it were, the very words with which it names that to which it urges us to attend. Writing, then, is not vibrant life, but neither is it a docile artifact. For better or for worse, writing has force, inflecting our perceptions and deflecting our attention away from some things and toward others. "Language never replicates extratextual landscapes," Lawrence Buell freely acknowledges in *The Future of Environmental Criticism,* "but it can be bent towards or away from them."[26] Yet it is only to the extent that it does not hold us spellbound by its own verbal constructions, luring us into the belief that vibrant life really does lurk right there in the text, that poetic language has the capacity to interrupt our reading and turn our gaze to the more-than human world beyond the page (which, needless to say, we can only ever perceive with human, all-too-human eyes, eyes that have learned to look in certain ways, moreover, within a world of human words).

The genealogy of negative ecopoetics is, in part, Romantic, and as such is intimately entwined with the Romantic revaluation of materiality.[27] Let me turn, then, to "The Tables Turned," Wordsworth's early manifesto of Romantic ecopoetics, which opens, paradoxically enough, with an exhortation to quit reading:

> Up! up! my Friend, and quit your books;
> Or surely you'll grow double:
> Up! up! my Friend, and clear your looks;
> Why all this toil and trouble?
>
> The sun, above the mountain's head,
> A freshening lustre mellow
> Through all the long green fields has spread,
> His first sweet evening yellow.
>
> Books! 'tis a dull and endless strife;
> Come, hear the woodland linnet,
> How sweet his music! On my life,
> There's more of wisdom in it.
>
> And hark! How blithe the throstle sings!
> He, too, is no mean preacher;
> Come forth into the light of things,
> Let Nature be your Teacher.[28]

Admittedly, the language and sentiments tend to sound corny in the twenty-first century—in fact, it's impossible to recite this poem, as I recklessly persist in doing in my first-year Romanticism lectures, without a note of parody. But there is one word here that prevents us from discounting the whole thing as hopelessly kitsch, demanding rather that we revise our too hasty assumptions about what went before, and that is "things." We have been bouncing along merrily with Wordsworth's folksy meter and conventional lexicon when suddenly, in classic Wordsworthian manner, we are tripped up by an expression that is, on reflection, very queer indeed. In case you didn't notice, and it is such a discrete divergence that you could easily miss it, it's not the "light of day" that we're being summoned forth into but the "light of things." The light of *things*? What on earth is that supposed to mean? In what sense are we to conceive of things as having their own light, as distinct from being illuminated from the outside? What would it mean to expose ourselves to this light, which is not the light of the setting sun, or of moon or candle or electric light bulb, although all those things too must be assumed to also manifest this peculiar other light? And how might we appear to ourselves in this queer other light, the light of things, of which we too perhaps are such: things, that is, with our own light?

On closer inspection—and as Geoffrey Hartman taught us, we need to look at Wordsworth's verse very closely indeed—this is not simply a call to head outside and take an evening stroll. Following Rousseau's *Reveries d'un Promeneur solitaire* (1780), this was already a well-worn trope by the late eighteenth century. The speaker of the poem, it is true, appears to have donned a Rousseauian mask, as suggested by the programmatic exhortation to "Let Nature be your Teacher." But the line before that takes us into new territory, philosophically and poetically. In fact, although the speaker clearly does want his friend to get a breath of fresh air, we as readers do not necessarily need to get up and go anywhere in order to heed the call of this poem. For what we are being asked to do is not necessarily to go anywhere but to perceive and relate to things differently, that is, to enter into the "light of things." Wordsworth does not tell us exactly what this is, of course, but he does provide some hints as to how we might come by it. The first hint is negative: it tells us how the light of things is liable to get blocked:

> Sweet is the lore which Nature brings:
> Our meddling intellect
> Mis-shapes the beauteous forms of things:—
> We murder to dissect.

Implicitly, of course, Nature's l-o-r-e is being contrasted here with the L-a-w of Nature as disclosed by Newton et al. Now, this should not be assumed to imply a hostile attitude to Bacon's *novum organum* and the type of science that it spawned per se. What Wordsworth does seem to be saying, though, is that neither empirical investigation nor rational reflection, as purveyed, perhaps, by the books that the speaker wishes his friend to put aside, should constitute the only and certainly not the primary way in which we relate to what he once again simply—and marvelously—calls "things." How else, then, might we relate to them? This is suggested in the last two lines, where we are given a positive hint as to how we might put ourselves in the way of that queer other light: "Come forth," the speaker once again exhorts his friend, but now he adds, "and bring with you a heart / That watches and receives." Far from insisting that we don our hiking boots, then, this text is suggesting that we still ourselves sufficiently to allow things to disclose themselves to us in their own way and their own time: this is, in the first place, a question of attention rather than action. To allow yourself to be illuminated by the light of things you will need to surrender for the moment your perhaps perfectly legitimate desire to objectively know and instrumentally use them, and position yourself instead as the recipient of whatever it is they might have to reveal to you, perhaps surprisingly, even amazingly, that is to say, in ways that exceed your expectations, comprehension, and capacity to respond adequately to their appeal.

Let me stress that this is not simply a matter of pitching aesthetic distance against rational inquiry and practical involvement. On the contrary, Wordsworth's verse seeks rather to call its readers, as the speaker calls his friend, into a risky physical proximity with all manner of things, a proximity, moreover, that carries a burden of ethical responsibility. As Adam Potkay has shown, "thing" or "things," words that occur no less than 439 times in Wordsworth's corpus, are key for this Romantic poet.[29] Moreover, Wordsworth deploys this term in a markedly different manner both from Samuel Johnson's authoritative *Dictionary* definition of 1755, according to which "thing" designates "Whatever is; not a person," and from William Blackstone's prototypically modern usage in his *Commentaries on the Laws of England* (1765–69) as "a being without life or consciousness; an inanimate object, as distinguished from a person or living creature."[30] By contrast, "Wordsworth uses *things* in a way that blurs distinctions between persons and non-persons, between entities and events."[31] In so doing, Potkay writes, he "borrowed from but gestured beyond Shaftesburian natural religion and Spinozan pantheism in imagining a joyous affection and non-appropriative stance towards natural things"[32]—a stance that foreshadows Silvia Benso's contemporary "postanthropologocentric" ethics of things in general, whether crafted, manufactured, or naturally occurring.

Bringing Heidegger's thinking of things as gatherings of the fourfold of earth, sky, gods, and mortals into a mutually corrective conversation with Lévinas's thinking of ethics as the "dimension within which a nonviolating encounter with the other can come to pass,"[33] Sylvia Benso passes beyond both Heidegger and Lévinas in proposing an ethics of things, understood as a response to the "facialities," as she terms it, of nonhuman others:

> Facialities invoke the intimation of signification of a face, and yet the vagueness of a cluster of meaning the demarcation of which remains blurred, fluid, porous to a continuous, osmotic interchange between inside and outside that mobilizes boundaries, and therefore definitions. . . . Facialities evoke the possibility of the existence of faceless

faces, which, despite their facelessness, are yet endowed with the intimating power of the face to demand an ethical response.[34]

Citing Benso's description of her own project, Potkay claims that Wordsworth too

> aims at restoring things to a preeconomical horizon of festive appreciation and celebration within which things can be encountered in their facialities and tendered—that is, treated with tenderness—because of the generosity of their self-giving, as if their alterity were a gift.[35]

Tender responsiveness to things in their fourfold givenness, Benso cautions, neither cancels out my ethical responsibility toward the human other nor implies indiscriminate approval of everything: while we might marvel at a nuclear missile as an extraordinary thing in its own right, in view of its potential to maim and destroy a myriad of both human and other-than-human beings, we might well decide that we would do well to dismantle it. Similarly, an awestruck appreciation of the phenomenality of earthquakes certainly does not mean that we rejoice in the destruction and suffering that their unanticipated arrival might occasion those who dwell near the shifting fault line.

Potkay sees a precursor of Benso's notion of faciality in Wordsworth's Spinozan-inflected redeployment of the earlier physicotheological trope of the veiled "face of things," which encoded a view of nature as the locus of a God-given order and splendor that could be glimpsed, but never fully known. Somewhat surprisingly, he does not discuss the strange spin that Wordsworth puts on "things" in displacing "face" with "light" in "The Tables Turned," for it is arguably here that the extent of his departure from earlier conceptions becomes most evident, in the radical subversion of the spirit-matter dualism that is implied by his attribution of luminosity to physical entities and encounters. There are a number of ways in which this odd turn of phrase could be contextualized and interpreted. Recalling Shaftesbury, the "light of things" might be understood as the trace of the glory of God in his creation. Following this thread, we might arrive at the contemporary ecotheology of "deep incarnation," whereby the enfleshment of the Word is understood to entail the entry of the divine, through Christ, into the whole fabric of earthly existence.[36] Alternatively, it could be read from the Spinozan perspective that was possibly closer to Wordsworth's own radical thinking at this time,[37] as an affirmation of materiality per se as always already irradiated by the spirit of which it is the expression: *deus sive natura.* Following this line of interpretation we might reframe Wordworth's call in terms of Jane Bennett's neohylozoist notion of "thing-power," that is, "the curious ability of inanimate things to animate, to act, to produce effects dramatic and subtle,"[38] or of Freya Mathews's neopanpsychist ethos of erotic encounter with material entities that are always already imbued with mindlike qualities.[39] Taking this path brings us into a field burgeoning with all manner of "new materialisms" that provide a necessary corrective to the narrowly sociopolitical and economic preoccupations of the older materialism with which I began.[40]

Whatever theological or metaphysical concepts might be brought into play here, though, the key point to note from an ethical perspective is that we are only able to get a glimpse of a thing's luminosity if we refrain from construing it as a mere object, "to which," as Benso writes, "the same reacts with a lust for power and domination."[41] Greeting things in their "fourfold" givenness, locating ourselves as bounded beings in the relational space that they illuminate, a space that bears traces of an "immemorial past in which the earth and sky, the divine, [. . . and] other mortals have interwoven their existence,"[42] we might catch what Benso terms a "glimmer into the beyond." In Benso's analysis, this glimmer is afforded precisely, and paradoxically, by the opaque materiality of things, which, if accepted as such, "suspends the power of domination on the side of the I, neutralizes the intentionality of its appropriative movements, and opens the I up to things in awe, admiration and wonder." Perceived in this way, things "in their impenetrability always refer to a beyond of which there is no possession but traces in the very things."[43] Rephrased phenomenologically, we might say that the light of things is what appears when we acknowledge, as Jean-Luc Marion would have us do, that "the given always shows itself too broadly for the scope of our grasp."[44]

Recalling the earlier meaning of "thing" as "meeting" or "meeting place," Wordsworth's peculiar "light of things," a light that, unlike Newton's, is not susceptible to mathematical analysis, might then be understood as appearing when and where we encounter other beings in their faciality. This other light, then, pertains both to the event of the meeting and to the things that we meet in the space of such an event. Echoing the phrase to "light upon something," Wordsworth's odd formulation foregrounds the moment of surprise, the unforeseeable and unbiddable quality of such encounters, when things that a moment ago we might barely have noticed suddenly impress themselves upon us in their very alterity as the locus of an ethical appeal. It is in meeting with things in the light of their faciality that we are best placed to apprehend their "beauteous forms." Such meetings, as Mathews stresses, and as Benso too acknowledges in her own, more Lévinasian way, have an erotic dimension. However, this eros is ethically constrained rather than boundlessly appetitive: interrupting the pernicious opposition of Eros and Agape, it is of the kind that desires the flourishing of the other in their alterity rather than their seamless assimilation to the self. To enter into the light of things, in this reading, is to place oneself at risk of being called into an ethical relationship with another whom or which one can no longer with a clear conscience "murder to dissect," or, to recall another key text of Wordsworthian ecopoetic ethics, namely, "Nutting,"[45] greedily "ravage." As the concluding lines of that poem make plain, moreover, this has nothing to do with cordoning things off as "untouchable," as in the aesthetics of so-called wilderness; on the contrary, this text calls us into active contact with things, inviting us to take pleasure in them and to participate with them in the joy that, as Wordsworth affirms elsewhere, "all things" seem to manifest if allowed to exist according to their own lights. If they are to do so, though, it is crucial that we respond to their appeal with tenderness, as Benso puts it, and this is Wordsworth's advice also: "Then, dearest Maiden, move along these shades / In gentleness of heart; with gentle hand / Touch—for there is a spirit in the woods."

It is only on the basis of a such a fundamentally ethical stance toward things, human and otherwise, one that, in ecotheologian Denis Edwards's words, "recognizes the limits of what we can claim to know, that accepts the mystery of the other in humility,"[46] that the knowledge gained through empirical investigation and rational reflection might not only be sound but also do good: *Ethos* before *Logos*. But what of *poiesis*? The most obvious point that might be made here is that the poem is of course itself a thing, and, whether encountered as marks on a page or sounds in the air, a material thing at that.[47] Moreover, the poetic text, understood also as a locus of potential meaning, has its own luminosity, which appears only when we register its semantic opacity, its resistance to our desire to assimilate its words seamlessly to a preconceived horizon of interpretation: a luminosity that, in the case of "The Tables Turned," I have ended up eliding in my eagerness to utilize it as a case in point for the theory of negative ecopoetics! And yet it is precisely on the opacity of the text that negative ecopoetics hinges. For if the light of things appears only in an embodied encounter with others in the modality of respectful receptivity and tender touch, then the poem can at best indicate how we might come in the way of it, without being able to mediate this light in itself. This is why the speaker in Wordsworth's ecopoetic manifesto exhorts his friend to set aside his books of Art, no less than those of Science:

Enough of Science and of Art;
Close up those barren leaves:
Come forth and bring with you a heart
That watches and receives.

But of course, it is only by means of such "barren leaves," a metaphor that, in foregrounding the materiality of the text, deftly undercuts the dubious opposition between nature and culture that has been invoked by the speaker hitherto, that the author, Wordsworth, issues his call to us, distant as we are to him in time as well as space, to "come forth into the light of things." What this suggests, among other things, is that the relationship between ethics and phenomenality is two-way: faciality discloses things as ethically considerable, but faciality appears only when we approach things in a certain way, a way that already embodies a minimally ethical move, namely, away from objectification, instrumentalism, and commodification, a move that is itself at least as much a cultural achievement as it is a natural capacity. In this regard, ecopoetry, understood as that kind of writing that responds to, without being able to replicate, the experience of entering into the light of things, and in so doing invites readers to take the risk of doing so themselves, is no less indispensable as it is inadequate.

In my admittedly rather trusting, if regrettably appropriative, discussion of "The Tables Turned," I have suggested that what matters when you enter into the light of things is not what you are going to get out of it but how you might be called on to respond ethically to others, human and otherwise, as a consequence. In so doing, I have opened a gap between the author and the speaker, especially in the latter's more Rousseauian (and perhaps also Spinozan) moments. Like James Phillips,[48] I am increasingly persuaded that the Wordsworthian sublime is in fact more "fraternal," than "egotistical," as Keats unkindly termed it, radicalizing the brotherliness that was to have been brought about, but that was ultimately betrayed, by the French Revolution, by extending it democratically to places, animals, and things, as well as people. But I suspect there might be an unresolved tension lurking in "The Tables Turned," namely, that between the call to "bring with you a heart that watches and receives" and the construction of nature not just as teacher but as a moral resource:

She has a world of ready wealth,
Our minds and hearts to bless—
Spontaneous wisdom breathed by health,
Truth breathed by cheerfulness.

One impulse from a vernal wood
May teach you more of man,
Of moral evil and of good,
Than all the sages can.

Let's face it: Wordsworth does seem to want us to revalue the life and light of our earth others for their own sake, but he is also keen on taking something away from his encounters with them by way of realizing his own striving (that is, *conatus*) to live more fully and freely: think of what he makes of that "host of golden daffodils," for example.[49] The contemporary Canadian poet Tim Lilburn, by contrast, seems to me to draw closer to Benso's "ethics of things" in his endeavor to practice a form of poetic attention that, as Alison Calder observes, "seeks not to appropriate the world, but to stand alongside it."[50] As Lilburn puts it in his essay collection, *Living in the World As If It Were Home,* this "involves submitting to be disarmed and taking on the silence of things, the marginality and anonymity of grass, sage, lichen, things never properly seen."[51] Far from offering a "world of ready wealth," things are disclosed by Lilburn precisely as withholding whatever meaning and order they might have in themselves from the poet, who is, after all, only human, and constantly at risk of seeing only himself in the other: "The grass is a mirror that clouds as the bright look goes in," concedes the speaker in Lilburn's "In the Hills, Watching."[52] This does not mean, though, that the things to which Lilburn's verse bears witness, however inadequately, are devoid of faciality. On the contrary. But, as he writes in a poem titled, axiomatically, "There is no presence," "What glitters in things is a mountain, it can't be held in the mouth."[53] Nor can this glittering even be glimpsed if you believe that the world "is there to do with as you will."[54] What the glittering signifies is that while there is "no presence" in the guise of an object to be possessed, there is what Benso terms "presencing," namely, in the event, or perhaps even the trace of the event, whereby something is glimpsed precisely as ungraspable.

Lilburn's most recent collection is called, deliciously, *Desire Never Leaves.* The desire in question is twofold: to fully know the other from the inside out, as it were, to get inside them or become one with them, and then to render in words what you have experienced with them. There is no end to this desire, for it can never be fulfilled:

> Contemplative knowing is not a feeling, a rest, a peace that sweeps over one, reward for the ferocity of one's romantic yearnings, one's energetic Wordsworthian peerings. Contemplative knowing of the

> deer and the hill must gather about the conviction that neither can be known.[55]

Contemplative knowing also requires grasping that each of them "exceeds its name."[56] Lilburn's theologically informed post-Romantic ecopoetics of the *via negativa* effects an implicit critique of the narcissism of consumer culture precisely by bespeaking the resistance of things to our desire for revelation, entailing the adoption of "a stance of quiet before things in which your various acquisitivenesses—for knowledge, supremacy, consolation—are stilled, exhausted before the remoteness, the militant individuality of what is there."[57] Here is another stanza from "There Is No Presence":

> You are good but no blond disc in the grass for you, none, no bone
> of light, no little palate or gland of stupid but shining
> intelligibility, the pure bride, none, none for you, in the grass prong.
> A glacier of night
> shoved through the centre of things. Juniper hard with absence.
> You are alone in the world: the flab of the river
> is anarchic, the water is feathered with ignorance,
> a dangerous mirror that makes your face darkness throwing its hair.[58]

"You are alone in the world": does this not risk reinstating human apartness, the toxic legacy of that dreaded reason-nature hierarchal dualism, which ecophilosophers such as Plumwood have held in large part responsible for our ecosocial woes? Potentially, but not necessarily. Lilburn is not denying mind to matter unequivocally but rather accepting the limits of human consciousness and facing up to radical nonidentity. Nor does this insistence on the nonidentity of self and other, word and thing, necessarily set us apart from the world: other things too communicate in their own ways, such as the pumpkins, which, in Lilburn's poem of that name, "sing, in the panic of September / sun."[59] The rhythms and sounds of human speech, moreover, in their sonorous materiality, are themselves continuous with, and can sometimes be made to echo, and certainly to sing along with, the more-than-human music of the world. But most of the communications that biosemioticians[60] tells us are ceaselessly passing among our earth others are not intended for our ears, even though we might revel in listening in on those that we can apprehend. To imagine that we can tell how a place is "when our backs are turned," to quote James Galvin,[61] is to elevate ourselves to the position of God. The only way to avoid such hubris, and to honor earth's glorious plurivocity, is to acknowledge that its song cannot be translated without loss into those merely human words by means of which we might nonetheless participate in the choir.

In drawing to a conclusion, I want to return to the sociopolitical considerations with which I began, by stressing that the movement out into "the light of things" to which ecopoetic writing invites us opposes the logic of capitalism at the most fundamental level, that of its treatment of materiality, whether as "standing reserve" awaiting transformation into energy and the commodities whose production it fuels or as manufactured goods awaiting purchase, disposal, and replacement. To call capitalist society materialistic is profoundly misconceived, for the true love of matter, as Mathews amply demonstrates, is utterly incompatible with consumerism, engendering a cherishing of things, whether or not they are of our own making, that is oriented toward an ethos of conservation and celebration. Capitalist consumerism, by contrast, cares nothing for matter in itself, while fetishizing commodities on the abstract basis of whatever we fancy they stand for, before trashing them in favor of newer and shinier ones as soon as we feel they have ceased to serve their purpose as objects of display or fantasmatic self-projection. It would be hopelessly idealistic (in the philosophical sense critiqued by Marx) to imagine that an ethics of things such as that proposed by Benso, and instantiated ecopoetically, could be widely embraced under these socioeconomic conditions. Until such time as global capitalism collapses under the weight of its own contradictions—the most profound of which might well turn out to be that between what earth's biosphere requires and affords and what growth economics demands and transforms—or, more optimistically, is democratically transformed into a social order that is more compassionate, just, and genuinely sustainable, ecopoetry can nonetheless help to hold open a space for an ethics of things that bears the promise of a different way of living on this earth and beneath this sky (for however long that remains possible, both individually and collectively). It would be no less futile (if potentially cathartic) to hurl Lilburn's pumpkins at Exxon-Mobil as it was for Enzensberger to shoot sparrows at canons. Yet to withhold our praise from pumpkins, to shoot down all amorous talk of our earth others, now, at a time when we are becoming ever more narcissistically entranced by things of our own making, some of which, moreover, are tearing apart the very fabric of the more-than-human mesh into which our own lives are woven—to do this, as Enzensberger insisted, would be to fall into the opposite error.

Festive celebration, however, is not the only mode in which ecopoetics might contribute to the cultivation of an ethics of things. In the face of ecocide, another kind of negativity is also called for: one that bears prophetic witness, in grief and anger, to the violence of objectification, instrumentalization, and commodification that has attended the denial of spirit to matter and of ethical considerability to other-than-human things.[62] As a gesture in that direction, I want to conclude, therefore, with the words of another Romantic poet, John Clare, who in protesting against the privatization of common land in his poem "The Mores" rages prophetically, as rage we too must do in our own far darker times, "against the dying of the light":

> Fence now meets fence in owners' little bounds
> Of field and meadow, large as garden grounds,
> In little parcels little minds to please
> With men and flocks imprisoned, ill at ease.
> . . . .
> Each tyrant with his little sign
> Shows where man claims earth glows no more divine.[63]

The Angel and the Storm

"Material Spirit" in the Era of Climate Change

TOM COHEN

> The world has more than one age. We lack the measure of the measure. We no longer realize the wear, we no longer take account of it as a single page in the progress of history. Neither maturation, nor crisis, nor even agony. Something else. What is happening is happening to age itself, it strikes a blow at the teleological order of history. What is coming, in which the untimely appears, is happening to time but does not happen in time.
>
> —**Derrida,** ***Specters of Marx***

It is *bad timing* for the global economic system to enter a self-feeding black hole—at least from the perspective of "climate change." The economic implosions of the credit collapse have, essentially, foreclosed any geopolitical will to address the gathering indicators of ecocatastrophic logics, had that ever been plausible. The interplay between the economic and ecological, the "eco-eco" disaster, tends to occlude the exponential curves of issues that lie outside the screen—collapsing marine life, mass extinction events, "peak" everything (oil, humans, water . . .), projections of "population culling," and so on. The Ponzi scheme of hypermodernity extending the depletion of reserves, the burn-off of futures regarded as disposable capital, sometimes parallels that of critical theory agendas today—caught in the recirculation of twentieth-century masters who did not address or anticipate ecocatastrophics generally. There is a curious structure to any "present" passed various tipping points that alter eons going forward and anticipate mass extinction events and disappearing futures. Into said "futures" megadebt is dumped, reserves and generations despoiled (water, oil, biodiversity). Such is the disaster porn mantras we are routinely fed, and routinely turn into mass entertainment vehicles to normatize. It is amusing to recall the neoliberal premise that a global "free market" heralded in the nineties. The collapse of credit mirrors, in the critical discourses of today, one of credibility in the referential models and contaminated agendas that partook of this parenthesis, which has now crystallized with the term *anthropocene,* a geologically marked era of humans, implicitly catalogued as if after the fact. These mutations of the biosphere seem never to have been quite anticipated in twentieth-century theory or critical culture (which deployed the term "materiality" liberally and insistently).

With tipping points passed, a collective *we* appears as if on the inside of a *time bubble*—at once too late, and yet not yet fully arrived. What does the phrase "material spirit" signify in what might be called the late anthropocene? What, even, would "materialistic spirit" signify before *other materialities* (the biosphere, energy, biomutation, weather), or from a position in which zombie logics and labels proliferate (zombie banks, zombie democracy, zombie politics, and so on) for which no traditional "enemy" declares itself to form resistance before? The dilemma of the Occupy movement emerges here, say, within a totalization or capture of various systems—global banker hegemony, postdemocratic mediacracies. One can be excused for asking this question, still, of a twentieth-century text if not icon for this problem, if in order to index where we stand in relation to it today. Benjamin's pop trope of an Angel of History in his "Theses" is one such text. Derrida's *Specters of Marx* is another, particularly as it appropriates the former to propose a spectrology—a recasting of both materiality and spirit in their way one more time. What one finds is not only that Derrida's "democracy to come" and use of weak messianism regresses from Benjamin's text, but that it gets rhetorically caught in the angel's dilemma.

What interests me here is not how this twentieth-century "angel" adapts to an era of climate change. One is alert to the fact that Benjamin's fable of the angel is dominated by the figure of the "storm," a force beyond sovereignty. This text has been read in the past to support one or another form of *angelicism*—at first the Marxist angel and the Kaballist angel, then a deconstructive angel. To read Benjamin under the auspices of an era of climate change is to ask if there has not been a misreading of this angel all along.

1

Bruno Latour uses the specter of ecocatastrophe as the definitive closure of what he calls a "Modernist parenthesis" in an essay diverted through the film *Avatar* read through Gaia theory. He means by this a preoccupation with sorting out local histories, *anteriority* as such, cultural memory, catastrophes past, and so on—as if never turning to what arrives ahead, and he necessarily forms a specular relation to the "parenthesis" he wants to close. (It has always been a "modernist" gesture to dream the closure of itself, a zero-degree departure—here forced from without differently with the prospect of extinction appearing before unmodifiable limits.) In the face of this he proposes to close out the figure of the future, as well, as a misleading construct, together with the dedication to back-turning legacies that defined the "modernist" enclosure. Even so, he finds his way back to the "tired" trope of Benjamin's angel to make his point, even though he has no wish to go there (or "embrace" it):

> I want to argue that there might have been some misunderstanding, during the Modernist parenthesis, about the very direction of the flow of time. I have this strange fantasy that the modernist hero never actually looked toward the future but always to the past, the archaic past that he was fleeing in terror. . . . I don't wish to embrace Walter Benjamin's tired "Angel of History" trope, but there is something right in the position he attributed to the angel: it looks backward and not ahead. "Where we see the appearance of a chain of events, he sees one single catastrophe, which unceasingly piles rubble on top of rubble and hurls it before his feet." But contrary to Benjamin's interpretation, the Modern who, like the angel, is flying backward is actually not seeing the destruction; He is generating it in his flight since it occurs behind His back! It is only recently, by a sudden conversion, a metanoia of sorts, that He has suddenly realized how much catastrophe His development has left behind him. The ecological crisis is nothing but the sudden turning around of someone who had actually never before looked into the future, so busy was He extricating Himself from a horrible past. There is something Oedipal in this hero fleeing His past so fiercely that He cannot realize—except too late—that it is precisely His flight that has created the destruction He was trying to avoid in the first place.[1]

Latour's turn is provocative, but might want to take account that the moment of a cognitive turn into the future—or, absent that, what he calls man's "prospects," a Standard & Poor's downgrade—coincides with not being able to address it either. Yet it is instructive, since it displaces the manner in which the "tired 'Angel of History' trope" has been most often rendered, that is, as a figure of pathos and as a hero within Benjamin's weaponized bestiary of terms and figures. Robert Lehman attributes to him what is called an allegorical function, as the one who sees the "dead letters" of history and is resoundingly materialist: "Benjamin's *Angelus* sees the dead letters out of which every epic history is written, the linguistic *corps morcelé* that remains when the time that imbues (written) history with life has been (allegorically) subtracted; he is, in this sense, the perfect materialist historian."[2] In a related vein, Beatrice Hansen, in her important work on Benjamin's "other history,"[3] reads the angel as Benjamin's counter-Zarathustran agent, indexed not to an *Übermensch* but to a "creaturely," nonhuman and inorganic zone, finally. Yet the angel's profile changes as we rotate into the twenty-first century. The entire text seems to alter its sense when we see that, rather than being a hero, the angel as Benjamin cites him is a mute *pantalone,* a dissimulating façade less endowed with translational powers than an autoexterminating angel—to the extent the trope of the angel is not self-evidently that. One hears the term angel differently from the position of the theologically hemmed masses looking toward his face, the unawakened dead of debris, or from the "storm" coming from the future, not to mention citing, already, Klee.

2

Benjamin mobilizes what is called a "materialis*tic* historiography"—that is, not *materialist* in its Marxian appearance. The practice points at once toward anteriority, memory programs (such as historicism), and modes of inscription ("materialistic historio*graphy*"). Benjamin's "Theses" is read not only as the precursor of *Specters of Marx* but of the latter's attempt to read "materiality," and perhaps spirit itself, as a matter of technics, *spectragenics,* and preoriginary inscriptions. What Derrida omits is a logic in Benjamin that turns a different way, that appeals not to the socius but to the biomorphic horizon of terrestrial or "organic" life indifferent to human time. This omission—the lack of any reference in his "ten plagues" of the new world order to any form of ecocatastrophic logics under way—retracts selectively Benjamin's less bounded implications. How does a *mnemonic politics* (a "politics of memory") reorient today toward *other materialities* that are subject neither to trope nor to conceptualization, anarchival, for which there is no cultural memory or inscriptions to reference?

A riddle emerges. Benjamin's Angel of History seems not only to ruin *history* himself by just being there (Latour's thesis) but to ruin the project of the "Theses." He cannot stop destroying, including and beyond himself. Having been called not only to redeem the hordes of undead beseechers (or readers, essentially), he knows it is a scam responsible for the acceleration of their undoing—angelicism itself being the signature of a theotropic reflex, a perpetual organicism and desire to make whole. He "wants to" play his role, we are told, but is whooshed away by a storm from the future. Despite the text's *Sturm und Drang,* or because of it, we may not see how foppish the angel is to Benjamin's eye: impotent, his audience of ruined souls is expectant, demanding to be made whole—they have a reading of him he cannot sustain; without divine or any backing, his costume's main accoutrement, wings, is his undoing, pinned by the storm; and then, put into a dissimulating relation to his audience, whom he would have wanted to satisfy but cannot, he *bolts.* That is, due to the dual prism of the conceptual traditions Benjamin is not merging, as readers look for, but taking down—theological-spiritual, Marxist-theological materialism, out of which Phoenix something called *materialistic historiography* would rise—we may not note that the figure is not ennobled or tragic but, in advance, stripped. It already cites or tropes Klee's own wire-grid, "new," incandescent graphic.

Yet the "angel of history" puts the project of a *materialistic historiography* in advance into question. At stake is a *torsion* between the "materialistic historiographer" that Benjamin conjures as the hyperbolic agent of historial intervention and what he reads in or into Klee's angel. This new and last *angel of anthropomorphism* falls away before what is called a storm, before the other materialities we will associate here with "climate change." Klee's angel must be costumed up one last time, given wings, and pushed out before the curtain to play his role, but he barely wants to, knowing what he does. There the wreckage of the past looks toward him to make things whole and precisely misreads what he signifies. There is a sort of reading trap that he enters, one formed by the expectation of readers, say, looking for the Marxian angel, or the Jewish angel, or the deconstructive angel—before he will be swept away, unable to address or resolve it. What is more interesting is that the angel's depiction undermines in advance the task of the *MH* (*materialistic historiographer*), squares off against it, making the "Theses" a suiciding text as its condition (only incidentally followed by Benjamin's own). I will divert this war zone within Benjamin's text to ask where Derrida appears not only to repeat this instability but to rhetorically regress from it, say, in his attempt to simulate for his readers "the political," or maintain that the house is an economy of mere ghosts.

3

Benjamin's *angel of history* stands looking back at the wreckage of the past. He wants to intervene in some way, to give a theotropic or Marxian interpretation that would answer the expectations of the multitude looking to him and make "whole" again the dead, but is interrupted. Rather, he is overwhelmed by what is called a "storm" that catches his wings. The use of this word is signal. And it opens the text to the climatic horizons and other materialities at work today. And he abandons his post:

> This is how one pictures the angel of history. His face is turned toward the past. Where we perceive a chain of events, he sees one single catastrophe which keeps piling wreckage upon wreckage and whirls it in front of his feet. The angel would like to stay, awaken the dead, and make whole what has been smashed. But a storm is blowing from Paradise; it has got caught in his wings with such violence that the angel can no longer close them. This storm irresistibly propels him into the future to which his back is turned, while the pile of debris before him grows skyward. This storm is what we call progress.[4]

This new angel loses his balance, the storm "caught in his wings with such violence that he can no longer close them." But the word "storm" is more significant than the word "progress," recurring three times as the subject of a sentence, compared to which "progress," supposed to be a punch line, is merely "what we call" that. Among else, the passage opens a purchase on weather, geological force, climatics.

This new angel poses a question by having no power at all. For one thing, he dissimulates. Eyes are on him, and the projected reading of him that is desired is something he'd "like" to supply but cannot. In fact, he's out of there. He appears unable to speak and unable to abandon the past that is a "single catastrophe" ("the pile of debris that grows skyward"). The trope of *debris,* repeated, underscores a field of waste and garbage separate from but linked to acculation. He "wants to" stay at his post and "make whole" this wreckage but he cannot, and not only because a greater violence draws him away. He might seem momentarily a sort of *materialist angel* as he is torn toward a future from behind, dissolved from his role and function. He was there to serve humans, *he looks human.* The angel of history should not have to be concerned by a progressive future. History as a figure here flips direction from tending the archive, narrative, and *anteriority,* where the "materialistic historiographer" of Benjamin's "Theses" plies his trade (a sort of Marx-inflected Zarathustra), to something else. But the new angel, who is also the last, must turn from even that.[5]

Why does the angel part company with the *MH,* though, by abandoning anteriority as a catastrophic heap? Or rather, why does Benjamin's "Theses," set to articulate the performative premises of the MH, turn against itself and create an angel of history that is first mocked (as if an "angel" of historicism) and then seems to interrupt the MH's orientation toward anteriority because of a *storm*? One answer to the question—that is, what separates the angel of history from the materiality of inscriptions?—appears in the later section 18 of the "Theses," which appeals to the nonanthropomorphic order of biological and terrestrial "time":

> "In relation to the history of organic life on earth," writes a modern biologist, "the paltry fifty millennia of *homo sapiens* constitutes something like two seconds at the close of a twenty-four-hour day. On this scale, the history of civilized mankind would fill one-fifth of the last second of the last hour." The present, which, as a model of Messianic time, comprises the entire history of mankind in an enormous abridgment, coincides exactly with the stature which the history of mankind has in the universe. (263)

The "time" one invokes here is a different and wild time-space, the utterly indifferent nonanthropic expansion of terrestrial mutation through inorganic and organic forms, and before. The perspective could be called that of a prehistorial trace, and accords discretely with the way Benjamin uses "prehistorical" elsewhere as an always contemporary logic that can surface (in Kafka, for instance). The latter bursts the nanometrics of a human present.

The angel's gaze is compromised by the weather, or *temps*. This *storm* within time pushes aside his programmed desire—theotropic or Marxist—to make the catastrophe of human history somehow "whole." It sweeps him into a future acceleration that should not be his provenance. But his wings are pinned. The image bears the logics of a rape. This interface as if between a caesura within the artefacted structure of memory and the natural mutations of an earth brackets what would today be called the "anthropocene era" (as if with a backward glance at it). It is drawn instead toward a certain explosive contraction or outside oblivious to the *anthropocene* parenthesis, its exponential accelerations, its wars, its "progress." Its disappearance. The *temps* of temporalizations and climatics intertwine, a *tempest* in Shakespeare's usage. Earth had ever been positioned between contesting temporal forces—geological shifts, meteoric impacts, microbial irruption, abrupt extinctions, new niche species. In the *anthropocene* era, as it is now named, earth witnesses the sixth mass extinction event—yet the first accomplished by a biological form, a linguistically endowed organism.

4

So the *angel of history* is disarticulated by a storm of logics that precede cultural memory altogether. He dissolves into the force of a terrestrial mutation that turns its face from the rising debris of human history. It is no longer about the crowds of beseechers, the unawakened dead wanting redemptive meaning, nor about some "otherness of the other" ethically reconstituted. It isn't about the home or man so defined. The more the latter is centralized, in fact, the more the suicidal spiral accelerates. The autoexterminating angel does two things that the MH cannot. *It* requires other metrics of time or even "presents" than either the notion of presence or its antipode, the caesura of the nonpresent, provides.[6]

Late in *Specters of Marx,* Derrida puts on display a running if cryptic subtext he had been in dialogue with, or wished to appropriate. It emerges when various formulations, like that of a "democracy to come," nonexistent and never to arrive, appeal to Benjamin's figure of *weak messianism*—a messianism without the messianic which retains, nonetheless, the structure of the "promise." In late Derrida this devolves to various double gestures that appear to mobilize this affirming *promise without promise* as a rhetorical glue: the labyrinth of hospitality (never abandoning its envelope inversions, appealing to an "absolute" variant), the rhetorical appropriation of the term "justice" (assimilated to deconstruction), the entourage of a "democracy to come" (at the moment an era of democracy palpably closed), the hyperbolic deployments of the Lévinasian "other" and conjurations of mourning—moves susceptible to deconstruction by an early Derrida, on which he perhaps counted. Why does Derrida not just let the "messianic" go altogether? Why pull back from, say, the reading of de Man that, in Benjamin, there is nothing messianic whatsoever at work—not just one without religion, using the *X without X* formula Derrida had come, "perhaps," to phone in too routinely? Derrida's redeployment of "weak messianism" is generous, negatively framed, but one cannot reinitialize the phrase without an uncontrolled literalization. Entering "this war of messianic eschatologies,"[7] one wishes "to open up access to an affirmative thinking of the messianic and emancipatory promise as promise" (75). In "this desert-like messianism (without content and without identifiable messiah), of this also abyssal desert, 'desert in the desert'" (28), we hear that itself, "perhaps, a certain experience of the emancipatory promise, it is perhaps even the formality of a structural messianism, a messianism without religion" (59). Any *perhaps* includes a perhaps not. Nonetheless, one totalizes this possibility since it keeps the future, supposedly monstrous and incalculable, open: "Was not Abrahamic messianism but an exemplary prefiguration, the pre-name [*prenom*]" (167), and one does so in order to ask, "Can one conceive an atheological heritage of the messianic?" (168). What, however, if Derrida finds himself caught—in any case, before the dawning era of climate change—in the position of Benjamin's angel as he is undone by a "storm"? Moreover, what if any calculation of "the debt" and its relation to mourning did not anticipate derivatives, high-frequency trading algorithms, sovereign default? Thus Derrida would turn to the problem of terrorism following 9/11, the import of the strike and America's suicidal autoimmune recoil (since played out, effectively handing Osama a win), but would again, as in *Specters*' "ten plagues," occlude or ignore the horizons of twenty-first-century climate change and ecocatastrophic accelerations.

5

The "Theses" come into contact with *Specters of Marx,* then, at two points: where Derrida's transposition of Marxian *materiality* into spectragenics pointedly echoes that of the "materialistic historiographer" and where his use of *weak messianism* appropriates, or misappropriates, the text directly (Derrida links the phrase to a nonexistent "democracy to come"). The new angel of history does not carry a message, does not witness, is not able to redeem. He is himself, a sign without a sender, interrupted. Ever facing the past, as the debris and wreckage of human events pile up at his feet, he is simply blown away by what is repeatedly called a storm from the future.

If the angel is linked, etymologically, to a messenger and message itself, a figure of media, he comes to supplant any individual content or message, like Gabriel coming to signify "annunciation." Or, say, an emptied form of promise. Yet the faces of the multitude of the dead turn toward him, look at his humanized face, expecting an answer or affirmation that will make whole the wreckage, redeem its debris. This Potemkin angel is also the prototype for the bewildered destruction of a self-anthropomorphized "subject," the *artifice of a subjectivity* at all, Latour's man in the "Modernist parenthesis," likened by him to Oedipus. He is trapped between a performance that is demanded of him and what is pinning his wings—he is trapped by an expectation of a promise contradicted by what he *knows.* Even the trope of the angel is comic, costumed in mythical attire, stuck with wings that will undo him, like a clown if one considers, as Benjamin does, the pretense of biblical attire and its absurdity.[8]

He is the locus of more than a contradiction. The performance required of him by his readers, that of conveying a healing secret, of being the messenger of the *Spirit,* is poetic. Formalized, his wings still attest to flight and he is given nonetheless animal *accoutrements* (wings with feathers). In popular culture today the angel appears fallen into the quotidian, more like the vampire (banally familiar and integrated into society in, say, *True Blood*). At a certain point the figure of the angel's planned obsolescence—as messenger, sign, promise—dissolves back into the matter it was intended to exceed. The phrase "materialist spirit" drifts back toward the nonhuman broadly, where personification is withheld and from where the construct of the human is as if viewed inversely as thing. The human-on-human twentieth-century model of war (with an enemy other) is today collectivized as a species in relation to a war with itself, its world, technics, terrestrial "life," with time. The new angel as the last anthropomorphized mediator with the appearance of a human face and form might be thought to yield, momentarily, to a *counterinspiriting of the anorganic.* One should resist any temptation to cast this as "apocalyptic." What is implied by climate change is, on the contrary, *banal,* the consequence of displaced biomass and waste, utterly material, the accelerated despoilments of the hyperindustrial and global era, related to oil, microbes, life forms, and technologies.[9]

6

If this last angel recedes, *abandons* his place as anthromorph and go-between, he takes *face* with him—the beautiful androgyne barricade before a set of interacting trace-chains and viral events without personification. This makes any materialist spirit in the era of climate change elusive, dispirited. In the revocation of face, the materialist spirit is apparent not in soaring resistance to capital or to transcendental or idealist pretexts but in a sort of depersonification and banalization of a "materiality" understood outside embodiments or binaries, as life shapes and inorganic formations, molecular shifts, translations of biomass to energy or light. The angel's face is pulled away.[10] One shifts from a time in which "shock" represented a counterstroke to a time where one encounters, from without, geomorphic events that require different categories of duration to enter perceptual memory—for instance, the cinematized inertias of glacial meltoff. The latter can have the cataclysmic effect of a meteor impact or nuclear winter yet is not representable by shock, blasting, or the perpetual "out of jointness" of a nonpresent present. The *artifaction* of any nonpresent "present" partakes of structures that can be stretched or applied otherwise, as occurs in other life formations that subsume different temporalities and speeds (the mayfly, the sloth, the amphibian). What the disappearing angel revokes, with face, is any possibility that the MH's interpretation of his project can be coherent.[11] The problematics of *hospitality*—to return Derrida to this discussion—appear here degraded if not revoked as the "eco" is turned (inside) out.

What was called "metaphysics" was a cover for a *semantic-behavioral model* once linked to tribal preservation and later transferred to acquisition, property, eating, *seeing* itself. That is, it would be bound to a compulsive interiorization, along with habits of personification and community construction ("*we*'s" depend on exclusion and enemy others). This empty production of "interiority" through consumption is displayed in the obese bodies of airports and malls in America today. The "new angel" goes a step further than Benjamin made apparent to those who read him as, indeed, some "Angel of History," that is, read still from the position of the unawakened dead. His human face recedes irreversibly, breaks into digital points. "Materiality" arises here as an avenging specter that brings the outside of the archive, the point at which its limit as human archive is exposed to mutation, together with micrological marks precedent to any memory formation.

Two points, again. One here suspends Derrida's oft-literalized ban on addressing "the future" as what, by definition, would preempt the latter from arriving. It was not that metaphysics was installed, say with the Greeks, at which point hermeneutic reflexes, communal investments, and transcendental signifiers were released into the injustices of history. Rather, *metaphysics* would be the name for a perpetual relapse bound to a collective semantic compulsion to restore an *eco* and the repetition of language seeking to establish the same: the compulsion to interiorize, the autoimmune. This is what the angel abandons or is abandoned by, including being an angel. "Presence" was not decreed by metaphysics but constructed as a perpetual disappearance by the technics that had made it impossible. Thus *it* leads, more or less calculably, not just through monotheistic formations and the reversible idealist-materialist axis but to melting glaciers, the credit collapse, extincted life forms. Today this viral effect shifts from the fratricidal wars of imperial states and tribal others to the postglobal, totalized, invisible, autogenic wars of the "human" collectively with its "outside," itself, and its disappearing futures. Such allochronic wars, *time wars,* remain indifferent to phenomenological discriminations.[12]

7

One arrives at the "materialistic historiographer's" dilemma: to displace archival programs, to open alternative possible "futures" to those seemingly prescribed, or totalized, the MH must alter anteriority violently, "blast" or activate a dormant trace or force of use to the present, and reinscribe the archive from which such would then emerge. This might take the form of shifting from one hierarchy of memory and reference—say, a period analysis—to a larger frame or event that, for the present's purposes, accounts for it. But to go parabolic, as Thesis 13 does, however, lets fall away those intrahistorial telescopings before what can certainly not be called an other, an absolute other, an otherness of the other, or any of the alterity declensions recently fetishized to maintain the semblance of the one doing the naming, extending, recognizing, incorporating. The MH's would be a "politics of memory" (the update offered by *Specters of Marx*).[13] The angel's removal unbalances the "materialist historiographer" before he is in place—which, in a sense, he never is—by precipitously removing the three things presupposed: personification, an able gaze, and an archival mediation. Something arrives from behind or outside the archive as conceived.

So the angel betrays his post. As the last humanlike intermediary and mytheme, a messenger for an unrepresentable other that has more in common with oil than it does with a "god," he takes with him *personification* and *face.* The parable of the "new" angel of history is not about the latter's impotence but about the destruction that the positing of him in this position has itself facilitated as the dolled-up version of a formalized if void sign. The question of any contemporary materialist spirit in the era of climate change moves to the obverse side of this screen. It oscillates between where the MH works the archive and the disappearance of the last anthromorph and mirror. It would perhaps switch sides, side with the rebellion of the molecular and the biomorphic against the anthropocene parenthesis—opening to a disintegration of representation beyond "life" or life forms as organized by memory.

The materialist spirit splits, in the "Theses," between the MH (material*istic* historio*grapher)* and the void created by the new angel of history's farcical depiction. This split further harasses the "Theses" from within. It in turn doubles any possible extension into a split screen as well—in which the position of the angel would be maintained, with "weak messianism," the future held as if open, and this to perhaps placate the faces turned expectantly. On the one hand is the work of archival transformation, of altering the import and reading of it, of blasting other pasts into different configurations of time; on the other, there is a falling away of representational borders. As remarked, the "Theses" never does name the gathering cloud of Nazism as the "enemy." The "enemy" is *historicism,* a received temporalizing and a knitting together of "facts" that, thinking it adds to Enlightenment order, fuels the furnace of a closing era. Similarly, the aims of eugenic wars of the twentieth century have simply been transferred to nanoscience and the hyperwealthy of the twenty-first anticipating, amid a neofeudal consolidation, a coming "population culling." Benjamin refused to situate the MH's dilemma in the absurdly extreme historical moment of the Nazi takeover of Europe—which he read as symptomatic, not unusual, contingent, and preparatory at best to the broader war between the species and itself, or the terrestrial life it portended.

The MH's strategy is to seize on the nonpresence of time to itself to "blast" potentially new mnemonic grids, conceiving of temporal threads as a plasticity. It would reanimate temporal forces archivally dormant. Yet as the eviscerated angel disappears before a set of inorganic expanses, the MH is tugged toward a non-site at which a sheer anteriority of trace interfaces with that "materiality" which approaches outside of the archive and is constitutive of it (marks, sounds). The figure of inky inscription segues to the histories of stone carving and carbon, to pencils and toward the pools of oil where liquefaction occurs and, in turn, ancient organic decay becomes "light." The historicism that Benjamin attacked is a program for managing time and reference. It has affiliates and other names (empiricism, causal genealogies, utopism). What Benjamin meant by historicism then bears a remote analogy to the veer of critical energies in the 1990s to new historicisms, "history," and politically astute culturalist studies, which embraced representationalism with a certain triumphalist faith that strangely paralleled the neoliberalist orgy it "politically" critiqued.[14]

The angel of history decamps from angelicism and history. There is nobody left at that post—the last anthropomorphic phantom and mediator with a human face turned toward it from *the other side*. The angel abandons its contract of representation and teleological pretense. And it is no longer the MH who can be entrusted alone to summon and manage archival blasting to keep open still virtual futures. At a certain point, say "tipping points," archival strategies dwindle before what arrives as if from the outside of the archive (though generated from it, as consumption, perception, grammatization, the Ponzi scheme of resource depletion). Benjamin's "Theses" breaks with and against itself or its politically recognizable, performative apparatus as weak messianic time is tested by what exceeds it. In a sense this is irrelevant, for its condition was impossibility to begin with. It accords, in the "Theses," with the core of an analysis that, against logic, did not take the Nazi overrun of Europe as its target or even reference: rather, it regarded that from afar, the course of organic life on earth (as a place-holder) as another possibility or symptomatic (of which, Benjamin notes, no one should be surprised). He is gazing not at the human and techno-warfare of his own moment. The point of "reference" shifts decisively: if there is a "new angel" to be indexed to the human compulsion to deferral narratives, Ponzi schemes of reserve (including conceptual faiths), personification, and so on, it is the non-angel, a materiality without body, disclosed by Thesis 18—or, in today's lexicon, "climate change."

Today this appears clearer: the fratricidal world war between two poles on the Enlightenment epistemopolitical spectrum, fascism and democratic market capitalism, gives way in the amnesiac "global" moment to follow before the disclosure of the underlying war between human autogenesis and the mutations of terrestrial, infraorganic, and technomaterial forces of time-space and "life" as an effect. Across this band human modernity or dominance of earth is an infinitesimal point in a plastic continuum. The war between peoples and nations, endless historical vendettas and doublings, is as if countered from without: it is now one between the totality of a linguistically defined species and its supposed exterior, its ideational premises, it molecular sustenance. It is the autogenic war under way when passed "tipping points" put a present in a self-feeding time bubble with calculably disappearing futures and specters of autoextinction. This is the horizon of "organic life" that Benjamin's text hails against the ideologies of human history.

While it is not clear that survival or disappearance means anything in the broader context of life forms, it brutally interrupts any model that depends on the possibility of alternative futures to those programmed. It opens the question less of an *outside of the archive* ("the"?) than where what is called archive backs into or touches other or allochronic archival orders not accessed in script. *Reine Sprache* as a virtual meltdown of language forms to their micrological atoms, which they all share, continues the meltdown until it permeates all life formations as contesting forms of embattled semiosis, proto-mimetic, "evolutionary," precisely not linked to the anteriority fetish and archival self-situating of the human empire—easily captured, from within, by media streams and telecratic repetitions. The "new" dispensation opens different questions about "justice" and different definitions of "life" than those of interhuman struggle, repression, resentment, and consumption. It remains interesting that Derrida, or the "late Derrida" as we say, never turned explicitly from his address of ethics or religion or politics to address climate change—as if it were the calculated blind or constitutive limit he warded off. It is also the case that something in *deconstruction,* a nonhumanist and undeveloped side, not "political" in the then public sense, might seem to lead precisely there.

8

The MH runs up against two obstacles. The historicism that Benjamin attacks bears a remote analogy to, and genealogy with, the critical energies in the 1990s turned toward new historicisms, returns to "history," and politically astute culturalist studies, the overfetishization of a supposed "other" or "otherness of the other" one was to enter, commune with, or absorb. Embracing sophisticated representationalism, it appears to have accompanied without a hitch the triumph and implosion of neoliberalism and the credit and credibility crisis that, today, absorbs, defers, blinds, and accelerates any address of the ecocatastrophic.

The *last* angel of history is carried off by a *storm* from the "future"—which signals the latter's dissolution as a commodity. The face of that storm of "progress" includes the increasingly compressed acceleration of human times—the exponential curves outbidding themselves, today, as with the suffusing of the global economies with megadebt. These are required by hyperconsumption in a "growth" economy, and the vortex of financialization and derivatives (the Ponzi schemes of debt and reference), a vanishing time bubble of "peak everything" (oil, humans, water). The second face of the storm is, in a sense, the storm of extreme weather itself—that is, a force outside any model of sovereignty. Something happens, Derrida begins by suggesting in *Specters of Marx,* not in time but *to time:* "What is happening is happening to age itself, it strikes a blow at the teleological order of history. What is coming, in which the untimely appears, is happening to time but does not happen in time." The Potemkin façades of theoretical nomenclature dissolve to disclose the era of the irrelevance of "eras," the implications of the term anthropocene. There is more than a vague sense in which this category interferes with emancipatory or utopic desire (the polity of man), as it does with any "weak messianism" that a hypothetical late deconstruction would want to recirculate or strategically market.

The vaudeville angel of history gestures toward a Judeo-Christian and utopist Marxian repertoire but negates both as part of an implacable charade. It pivots the legacy of spirit and of materialism off one another, disassembling both. It is not that the Christo-Marxian adventure would be the cause of the *anthropocene* error but that the latter implied a theotropic mechanism linked to language (the promise, say). That theotropic reflex or relapse would have required these or other narratives to cover it in any case, and would devise innumerable alibis to cover its voracious consumptions, wars, virtual genocides, and biospheric depletions.

This last angel, rather like a "last man," abandons contracts of representation and teleological promises. He does so by force, not choice (the storm), though he is written as dissociating himself from the performance of a promise the others, his readers, turn to him for (or so he thinks). He "wants" to continue, more or less, if only to assuage his readership and undead fans (what, to take advantage of an aside, replicates what "late Derrida" appears doing by degrees, and which his appropriation of *weak messianism* is as much an emblem of as "hospitality"). And since this last new and new last angel is but a caricature of cognitive subjectality, the angel mimes a certain "human" simulation or conception of consciousness.

Benjamin assigns the *MH* a task, but then produces a countertext that buckles the already compromised thread of *weak messianism*—which would not happen so simply by Derrida's *X without X* app. The latter becomes autotelic, since it must keep the future open for anything at all to occur, even as failed, but does so without any possible messianism whatever. *Weak messianism* implies: act as if messianic time opens the future, even though the structure of temporality guarantees nonarrival, perhaps the opposite of the desired, and the pretense is irreal. So the never-to-be messiah is similar to the angel of history as he is forced to abandon his position, which was faux all along—taking face with it. If the storm from the future seems one of exponentially accelerating technologies ("progress") it is also the violence of a sheer technics of organic life on earth. The angel ups the ante against the MH, in effect, by making his task pointless—which he seems to regard only as an ultimate test and provocation. For human institutions to evolve ideally, like any premise of democracy, they would need to have sufficient energy, water, and transport, and to be free of *absolute* threats or that the system itself was not in a suicidal phase. That is, it would have to not be in a pretended permanent state of exception that would become unexceptional. The "Theses" undermines its own program as the condition of its (im)possibility, but what disturbs is that it floods and dispossesses.

Thus, it is not the MH who can alone be entrusted to manage archival blasting or keep the future open to arrive. He cannot keep open still virtual futures. He is not facing a historicism that can virally reconfigure endlessly, like the fiction of metaphysics itself. Benjamin has his angel transition to where the MH cannot ostensibly go: to a materiality so precise it burns off all traditional uses of the word (one argument in Latour's piece is that the term "materiality" needs to be dropped altogether), a metrics whose resistance is its nontranslatability back into any of the terms in circulation. If there is a palpable agency in the absence of the personification machine, that might be the granular, mud, oil, the border zones of the anorganic. It would not curtail the domain of the animal as that without language or, in turn, raise animals to "subjects," but view language as nonhuman (as Benjamin does in "The Task of the Translator"), a "biosemiosis" that pervades animation.

Hamlet's father's ghost is but the occasion for the *visor effect* itself—without face, without paternity, the visor effect looks at one before one looks, without person or subject behind it:

> The perspective has to be reversed, once again: ghost or revenant, sensuous-non-sensuous, visible-invisible, the specter first of all sees *us.* From the other side of the eye, visor effect, it looks at us even before we see *it* or even before we see period. We feel ourselves observed, sometimes under surveillance by it even before an apparition. Especially—and this is the event, for the specter is *of* the event—it sees us during a *visit.* It (re)pays us a visit [*Il nous rend visite*]. Visit upon visit, since it returns to see us and since *visitare,* frequentative of *visere* (to see, examine, contemplate), translates well the recurrence of returning, the frequency of a visitation. (101)

One must discriminate here. There is the *visor effect,* and there is the fact that the visor effect makes us posit a who or "it" behind the visor—when in fact it is this effect itself, without subjectal force (not, say, the ghost of a "father," hence Horatio's just suspicion), and without in fact all the stagecraft suggested here (it "sees us," it "repays us a visit," and so on). The visor effect covers and shreds face, offering intervals and bars, a semiosis precedent to letteration or word. Exoskeletal, it precedes any "face" projected behind it to create an intentional and answerable (human) other.

What looks in advance is called an *it.* Or rather, *it* is not even an "it." It implies the intervals of the war helmet's metal visor, not eyes, whose alternations manifest *spacing* as the bare rhythms preceding phenomenality or semiosis. It precedes alphabet or sign. All of this does not deter the MH, since the specter of extinction is irrelevant to the archival and angelic wars waged from within—even if that archive were to turn against it(self), sicken of itself, or suicide one of its programs. Here the question of "justice" is unwieldy, since instead of negotiating human decisionism, or the "otherness of the (human) other" in its situational and legal variations, it turns against an entire criminal acceleration of the human as constructed, as the organism who consumes "life" and creates for itself faux interiority, iconic angels, in the name of what is outside it. Derrida looks back (say, from the rim of the archive) to better manage the expectant readers, to engage their communal expectations, as if to keep open their (or deconstruction's) institutional future. This permeates the phantom of a nonexistent "democracy to come."

9

Thus the supposedly "new" angel of history turns into the dispirited *non-angel of climate change.* Face no longer adheres, and the programmed relapse of reading is mimed by the fable of the angel's relationship to the undead—taking their supposed desire for redemption, anyway, as a pretext for dissimulation.[15] What is discarded is not just "historicism." The *angel who is not one* is essentially left holding the bag of a Ponzi scheme logic and a systemic con. It is, like the storms or global warming or the economic and ecological accelerations (the eco-eco disaster), irreversible, a one-way street.

What Thesis 18 discloses, however, is a scene without mourning, which the angel clearly has no time for. What it also does without doing anything is situate politics in the twenty-first century in the epistemographic mutations and wars, in which the possibility of reinscribing preoriginary or default settings of perception, reference, and time intensifies.

Is it Derrida's rhetorical strategy, in *Specters of Marx,* to keep the ghost of angelicism alive ("a politics of memory"), and to do so by recasting the figure of "weak messianism"? Even regressing from what Benjamin's text does with it? He calls it spectrology or hauntology or spectragenics. But the ghost, he reminds us, always comes from the future. It is a compromise, he thinks, suited to the moment, the triumphalism of neocons after the fall of the communist East (as if that were "Marxism"), in the face of the sly efforts on the stalwart left to appropriate that as an endless future of "formal democracy." He addresses in his "ten plagues" of the supposed new world order that never arrived only human-on-human politics. He occludes reference to the ecocatastrophics that drives the collective game board at a critical juncture "in" time. The gothicism exploited by the metaphor of haunting, its *literariness,* seems to have bracketed its currency or value—despite the brilliance of its formal summary of all Derrida might have had to say, finally, about phenomenality and the event. Derrida refuses the names of *matter* or *materialism* altogether as suggesting idealist ontologies displaced into a narrative mobilized by social justice and diverted into a utopian creed. Responding to the triumph of neoliberalism, Derrida is directed by the occasion—by his own mercurial *contretemps*—which, in this, exemplifies a running contamination in "late Derrida." In two decades one has witnessed the implosion not only of free-market capitalism, "American" power, the energy infrastructure, and the premises of continuity with the recent past ("history") altogether—a rupture, dispersal, devolution, and acceleration of threats now irreversible in nature, all extending beyond not only the premise of borders and homelands, but also of species and econometric models, with a corresponding doubling down and consolidation of neofeudal global orders (the exponential and irreversible division of wealth, a *virtual* species split).[16]

What could with intricate modifications be called the "late" Derrida's faux angelicism juggles the "secret" that the arc of human modernity rested against a terrestrial other that was open to view yet irreducible to the rhetorical treatment of an otherness of the other. In this regard, "late" Derrida was not deconstructive enough. Turning again and again to deconstruct human institutions, he chose to occlude the emergent parameters of irreversible and catastrophic climate change and terrestrial mutation.

10

A recent work challenges the general drift that the canonization of a "late Derrida" has taken in an interesting fashion, essentially splitting the "Derridas" into autosubverting columns folded back and rhetorically autocontesting in implications for the direction, or formations, that would settle into in various readerships. What is striking is that the deceived readership, or those accounted for here, would be those technically "closest" to him (translators, dedicated exegetes), in a manner that raises questions. The questions it raises takes numerous partial forms, including that of Derrida's rogue rhetorical strategies and anticipating, perhaps plotting, of an autoimmune phase of consolidation of a certain "deconstruction" (implicitly vacated, a deconstruction without "deconstruction") whose intent would be, in part, that of anchoring various threads of his production in traditionalist and high humanist canons, academic mainstreams, as a certain phase—a calculation of canonical survival beyond death, at a price. The narrative of this would involve what is misrepresented as his *turn* to ethics, religion, and political institutions in his "later" writings—even where Derrida remarked refutes any "turn" as such, and so on. In *Radical Atheism: Derrida and the Time of Life* (2008), Martin Hägglund indirectly posits that the general humanization of deconstruction was, to leap ahead, a rhetorical feint by which Derrida strategized inserting a logic of the trace into twentieth-century humanist and institutional thought as a series of contamination. The title is potentially misleading, to the degree "atheism" remains a theotrope itself. And the approach remains bound to the insistence on a Derrida who can be faithfully restored by valorizing early moves, that a certain "Derrida" can be repurged from a trail of mild recuperations, retheologizations, and regressions undertaken, nonetheless, in his "name."

It would be out of character if Derrida's text were not internally contested by different, clashing itineraries (as Derrida allowed at the end, in another context, "I am at war with myself"). Such would accord with his own late reflection that after his death, within two years, there would be nothing left of his trajectory, despite awareness of the networks of disciples, translators, and interdisciplinary extensions he left in his wake—the latter, he would know, destined to enact a programmed version of an autoimmune formation he understood. The more interesting question isn't that between an "early" or "late" Derrida but whether keeping the angel in play, technologized as specter, involved a miscalculation or a contamination. The rhetorical moment that marked this dossier in Derrida after all—that of wedding deconstruction to "justice," and this for an American cadre—seems as much a flirtation with bad faith as a gesture of rhetorico-political despair at the community's then lackluster fortunes or resilience.

According to Hägglund, a pattern emerges. The general drift of Derrida's more prominent commentators had been to normatize and reinscribe the violence of Derrida's itinerary in a more or less hybrid restitching or translation *back.* The now routine attributions of "negative theology," the buoyancy of an "ethical" motif (departing from Lévinas), the invitation to proactively mark a politics and religiously nuanced invocation of difference, and so on—all relapse to categories Derrida essentially blocked, yet rhetorically put in play. Lévinas's use of face to denote the human other explicitly becomes, instead, a strategy of Derrida's in his late phase not unlike the use of Marx in *Specters of Marx,* in part to lure and contaminate a rich philosophic discourse that would then be bored through by a differential calculus that exceeded and vacated these referential traditions, yet which the individual critics (the list is too broad to personalize here) could not not recuperate and normatize.

Hägglund reverses the narrative pretext which "Derrida" developed from a deconstruction of "metaphysics" to a turn toward the institutional and humanist discourses of ethics, religion, law, and so on, making the latter appear contaminating colonializations that would have to shed their precepts and be read through the irreversible premises of the earliest conceptual dispersals of time and trace still. He situates this by returning late figures such as "justice" or "democracy to come" to deliteralized strategies of rhetorical maneuvers that would pay the price of literalization to seed a resistant discourse that would take a generation or more to shake out, essentially marking Derrida as having, so to speak, *played* his disciples as carriers (an exception to this, and exemplification, would be the bare-fisted treatment of Nancy in *On Touching*). "Justice" would return to its Greek sense of a sort of *eris,* a scene of war, the Chinese laughing Buddha's glee at all annihilations that occur. One wonders why this book had to be written, so obvious is it from a distance, and it is a testament first to the calculated (academic) relapse against which Derrida aimed at a future reader. The normatization and faux theologization of Derrida would occur not in the polemics of his most iconic enemies (an Eagleton) but through his translators, *extenders,* "friends."

But Hägglund's use of Derrida's reading of any nonpresent as the fulcrum or wedge here leads to a premise of "survival" as the overarching drive of this difference, guaranteeing nothing, inscribing no decision in justice as such—only negotiation and risk, betrayal and contamination. Hägglund's reliance on the "autoimmune" complex nonetheless deletes the suicidal variation that Derrida came to mark as its logics intensified and would be applied to the "terrorist" effect in America he lived to analyze. But it is not my aim here to indicate the limits Hägglund must subscribe to, including the commitment to extending legacies, the possibly weak Darwinianism (as opposed to weak messianism) implied, or the deletion of a "death" drive from the "time of life" his subtitle names.

Derrida eschewed the term *material,* and when compelled to address de Man's covert "Benjaminian" trope—"the materiality of inscription"—recoiled to his *X without X* formula, calling it a "materiality *without matter.*" Whatever *inscription* might pretend to name, it gestures toward the non-site (Derrida would later call it *khora*) where mnemonic programs emerge as consolidating responses to a preoriginary mark or mnemonic incision. The gesture implies a backloop in which—without authorship or control, since it would erase its own premise at that point—a prephenomenal dis- or reinscription would be posited, if not provided agency, out of which alternative epistemographic fields and decisions would be possible. This is the point of "risk," what is missing from the representations of deconstruction as a sort of theological commentary on "Derrida." To the extent that would not occur, there would be a relapse (de Man's term) or weak reinscription, like the normatizing examples Hägglund inspects in the adaptions of Derrida to political, ethical, or religious premises. The strategy would suggest one of generations—to gain entry to the institutional discourse hubs but let the generation of carriers get it wrong, still play out the half measures of the family.[17] It would be readable according to what limits too seemed prescribed to this apparatus: ecocatastrophics would be occluded, along with select zones (one might add to this list cinema itself, or the specter, for Derrida, of de Man, who had no use for "metaphysics" and read deconstruction as over upon its arrival).

Of course, it may be that what Hägglund wishes to correct—the inevitable dependence of this "survival" on academic writing, academic media, academic personalities, related debts and capital, the compulsion to fetishize "legacy," specifically Derrida's—both is inescapable and, inversely, feeds the autoimmune spiral. One would be tempted to ask of a certain "spirit of deconstruction" in the way that *Specters of Marx* claims a "certain spirit of Marxism" and suggest, today, a discrimination between maintaining deconstruction as a franchise (and tending, in programmatic fashion, to the *extension* of and tending to Derrida's archival produce and author-specific intervention) and a general rearticulation to what had animated "deconstruction" in its appearance or pursuit across the histories of writing. Plato, one may argue, was *ur*-deconstructive, yet would be formalized, with some Christian help, as Platonism, and so on. Could one then speak of a deconstruction without "deconstruction," without the presupposition of an entity, so named, that was the haven of a family or community in accord, presumed legatees, which "Derrida"—who would have it both ways—repeatedly cut off ("I am not of the family")? That would call for the act of anonymous dispersal, the forgoing of the entire apparatus of the great signature or thinker, interrupting the literalizations and betrayals (now prolonged) of supposed mourning—and turning toward the one domain, nonanthropomorphic, that represents the mutation that has arrived from without, the horizon missing from Derrida's itinerary (which requires analysis as a decision): "climate change." This is indirectly to ask again whether Derrida, in appropriating *weak messianism* from Benjamin's text to channel his project of a spectragenics, does not return, in a sophisticated rhetorical torsion, to the angelicism that, in Benjamin, the term itself relinquishes? This would imply, in turn, a rereading of Derrida's late strategy from the perspective of Benjamin's autoexterminating angel (who abandons his entourage), from the "storm."

11

Derrida's strategies for working the aporia of hospitality, of ethics, of contemporary politics, or religion, would silhouette a choice to participate in his own domestication (to control its future contaminations), much as the polemic with neoliberalism and occlusion of climate change frames the dated occasion *Specters of Marx* impersonates.[18] By tarrying among the aporia or pathos of decisionism and mourning, the shortcut appeal to "the otherness of the other" and human "justice," a certain narcissistic subject-effect was rhetorically kept in spectral circulation or as a faux contract.

The angel is not the one who sees. He is not an allegorical functionary, since he has neither powers nor meaning. He is a Potemkin angel, whose positing as "angel" had launched the catastrophe. He betrays the reading masses who are turned to his face, expecting any returns from their designated broker. The angel's position before the storm is embarrassing—wings pulled back, face disarticulated in impotence or horror, among else by how he is projected upon as savior by masses of undead readers.[19] Thus, the angel is not an allegory of Benjamin's "materialistic" hero or counter-Zarathustran, the *MH.* He is not a hero at all. He is not a figure of pathos, as one might read him coming out of the theophantic traditions. He is comical, retired but still in zombie circulation, like a host of Benjaminian words (messianism, materiality, history). The real subject of this dissimulating text is the "storm."

Thus "terror" at the rim of the twenty-first century's unraveling would require the still human face of the enemy, or at least a name (Osama, Saddam). Any *materialist spirit* today shifts from humans to a storm of processes indifferent to sovereignty, anthropism, face—that is, toward the nonembodied visor effect, that of a materiality that precedes the "letter" and animation.

12

> The specter, as its name indicates, is the frequency of a certain visibility. And visibility, by its essence, is not seen, which is why it remains . . . beyond the phenomenon and beyond being. The specter is also, among other things, what one imagines, what one thinks one sees and which one projects—on an imaginary screen where there is nothing to see. Not even the screen sometimes, and a screen always has, at bottom, in the bottom or background that is, a structure of disappearing apparition. (100–1)

Let us say, this time, the specter is of climate change. And let us say that the "structure of (a) disappearing apparition" coincides with a structure marking this biospheric mutation and the disappearance not of a past event or death but the organization, gone forever, of something called "life" as we know it. If so, then the agency of the spectral would be inverted, and could even seem to have been superseded by a kind of zombism of a broader scope. The disappearances in effect would overwhelm anything like discrete "mourning" and include not only the local conditions of human cultures but innumerable life forms—and prospectively the cognitive or writing center of the episode. Such a specter is what is then not visible because it perpetually shapes the "visible." It can't escape the *visible-invisible* nexus.

Derrida in *Specters* ignores this broader, other, ecocatastrophical disappearance to refocus on contemporary human domains and appropriate or spectralize Marxian "materialism." Here Derrida attempts to engage *politics* as of the world of men primarily, mimes the received terms of "politics" he would disown, appropriates a certain "Marx," engenders a "politics of memory" (up to a point). That is, he is so preoccupied in inhabiting the discourse presented to him that, in listing these "plagues," he occludes and avoids the most overarching one, that is, "climate change" itself, and the latter is allowed to persist as the invisible implicitly. Does Derrida partake of this late twentieth-century blind or, at very best, eschew it for scriptive-strategic reasons? Implicitly, the *archive* of life mutation exceeds that of *human* writing. From the former's perspective, perhaps, deconstruction and the "metaphysics" it must invent to stage itself are part, still, of the anthropocene.

One is left with a problem that could be put thus: Derrida's favoring of spectragenics, for all of its gothic seancing, for all its literary techniques and technics, manages to post itself as an extended humanism rhetorically—while adopting the positions of the spectral visitation. This is why, for some, it is difficult to extract from Derrida's political agenda more than the sense of "justice" of a "good liberal" (Jameson). In turn, the "*weak* messianism" he repositions here recuperates, for his own ends, what in Benjamin may in fact be no messianism whatsoever. Derrida is contaminated holding the angel of history in place as a marionette as long as possible. It suggests either the calculation of what his readership desires to cohere around "deconstruction," a decision it was not yet time for this, hence a rhetorical calculation, or else the limit of what he deemed archive was (something already within memory systems, canons, received programs). One could have wished that, rather than falling for the poker bluff of the other here, and covering his supposed textism, he had allowed the latter to run, hyperbolic and viral, into the orders of the anorganic—into a sort of *abiosemsis* without borders. Similarly, Derrida's favoring of "hospitality" elsewhere, as if it were an infinite labyrinth of inversions (and "absolute hospitality"), retains the specter of the "eco" for rhetorical uses, chooses to tarry in the ghost of a house that, "deconstructed," would be maintained as its own phantom.

If *spectragenics* blanked on this other logic of disappearances, if Derrida's "weak messianism" appropriates Benjamin's phrase by retracting it (we may contrast this with de Man explicitly, who simply remarks that there is "no messianism" whatever in what Benjamin purports), if Derrida had become too enamored of the *X without X* formula to remark its seepages and doubling against itself—there would, as in *Specters of Marx,* be a rhetorical gesture that plays to the terms he implicitly and elsewhere eschews nonetheless: *the* community, *the* politics, the "ethical," the "religious," "justice." The materiality or figure of the *materialistic* that Benjamin invokes and Derrida knows but would do without may accord with the storm that obliterates the "angel" or its theophantic caricature. Derrida in this respect remains in a conservative position before the logics Benjamin opens and de Man requires.

The angel of climate change is an *autoexterminating angel,* one that first destroys the angelicism of the sign, the premise of hermeneutic mediation, and the backturned posture of addressing (or not) the pleading faces of the zombied or dead. But what emerges from this conflagration within Benjamin's text, this rift in which a dissimulating non-angel is cast against the prospect of any materialistic historiography, deletes the messianic, tortured attempt to *play* the charismatic angel, the "just," and to play both sides rhetorically. Instead, the logics of the one-way street arrive, comparable to the irreversibility of catastrophic climate change unfolding today.

The Material Working of Spirit

J. HILLIS MILLER

It must have been the spirits that I drank last night . . .

—C. P. Cavafy, from an unfinished poem

The Invention of Material Spirit

"Material spirit." "Material!" "Spirit!" These two words taken together, or either word taken separately, are endlessly suggestive. That is especially true if you hear behind or beside them their semantic variants. For "material": "materiality," "matter," "immaterial," and so on, in all the different ways these words may be used in sentences, such as "It's immaterial what format you use." For "spirit": "spiritual," "spiritualism," "spiritualist," "spirituous," "spirited," "dispirited," "in good spirits," "out of spirits," and so on, as in "His indulgence in spirituous liquors kept him in high spirits." Cavafy's drinking of spirits embodied those spirits in his emotions and feelings, his materialized spirits.[1] The mind boggles, and the body faints at thinking of the complexity of this double labyrinth of inscriptions.

The phrase "material spirit" appears to name a concept. Claire Colebrook, in a recent brilliant essay titled "Matter Without Bodies," asserts, following Jacques Derrida, that

> A concept must have some factical material support, and this marks its inscriptive or textual materiality. At the same time, a concept is only a concept if it is repeatable beyond any of its actual instances. Concepts therefore have the force of an essential impossibility, for their meaning or repeatability gestures to an ideality that exceeds any context, any actual material instance; and yet concepts, because of

their materiality—are marked, scarred, deflected and contaminated by their singular conditions of emergence. The concept of matter, for example, can never be cleansed of its inscriptive history, and will always bear the traces of Marxist, metaphysical and humanist geneses.[2]

"The concept of matter"—that is almost, but not quite, a synonym for the apparent oxymoron, "material spirit." If the "concept of matter" is "an essential impossibility" because it must be, and yet cannot be, both absolutely universal and, at the same time, always marked by its inscriptive history, the history of the ways it has been used over time, how much more must this be the case for a double "concept" like "material spirit." This essay indicates some of the stages in that complex and by no means noncontradictory inscriptive history. My examples might be seen as a constellation forming itself around the invisible center of "material spirit" as such, that is, something so general as not to be marked by the history of its inscriptions. The latter, material spirit as such, may conceivably exist, but we cannot ever confront it as such. Material spirit, as Colebrook asserts for "matter," is always marked, scarred, by its inscriptive history. My spatial figure of a fixed stellar constellation, however, is misleading, since the stages of my essay form a logical sequence with an end in view. The logic of that sequence is briefly recapitulated in my last paragraph.

A dictionary gives a range of meanings for the words "material" and "spirit." As everyone knows, modern linguists say a word's meanings are its uses. The meanings of the words "material" and "spirit" are the seemingly endlessly variable significances they take on when used in a sentence or in a larger sign system, such as the Christian Bible or the gigantic textual conglomeration of zeros and ones in cyberspace. The phrase "material spirit" looks like an oxymoron. It is easy to take for granted, however, as the phrase implies, that no spirit exists or can exist, for human beings at least, that is not material in one way or another. At least that is what we tend to assume and what Claire Colebrook asserts, in commentary on Derrida, in the citation above.

A ghost or specter is a paradigmatic form of spirit. We call a ghost a "spirit," but to see a spirit is to see an "apparition," that is, something that appears, something phenomenal. Spirit must appear to be known and acknowledged. Ghosts are a strange mixture of materiality and immateriality. You can see them but not touch them. Though you can see them, you can also see through them to whatever is behind them. Spirits do not make reflections in mirrors. Material spirits are like that dark matter astrophysicists hypothesize. Though you cannot see or analyze dark matter, it gives material evidence of itself in distortions of gravitational patterns and of the expected speed of the universe's expansion. Dark matter is material spirit. Dark energy, also a subject of lively current debate among cosmologists, if it exists, would be a form of immaterial matter. Matter is energy in another form, as we know, and vice versa. $E = Mc^2$.

Saying yes to the flattering request or polite demand that I write an essay on these two words, "material" and "spirit," set side by side, an adjective and a noun, puts me face-to-face with a blank sheet of paper or with an empty computer screen. It leaves me confronting the anguish Stéphane Mallarmé famously described, as did Jacques Derrida at the beginning of "Psyche: Invention of the Other."[3] Suppose invention fails me!

"Psyche" is of course a synonym for "spirit," as is the wonderful German word *Geist,* cognate of English "ghost" and "ghastly." Derrida puts the anxiety or anguish of the blank page under the aegis of invention, in the double sense of "make up" and "find." "What am I going to be able to invent?," asks Derrida in the first sentence of his essay on Psyche, "Psyche: Invention of the Other."[4] That essay was given as a sequence of two lectures at Cornell in 1984 and then at Harvard in 1986. An invention like that essay might be called the materialization of spirit, as Derrida goes on to explain, though without using that formulation. An improvised lecture pulls spirit out of the air and turns it into material spoken words, vibrations in the air. This happens unpredictably for both speaker and audience. All lectures and essays, however, are in a sense improvised. They are at some point invented out of thin air swarming with spirits in the form of memories and vague ideas. You do not know what you are going to write until you write it. I am at this moment improvising, doing what I am talking about, feeling my way toward a dimly seen endpoint I want to reach. That makes my words not just constative, a description of what is meant by "improvisation," "material," and "spirit," but, quite properly speaking, performative, in J. L. Austin's sense of words that work.[5] My words on the computer screen do something by way of the enunciation itself. They materialize spirit.

"Spirit," in the sense of ideas for an essay, is, we would like to think, there already somewhere, floating around immaterially in the writer's mind or even in some strange realm of "otherness" that inspiration taps into or breathes in, as the word "inspiration," another word with "spirit" built into it, suggests. Inspiration breathes spirit into your body and embodies that spirit there. All you need to do is to write those inspired ideas down, copy them out, to make that spirit material in the form of words on the page or on the computer screen. The experience of writing, however, shows that this is not the way it works. That is not the working of spirit. The preexisting spirit is not lurking somewhere, in some hidden reservoir, waiting to be tapped into. You do not just copy down, mechanically, a preexisting discourse. Spirit comes into existence only when it is embodied in words. The embodiment creates what appears to preexist it, though actually projected by it, in a scandalous metalepsis, the cart before the horse.

We tend to dwell within a confusion between, on the one hand, thinking that thinking takes place in some immaterial, disembodied region within me, my "consciousness," or mind, or spirit, and, on the other hand, recognizing that thinking is always embodied in one form or another. That embodiment may be, for example, the minimal neurological-linguistic form of the constant interior monologue that goes on "within me," at least in my case. My thoughts are instantly worded, in however fragmentary and agrammatical a form. When you perform the act of writing, you are inclined to think you think first and then write your thoughts down, but you actually think by writing. Thinking takes place in the material form of those fingers that seem to type of their own accord on the keyboard, as is happening with me right now.

Derrida was reluctant to face this strange fact, as who would not be? He covered it over by means of all his talk, in "Psyche: Invention of the Other," about invention as a response to the call of "the wholly other," *le tout autre.* Some quasi-spiritual something, he felt, must be inspiring his inexhaustible inventiveness, the creative power that permitted him, for example, to write *Specters of Marx*[6] in a month (though he did reuse material prepared for seminars years earlier). In spite of Derrida's cover-up, his formula, "invention of the other," is Janus-faced. It can mean either that we invent the other or that psyche, soul, mind are inventions of the wholly other. This undecidability is generated according to a doubleness inherent in the word "invention," *inventio.* The word can mean both find and make up, as Derrida abundantly demonstrates. The equivocation also turns on the double genitive "of," invention belonging to the other, of the other, already part of the other, or invention *of* the other, making up the other. The "of" can go either way: invention derives from the other, belongs to it, is secondary to it, or, on the contrary, goes toward it, in a transitive act of creating something.

Improvisation, as Derrida knew, is an act of invention that is not only insolent, impolite, a breech of academic etiquette. Improvisation also says something about the conditions of novelty in writing and speaking. If it is new, it will upset institutions and ideas already in place. If what is said in a lecture were wholly predictable, however, it would not be inventive.

Therefore it would hardly be worth saying. Why hear something said that you already know? Invention, on the contrary, is the materialization of spirit that would not otherwise be able to work in the world.

> Here [continues Derrida, improvising a riff on that first sentence I have already cited: "What am I going to be able to invent today?"] perhaps we have an inventive incipit for a lecture. Imagine, if you will, a speaker daring to address his hosts in these terms. He thus seems to appear before them without knowing what he is going to say; he declares rather insolently that he is setting out to improvise. Obliged as he is to invent on the spot, he wonders again: "Just what am I going to have to invent?" But simultaneously he seems to be implying, not without presumptuousness, that the improvised speech will remain unpredictable, that is to say, as usual, "still" new, original, unique—in a word, inventive. And in fact, by having at least invented something with his very first sentence, such an orator [that is, as the word suggests, someone who breathes back out again what he has breathed in, "in-spired," been inspired by] would be breaking the rules, would be breaking with convention, etiquette, the rhetoric of modesty, in short, with all the conditions of social interaction. An invention always presupposes some illegality, the breaking of an implicit contract; it inserts disorder into the peaceful ordering of things, it disregards the proprieties. Showing apparently none of the patience of a preface—it is itself a new preface—it goes and frustrates expectations [*voici qu'elle déjoue les attendus*].[7]

Derrida here performs a variant of the work of words I ascribed to myself a few moments ago. In speaking of the insolence of telling an audience you have unfortunately not prepared a lecture and are going to improvise, though you haven't really much idea of just what you are going to invent, Derrida, no reader can doubt, is insolent. He performs the insolence of which he speaks. "You want to understand why improvisation is insolent? I'll show you. Here is an example of it at work."

Well, what am I going to invent today? After having primed the inspirational air pump, so to speak, with a resonant citation from Derrida, I can only hope for the best, since, though I have a proleptic glimpse or foreknowledge of my endpoint, I do not know just what track this essay is going to take to get there, just what spirits it will materialize along the way, just what spirits will use me, work my mind and my fingers on the keyboard, as the medium by means of which to become material.

"Material spirit": it is a wonderfully provocative (apparent) oxymoron. The phrase is a juxtaposition of seemingly blank incompatibles. The material, we assume, is dumb matter, solid, recalcitrant, like that stone Samuel Johnson kicked to refute Berkeley's idealism, or like what we may assume we can take for granted about the materiality of human bodies. "The materiality of the body" is a big theme in present-day feminist studies. We all know what is meant by that phrase. Of course the body is material. Spirit, on the contrary, is, well, spiritual: invisible, intangible, disembodied, immaterial. Spirit may be all around us, ubiquitous, but you would never know it, just as we are not aware of all those radio and television signals that are passing through our bodies at every moment, night and day. Nevertheless, we assume that unless spirit is in some way embodied, materialized, inscribed, it cannot be performatively felicitous. It will not work. It requires some form of tuner, something analogous to a radio or a television set, to materialize it in an inscription so it can work in the world. We need to use matter to get tuned in to spirit.

The idea that spirit can be, must be, materialized is to be found in many dimensions of Western thought and culture, for example in my initial citation from Claire Colebrook. Spirit's need for inscription is a ubiquitous presumption, so taken for granted that we hardly notice it. This presumption is like the hypothesis of what used to be called "the ether," or like the air we breathe. The assumption that spirit must be materialized to work is a material-spiritual presence among us. In all its many forms the same insoluble paradox or aporia of a two that is also, necessarily, one reappears. Though many examples of this exist, I shall begin with the most important, the *ur*-example, the arch-example, the one that has been there since the beginning of what we call "Western culture."

Verbum Caro Factum Est

Logos sarx egeneto. Verbum caro factum est. "And the Word was made flesh, and dwelt among us" (John 1:14). The model or paradigm of material spirit, at least in the West, is the Incarnation. John's sentences have called forth endless commentary, by Christian exegetes and others, for millennia. To recapitulate them here and comment adequately on them would take volumes. "This is the formula of the 'incarnation,'" says Jean-Luc Nancy of John's words, "by which God makes himself man, and that humanity of God is indeed the decisive trait of Christianity, and through it a determinative trait for the whole of Western culture."[8] All the other cases of what can be called material spirit, in our tradition, are based on the Incarnation. As Nancy goes on to say, however, the doctrine of the Incarnation does not mean that the flesh was there first and then was entered into by spirit, by way of an insufflation. John means, rather, Nancy says, that spirit itself became flesh, or, in John's original Greek, engendered (*exgeneto*) flesh: "If the word [*le verbe*] was *made* flesh, or if (in Greek) it *became* flesh, or if it *was engendered* or *engendered itself* as flesh, then it is surely the case that it had no need to penetrate the inside of that flesh that was initially given outside it: it became flesh itself."[9]

This was transubstantiation in reverse. In transubstantiation the bread and wine of the Eucharist become the body and blood of Christ, that is, the incarnated deity. *Hoc est enim corpus meum,* "this is truly my body," said Jesus at the Last Supper. Taking Communion is a way of eating and drinking spirit. In the Incarnation spirit becomes body, engenders itself as flesh. We then eat and drink God in the Eucharist. The Incarnation is the necessary presupposition of the Communion service. Without the Incarnation, no Eucharist. The Eucharist is a way of ingesting spirit because the body and blood of Christ, in what is called the "real presence" of these in the transubstantiated bread and wine, is the Word incarnate. Consuming the changed substance of the bread and wine is to ingest Christ, that is, God incarnate, spirit become matter, and so to become Christlike. Taking Communion is to be changed into what Gerard Manley Hopkins called an "AfterChrist." Hopkins converted to Catholicism from his family's Anglicanism because only Catholicism, he believed, believed in the real presence. Jesus was not a ghost walking in broad daylight, at least not until the Resurrection, when he rose from the dead, though just what form the risen Christ took is hard to define, as the story of Doubting Thomas in John's Gospel demonstrates. Jesus was a man of flesh and blood, born of woman, like you and me, and at the same time he was God.

As Nancy observes, theologians have tied themselves in knots through the centuries over the Incarnation, just as philosophers, most notably Heidegger in modern times, have tied themselves in knots over the word *logos.* Theologians have made truly superhuman efforts trying to account for this becoming or making or self-making that engendered Christ's double nature as man-God, as material spirit. Christ incarnate is the second member of the Trinity, which is made up of God the Father, God the Son, and God the Holy Spirit, "Theology," says Nancy, "has made superhuman efforts—one might quite appropriately say—to think this *becoming* that produces, in one sole person, two heterogeneous natures."[10] The efforts are superhuman because you would have to be a God or a man-God to think the mystery of the Incarnation. W. B. Yeats, or at least his persona "Ribh," calls the doctrine of the Trinity "an abstract Greek absurdity," that is, both inhumanly abstract and sexist. For Yeats, the true trinity is man, woman, and child.[11] It might be argued that the role in Christianity of the Virgin Mary in engendering Jesus is a way to rectify that bias toward masculine abstraction. Whatever those dry theologians may try superhumanly to think, Catholics can go on worshipping the Virgin as the medium by which the Word became flesh.

Nancy, in my judgment, does not pay enough attention, not, at least, in the passage I have cited, to the notorious fact that John does not say "God was made flesh," but "the Word was made flesh." Nancy at first says "God makes himself man," and then a little later "the word [*le verbe*] *was made* flesh,"[12] as if these formulations were two ways to say the same thing. In a peculiar way they are the same, but the way is definitely peculiar. Nancy's elision may betray something essential about his project to "deconstruct Christianity." He sidesteps a puzzle that has to do with language as a self-sustaining nonsystematic system or set of systems detachable from all referents, though always seeming to refer.

Well, what is the difference between calling God "God" and calling God "the Word"? The usual explanation, as most people know, is that the word "Word" in John's Gospel is a sign that, unlike the other Gospel-makers, those who wrote the so-called synoptic Gospels, Matthew, Mark, and Luke, John was deeply influenced by Greek philosophical thought, Gnosticism, Neoplatonism, and so on. John's Gospel begins with the words, "In the beginning was the Word, and the Word was with God, and the Word was God" (John 1:1). Well, which is it, John? If the Word came first, as an *archē,* a beginning before the beginning, there perhaps even before God was, was the Word then just "with God," or was the Word identical to God, as the verb-to-be copula "was" in the final phrase asserts? It must be both at once, assuming John knew what he was talking about, and wrote carefully what he meant to say. "Beginning" is *archē* in Greek, meaning, in this case, an absolute beginning and source of all things, existing before anything else was. The word *archē* is translated as *principio* in the standard Latin translation of John's Gospel.

Matters are not made any simpler by the fact that "Word" is *logos* in Greek. *Logos* is a complex word (in Empson's sense). It means not only "word" but also "reason," "mind," "measure," "ratio," "proportion," and "wisdom." *Logos* is a kind of ubiquitous interpenetrating spirit that holds material things together and keeps them in rhythmic harmony and measure, as in Heraclitus's definition of the materialized logos, fire: "All things are an equal exchange for fire and fire for all things, kindling in measures and going out in measures."[13] Philosophers and theologians, from Heraclitus down to Martin Heidegger, have had a superhuman field day with the word *logos.* Heidegger habitually, in his later work at least, for example in his Anaximander essay, though not in *Sein und Zeit,* relates the noun *logos* to the verb *legein,* which means, according to Heidegger, "to gather" in Greek. The *logos* is a gathering, *eine Versammlung.* It smorges, as Pogo would say, diverse entities together into one whole, while leaving them identifiably separate entities.

This, if I may dare to say so, is a good example of Heidegger's penchant for thinking in terms of etymological metaphors and for then portentously taking those metaphors literally. Heidegger abominated tropes. The Greeks, Heidegger avers, did not really mean "word" or "mind" or "reason" or "ratio" or "measure" by *logos.* They meant "gathering," whether they knew it or intended to mean it or not. The word's root did their thinking for them. They thought they were saying "word," but they were really saying "gathering": "Yet since the dawn of thinking 'being' names the presencing of what is present in the sense of the lighting-sheltering gathering [*lichtend-bergenden Versammlung*] which is how the *Logos* is thought and named. The *Logos* (*legein,* to gather or collect [*lesen, sammeln*]) is experienced out of *'Aletheia,* the sheltering which discloses. In the conflicted essence of *'Aletheia* is concealed the thoughtful essence of *'Eris* and *Moira,* in terms of which *Physis* is at the same time named."[14] That knits things together, all right! It gathers a whole set of portentous words pretty tightly, partly by way of hyphens, in a lighting-sheltering gathering, a gathering that hides and reveals at once. It is almost a little too neat. One wants, a little, to get out of the cave, wherein abides Heidegger's eternally revolving machine of words, into the sunlight.

Christian theologians usually assume that Christ, the second person of the Trinity, is the Word, the *Logos.* God the Father created all things by means of the *Logos.* He thereby holds them in measured balance. One might even say God gathers things together into the one creation. The Holy Spirit, the third member of the Trinity, is the name for the *Logos* as it is impalpably, immaterially present everywhere in the creation through God the Father's action in creating the world. He did this by means of Christ as *Logos.* The Holy Spirit can only work in the world by way of its embodiment in Christ the Word. This is the model, for us in the West, of material spirit.

The paradigm of the creation is therefore the Incarnation, in which the Word was made flesh or made itself flesh. The whole Creation in a sense exemplifies the Incarnation. The Creation is matter and spirit combined, *sarx* and *Logos* at once. The great Victorian English Catholic poet, Gerard Manley Hopkins, Jesuit priest, expounds the doctrine of the *Logos* in his poems and devotional writings, as in "That Nature is a Heraclitean Fire and of the Comfort of the Resurrection."[15] When the "tall nun," heroine of Hopkins's "The Wreck of the Deutschland," calls, in her extremity, "O Christ, Christ, come quickly,"[16] the poet comments, "Wording it how but by him that present and past, / Heaven and earth are word of, worded by."[17] All Creation is word of God, speaks for him, in a ubiquitous gospel or good news. You just need to look out your window or to go for a walk to hear or see the Word.

I conclude from the discrepancy between "Word" and "God" in John's formulation (they must be both identical and different) that some difficult-to-think issue involving language is always present in the doctrine of the Incarnation and in all of its derived forms, however secular they may seem. The aporia of the Word made flesh is perhaps impossible to think clearly, rationally, logically. You must take it on faith, as they say. Thomas Didymus, "Doubting Thomas," at the conclusion of John's Gospel, in the end believes he is face-to-face with the risen Christ without actually needing to put his hand into the wound in Christ's side. For him, seeing is believing; touching is not necessary, though at first he had wanted to touch. The risen Christ, however, says of this seeing-believing, "blessed are they that have not seen, and yet have believed" (John 20:29). That includes all of us since the Ascension of the risen Christ. To say God became flesh and to say the Word became flesh is to say two different things and at the same time to say the same thing. Some version of this aporia of the Incarnation is present in the many derived forms of it in the Western tradition, in spite of the evident heterogeneity of that tradition.

Another way to put this is to say that John's words manifest the irreconcilable interference of two different language systems, each with its own "God-term," to borrow Kenneth Burke's frequently used phrase.[18] On the one hand, to say "God became man" is to speak within a metaphysical, ontological, or, more properly, theological language system. "God" is the God term in this case. This system depends on the dualism between God and man, the transcendent world of spirit and the material world of nature and of natural creatures here below that God created by way of his "Fiat." On the other hand, to say "The Word became flesh" is to speak within a linguistic system that recognizes that all words must have some material base to work effectively in the world. The God term in this system is "Word." The word must become flesh to dwell among us and to do the work of salvation, ultimately by way of the Crucifixion. That, however, is not an exit from a linguistic system. It is rather an observation about language. It is a claim that all things are word of, worded by, the Word. All individual words are derived from the *ur*-Word, from Christ the Word.

Which of these two language systems takes precedence over the other? Which is the literal of which the other is a metaphor, or even an allegory of the other, in the de Manian sense? Is God really the Word, or is the Word really God? That may be impossible to decide, though much hangs on being able to decide. John says both that the Word was with God and that the Word was God.

The word "Word" is, for Saint John, a synonym and at the same time not a synonym for the word "God." "Word" is a word that is not a word. It is an *ur*-word for which all other words are tropes, just as Hopkins says all creation is word of, worded by, Christ the Word. Paul de Man in the section about the "Profession du Foi" of the "Savoyard Vicar" in "Textual Allegories" (the as yet unpublished 1973 draft of the Rousseau section of *Allegories of Reading*) uses the word "theotropic." "God," says de Man, is the only literally referential word. It is, hyperbolically or paradigmatically, what Burke calls "the God-term" that any system of language must have, even completely nontheological ones. The "God term" is the word that is both outside and inside the system at once. In the theological sign system "God" is the word that all other words are word of and that makes possible those other words in their (presumed) systematicity, their hanging together, their gathering.

Every linguistic system must have a God-term that cannot be defined by the other words. The God-term cannot therefore be defined, since it is the basis of definition. It just is. It must be taken for granted as a beginning, since it is the basis on which all the others words are to be defined and to function. Words that are worded by, words of, God are theotropic both in the etymological sense that they are turned toward God the Word and in the antithetical sense that they are tropes, metaphors, substitutes, for God. They are even, in the de Manian sense, allegories for the word God. They are, that is, displacements, substitutions, metaphors, tropes, turnings. In that sense all words but the word "God" are turned away from direct face to face orientation toward God. The theotropic is atheotropic, and vice versa. It is no wonder theologians have had to make literally superhuman efforts to understand these impasses in thought. You would need to be a god to do it. Here is what de Man says:

> On the other hand, referentiality is also, and simultaneously, the very movement of transgression or transcendence that prevents any judgment from being anything *but* a sign, compels it to turn always again into a signification that radically differs from it by its (fallacious) claim <of> to be a meaning. As such, referentiality is constitutively metaphysical, in the Nietzschean sense of the term as taken over by Heidegger and his best French reader, Jacques Derrida. It is also constitutively theotropic, since the only conceivable name for transcendental signification that would no longer be itself a sign, the only word that would have a truly proper meaning, is "god." The only

"meaning that one can give the word to be" (Profession, p. 571)[19] is that of "god." Yet, at the same time, the referentiality resulting from this paradigmatic denomination must lead to the performance of a finite, practical or, as we say, "historical" act—such as, for example, the acts performed or the emotion experienced by the readers of the second part of the Nouvelle Heloïse under the impact of their reading.[20]

The word "god" is generated by language out of its inescapable need to have a God-term. Nevertheless, the (aberrant) referentiality generated by this word, "God," the only word with "a truly proper meaning," that is, the only word that is not a theotropic figure for God, produces belief that this referentiality refers to something preexisting rather than being generated by a linguistic necessity. That belief in turn produces, no one can doubt in these days when religion is so politicized, acts or emotions in the "real world."

What We Call Ideology: Mystified Incarnations

The Incarnation is the *ur*-version of ideology, the name we give to mystified belief in materialized spirit of one sort or another. All the various intertwined machinal-ecotechnical-material-spiritual sign systems within which we live today are secular versions of the Incarnation: the global ecosytem that is suffering probably irreversible anthropogenic climate change; spiritualism as a cult belief still very much alive, incarnated in the mediums who practice it; assumptions about the materialization of soul in a body; cultural studies of various sorts with their focus on "the body" and on "material culture"; the immense teletechnological system of computers, iPods, cell phones, radios, television sets, cinema, and the media that, working together, so much determine the way we live now (my ironic reference is to Anthony Trollope's novel of that title); the global financial system, now in autoimmune "meldown," a subset of the larger ecoteletechnological machine; language, literature, and literary studies as yet another example of a machinal system dominated by derived incarnational ideas.

I say these are interwined "systems," but these systems are asystematic. They are never complete, and each contains contradictions within it that might be compared, as Derrida does in "Faith and Knowledge" ("Foi et savoir"), to the autoimmunity that can lead a human body to destroy itself through the working of its own immune system.[21] All these machines assume spirit must be materialized in order to work, to function in the world, whether for good or for ill from the human perspective. All are examples of what Jean-Luc Nancy calls the "ecotechnical," that is, the assumption that the whole world is an immense machine that has generated our bodies and plugged them in various ways into the "environment." Nancy's usage of the word "ecotechnical" is quite different from *Wikipedia*'s definition of ecotechnology as "an applied science that seeks to fulfill human needs while causing minimal ecological disruption, by harnessing and subtly manipulating natural forces to leverage their beneficial effects."[22] Nancy, on the contrary, says:

> Our world is the world of the "technical" [*la* "*technique*"], a world whose cosmos, nature, gods, entire system, is, in its inner joints [*sa jointure intime*], exposed as "technical": the world of an *ecotechnical.* The ecotechnical functions with technical apparatuses, to which our every part is connected. But what it *makes* are our bodies, which it brings into the world and links to the system, thereby creating our bodies as more visible, more proliferating, more polymorphic, more compressed, more "amassed" and "zoned" than ever before. Through the creation of bodies the ecotechnical has the *sense* that we vainly seek in the remains of the sky or the spirit.[23]

The phrase "material spirit" does not imply that it is impossible to think of one form or another of *immaterial* spirit. Nevertheless, as I have said, our tradition tends to assume that spirit, in whatever form, cannot work in the world unless it is embodied in some medium or other, some mediator. The emblem of this might be the folk belief in Ireland, reported somewhere by W. B. Yeats, that says the fairies, the *sídhe,* cannot play hurling (an Irish form of field hockey something like lacrosse) unless they have a mortal playing on each side. Without that, their hurley sticks would be powerless to strike the ball.[24] I mention this somewhat comically absurd example (who would be likely to believe in it today?) to suggest two things. The first is the way all the examples I have listed are versions of an (aberrant) penchant toward thinking of matter in organic terms. The prime example of matter is *sarx,* the human body, attached to some technological prosthesis, like those hockey sticks, or like language, or like the Internet. All the derived forms of the Incarnation are, however, not organic in the traditional sense of the word. They are not an inextricably assembled many in one, animated by "life." The derived forms of the Incarnation I have listed are not organic but are more or less complicated machines. This includes the human body itself, with its genetic programs and its automatically, autonomically functioning immune and endocrine system.[25]

What, exactly, is a machine? It is an assemblage of material parts not inhabited by any "spirit." A machine just goes on repeating itself, mindlessly, though perhaps with some tendency to destroy itself catastrophically, as in catastrophic climate change or in autoimmune self-destruction of the human body. Henri Bergson, in a provocative formulation at the end of *The Two Sources of Morality and Religion,* says it is humanity's primary responsibility to play its part in furthering "the essential function of the universe, which is a machine for making gods."[26] Humanity is here defined as no more than a prosthetic tool employed by the universe to get its essential work done. Derrida cites and comments on this formulation in various places in "Faith and Knowledge" ("Foi et savoir").[27]

My example of the supernatural hurling players hints at another feature of all systems derived from the Incarnation. All my examples, like the Incarnation itself, are forms of what might be called ideological belief, objects of faith, not of knowledge. You must believe in fairies, in the *sídhe,* in order to worry about whether or not they can play hurling. Marx in *The German Ideology* and in *Capital* asserts that all forms of ideological aberration, for example commodity fetishism, are based on religious ideology. Religious belief, for Marx, is the prime example of ideology. All ideological mystifications are displaced forms of the Incarnation.

What, then, is ideology? Paul de Man's definition in *The Resistance to Theory,* with its accompanying reference to Marx's *The German Ideology,* is succinct and accurate. This well-known definition says much in little. At least it is well-known to those who read de Man. "What we call ideology," says de Man, "is precisely the confusion of linguistic with natural reality, of reference with phenomenalism."[28] This sentence is highly compressed, elliptical, cryptic. It is not entirely perspicuous at first glance. "What we call" is an odd phrase. The "we" may be de Man himself, politely using the academic "we." He may therefore mean, "What I call." He may also mean, as is more likely, a collective academic "we." We all habitually use, in a sort of somnambulistic, ideological trance, the strange and inappropriate word "ideology." "Call" is also odd. I suppose he means that is just the name we call it by. It is an arbitrary label. This name is misleading in various ways. Its direct source is the "ideologues" of the post-Revolutionary period in France, for example Destutt de Tracy (1754–1836). Tracy, for example in his main work, *Éléments d'idéologie* (1817–18), referred "spirit" in the sense of human psychology and human "ideas" back to their material, physiological bases. The word "idea," however, has for us today not only Tracy's Lockean meaning but also misleading Platonic, Hegelian, and Husserlian associations, all different from one another in their use of the word "idea," and in their use of the word "spirit," too, as in Hegel's *Phenomenology of Spirit* (*Phäenomenologie des Geistes* in German; *Geist* as in *Poltergeist*). A *Geist* is a ghost. "Ideology" means, literally, the knowledge or study ("logy," formed from "logos") of ideas, as "theology" is the knowledge of God, or as Derrida's coinage, "hauntology," names the sciences of ghosts. Kenneth Burke's tautological word "logology" might be a better term for "what we (mistakenly) call ideology." The title of one of Burke's books is *The Rhetoric of Religion: Studies in Logology.* This might be paraphrased as "words about words," or "words about the Word." "The rhetoric of religion" names the ways we talk about God, by displacement, metaphors, metonymies, catachresis, and other rhetorical devices.

What we call ideology "is precisely the confusion of linguistic with natural reality, or reference with phenomenalism." Just what does de Man mean by these two phrases in apposition that, he claims, define correctly what we call ideology? Ideology confuses something that exists only in language with something that exists in material "reality," as that reality manifests itself phenomenally. All language is irreducibly referential, even though what it refers to does not always exist, as, for example, in literary works. Dorothea Brooke, the heroine of George Eliot's *Middlemarch,* can be encountered only by reading the novel. She does not have an extralinguistic existence. In a sense she is spirit without matter, a literary ghost, though she is embodied in the inscribed words on the pages of the novel.

Many, perhaps most, literary studies, especially current ones of the "cultural studies" kind, are examples of incarnational ideology in their resistance to the self-evident fact I have just mentioned. I do not exclude my own work. We cannot accept the idea that literary works inscribe referentiality without preexisting referents. The force of a literary work, we assume, must lie in its reference to some solid external material reality like the coming of the railroads (referred to in *Middlemarch*). Literary works must somehow be implicitly embodied by way of their referentiality. They must be materializable spirit rather than autopoeisis, the self-generation of a purely virtual reality, which is what they actually are. Paul de Man expresses this by way of the distinction between hermeneutics and poetics he makes in his lecture on Walter Benjamin's "The Task of the Translator." Poetics studies the way literary works mean, their *Art des Meinens.* Hermeneutics goes outside the literary work toward what it means, *das Gemeinte:*

> When you do hermeneutics, you are concerned with the meaning of the work; when you do poetics, you are concerned with the stylistics or with the description of the way in which a work means. The question is whether these two are complementary, whether you can cover the full work by doing hermeneutics and poetics at the same time. The experience of trying to do this shows that it is not the case.

> When one tries to achieve this complementarity, the poetics always drops out, and what one always does is hermeneutics. One is so attracted by problems of meaning that it is impossible to do hermeneutics and poetics at the same time. From the moment you start to get involved with problems of meaning, as I unfortunately tend to do, forget about the poetics. The two are not complementary, the two may be mutually exclusive in a certain way, and that is part of the problem which Benjamin states, a purely linguistic problem.[29]

The referential function of words cannot, however, be suspended. A given word or phrase or sentence always appears to refer to something, even if that something does not exist in "reality." Existing in reality is defined as being "phenomenally" present, that is, I take it, open to sensation, perceptible by one of the five senses. Ideology assumes because something has a name it must be somewhere or somehow visible, touchable, hearable, smellable, or tastable, or all five. That assumption is a confusion, an error, an aberration.

De Man gives a witty example of this confusion and of the difficulty of avoiding it a few sentences earlier: "no one in his right mind will try to grow grapes by the luminosity of the word 'day,' but it is very difficult not to conceive the pattern of one's past and future existence as in accordance with temporal and spatial schemes that belong to fictional narratives and not to the world."[30] The word "day" refers, but it has no luminosity, just as the pattern I think my life has, for example as embodied in an autobiography I may write, is "fictional," a matter of words, not something that has a real existence. We project an incarnation in materiality of our spiritual ideas, an incarnation that is illusory, that has no bodily form. That does not mean, as de Man goes on to say, that such illusions do not have effects in the "real" world: "their impact upon the world may well be all too strong for comfort."[31] Ideological illusions are performatively felicitous. They bring about wars, economic meltdowns, marriages good and bad, such as Dorothea Brooke's disastrous marriage to Mr. Casaubon, the passing of laws good and bad, and catastrophic climate change.

De Man follows his definition of "what we call ideology" with one of the most extravagant, most cheeky boasts about the usefulness of literary theory and literary analysis that has ever been made. If ideology is the confusion of linguistic with natural reality, "it follows that," de Man says, "more than any other mode of inquiry, including economics, the linguistics of literariness is a powerful and indispensable tool in the unmasking of ideological aberrations, as well as a determining factor in accounting for their occurrence."[32] It has always seemed to me a savage irony and a splendid example of the ideological mystification de Man is denouncing that this spectacular essay, now a classic of literary theory, was rejected by the MLA committee charged with putting together a collection of essays by various scholars on the different facets of literary study. De Man had been asked to write the essay on literary theory. Rejecting it was a big mistake, to put it mildly. "Those," de Man continues, "who reproach literary theory for being oblivious to social and historical (that is to say ideological) reality are merely stating their fear at having their own ideological mystifications exposed by the tool they are trying to discredit. They are, in short, very poor readers of Marx's *German Ideology.*"[33]

What is *The German Ideology* doing here, suddenly, climactically, but laconically, enigmatically? It is quite surprising, to me at least, to find de Man alluding favorably to Marx. It is impossible to know exactly how de Man read *The German Ideology,* since he never followed up on his hint by showing how he thought Marx's book should be read. The most distinguished reading of *The German Ideology* I know, however, is that by Derrida in *Specters of Marx.* This gives some idea of what is at stake in de Man's allusion.

Marx's goal, as Derrida shows, is an exposure of ideology as false incarnation. Ideology, Marx holds, is the aberrant assumption that spirit in the form of wacky ideas is materialized or can be materialized, just as God or the Word became flesh in the Incarnation. Derrida, following Marx, traces all ideological aberrations back to the notion of the Man-God, the material incarnation of spirit: "Is not the Christic moment, and within it the eucharistic instant, the hyperbole of *acharnement* [opinionated ardor, from *charnière,* hinge, point of junction] itself? If every specter, as we have amply seen, is distinguished from spirit by an incorporation, by the phenomenal form of a quasi-incarnation, then Christ is the most spectral of specters."[34] Derrida on Marx on Stirner on Szeliga, in the admirable chapter 5 of *Specters of Marx* ("Apparition of the Inapparent: The Phenomenological 'Conjuring Trick'" ["Apparition de l'inapparent: 'L'escamotage' phenomenologique"]) (124–76 [201–79]), is pervaded by the ghostly presence of theological figures. This is the case not just in Marx's language or Stirner's but also in Derrida's own vocabulary, or in what appears to be Derrida's vocabulary and not just ironic miming of Marx. *Es spukt* the language of the Incarnation in what Derrida writes.

Es spukt, as Derrida observes, is a wonderful and untranslatable German expression, just as is the word for "conjuring trick" (*escamotage* in French or *Eskamotage* in Marx's German). *Escamotage* is favorite word of Marx and of Derrida after him. It means "sleight of hand," as in the tricks spiritualist mediums play with tables, cards, and other objects that seem to move by spiritual impulsion, or that are made to disappear and then reappear again in spiritualized form, as hovering ghosts, like those worthless credit default swaps into which bankers and financiers, with the help of computer programs, turned valueless subprime mortgages, so that the bankers no longer knew who owed what, to whom, or how much, only that the derivatives made untold billions disappear by *escamotage:* "Now you see it; now you don't."

> The word *Eskamotage* speaks of subterfuge or theft in the exchange of merchandise, but first of all the sleight of hand by means of which an illusionist makes the most perceptible body disappear. It is an art or technique of *making disappear.* The *escamoteur* knows how to *make inapparent* [*rendre inapparent*]. He is an expert in a hyper-phenomenology. Now, the height of the conjuring trick here consists in causing to disappear while producing "apparitions," which is only contradictory in appearance, precisely, since one causes to disappear by provoking hallucinations or by inducing [*donnant*] visions. (127–28 [204])

As for *es spukt,* "its translation," says Derrida, "always fails, unfortunately, to render the link between the impersonality or the quasi-anonymity of an operation [*spuken*] without act, without real subject or object, and the production of a figure, that of the *revenant* [*der Spuk*]: not simply 'it spooks' [*ça hante*], as we just ventured to translate, but 'it returns,' 'it ghosts,' 'it specters' ['*ça revient,*' '*ça revenante,*' '*ça spectre*']" (133 [212]) One might say that *es spukt* is an equivalent of the Greek middle voice, neither passive nor active, though uttered in a language that does not have a middle voice. It is parallel to *es gibt* in German or *il y a* in French, both notoriously hard to translate. "It gives spookings." "There are spookings." English has the advantage over French here, since "spook" is a good English word, though a somewhat comic or apotropaic one. "Spooks" holds off belief in ghosts by giving them a funny Halloween name. A bit more seriously, we say, "He was really spooked!" to mean "He was scared to death." We do not mean that the person was scared necessarily by anything overtly spectral. We might say, "He was spooked by the doctor's diagnosis." Belief in ghosts, as in spiritualism, is a peculiar, somewhat twisted, form of displaced belief in the Incarnation.

What follows the passage on *es spukt* I have just cited is a good example of Derrida's use of language about the Incarnation proper to talk about something else. In this case Derrida, following Marx, argues that all doctrines of the ego, "the Cartesian *cogito,* the Kantian 'I think,' the phenomenological *ego cogito*" (133 [212]), including Stirner's ego theory as deconstructed by Marx, are versions of the Incarnation. Just how does Derrida articulate this connection? Is it just an analogy, or is the relation a kind of chiasmus, in which each is the figure of the other, the biblical Incarnation a result of reifying perennial assumptions about the ego, while modern assumptions about the ego are displaced versions of notions about the Incarnation ubiquitous in our culture? Does Derrida agree with Marx, as Marx seems sometimes not to differ essentially from Stirner (whom Derrida praises in passing as worth serious reading)? It is not all that easy to tell, since an accurate measure would depend on assessing the degree of irony in Derrida's miming of Marx, who mimes Stirner, who ridicules a certain hapless Szeliga. "The latter," says Derrida, "is reproached for the very thing that Marx reproaches Stirner for," that is, for finding nothing but a ghost in the self (134 [213]).

These fellows play hardball. The rule of the game they play is that you must show your predecessors in the line to be prime fools for believing in ghosts, whereas you are free of such superstition. Nevertheless, as Derrida demonstrates for Marx in relation to Stirner, if not for himself in relation to Marx, in talking about the last in the chain before yourself you are really talking, by secret transference and denial (*Verneinung*), about yourself. The pot, when it calls the kettle black, does not know its own blackness, but implicitly reveals it. The compulsive repetition and excessive joyous almost hysterical violence with which Marx performs his putdown of Stirner betrays the way his critique, as he secretly knows, returns in a boomerang effect on himself: "The deconstructive critiques that Marx will address to the Stirnerian 'historical constructions' or 'montages' risk coming back at him like a boomerang" (141 [224]). Derrida's words, performative enunciations, words as acts, are themselves another boomerang. They make sure the risk becomes event, both in revealing that Marx is obliquely criticizing himself and in even more obliquely, secretly, showing that the same thing can be said about Derrida. The conspicuous excesses in Derrida's deconstruction of Marx, the obsessive repetitions, anticipations, retrospections, and circlings back to similar points, the constant postponing refrain that says he is not doing the full reading of *The German Ideology* that would be necessary, indicate that Derrida cannot get Marx out of his head because he knows without knowing it that "Karl Marx, *c'est moi.*"

One might ask whether or not Derrida is a Marxist. He certainly gives Marx his due, both for his global political effect and for his intellectual power as an irreplaceable analyst of ideologies. Nevertheless, in one place in *Specters of Marx,* Derrida gets the last word and puts Marx firmly in his place, as Stirner had put Szeliga, and Marx had put Stirner. What is the point of disagreement? Where, in Derrida's view, does Marx go wrong?

The issue precisely has to do with the material workings of spirit. Marx, says Derrida firmly, is "pre-deconstructive." Marx, according to Derrida, bases all his critical work on a presupposed ontology that is never put in question. It is the ontological belief that we know what materiality is and that the material base in the form of raw materials, the workers' work to transform these into commodities, the oppressive class structure, capitalism and its institutions, underlies all the fantasies of ideology as a solid ground on which airy ideological structures, ghostly immaterial houses of cards, are constructed. I remember Derrida saying to me more than once how suspicious he was of the word "materialism" and its cognates. Derrida believed rather that materiality was something to put in question. In the end he opted for a "materiality without matter," a difficult concept that I cannot parse in this essay except implicitly, indirectly, in all I say about "material spirit."

Here is what Derrida says in *Specters of Marx* when he finally, almost at the end, comes clean and says just how he thinks Marx was a fool, befooled, the last dummy in the chain before him:

> . . . even as he remains one of the first thinkers of technics [*de la technique*], or even, by far and from afar, of the tele-technology that it will always have been, from near or from far, Marx continues to want to ground his critique or his exorcism of the spectral simulacrum in an ontology. It is a—critical but pre-deconstructive—ontology of presence as actual reality and as objectivity. This critical ontology means to deploy the possibility of dissipating the phantom, let us venture to say again of conjuring it away as representative consciousness of a subject, and of bringing this representation back to the material world of labor, production, and exchange, so as to reduce it to its conditions. (170—translation modified [269]).

Derrida goes on to say that "pre-deconstructive" "does not mean false, unnecessary, or illusory" (170 [269]). It does, however, characterize "a relatively stabilized knowledge that calls for questions more radical than the critique itself and than the ontology that grounds the critique" (170 [269–70]).

Once we abolish capitalism, the phantasmagoria of ideology, for example commodity fetishism, will vanish, says Marx. Marx's whole effort in *Capital,* according to Derrida, is based on an original conjuration or exorcism that attempts, necessarily without success, to abolish the ghosts of immaterial/material spirit that are always already there before human beings made the first table out of wood and will still be there when capitalist commodity fetishism (as in the assumption that everyone needs to buy a new car at least every two years or a new table to replace a perfectly good old one) disappears in the proletarian revolution, the revolution to come, that is certain to come. "Ontology," for example Marxist dialectical materialism, says Derrida, "opposes [these preexisting and always surviving ghosts] only in a movement of exorcism. Ontology is a conjuration" (161 [255]). It is, however, a conjuration that never works, just as there is no "deconstruction of Christianity" such as Jean-Luc Nancy hopes can be performed.

Ideologies, I conclude, are an omnipresent form in human cultures, especially in Western capitalist societies, of secularized Incarnation, that is, of material spirit. Ideologies are not just mystified belief in groundless ideas. They are ideas incorporated in the human body, in its feelings, speech, and actions, and then in the ecotechnical systems human beings collectively create on the "basis" of those ideological aberrations. Those prosthetic systems include the whole earth as an extension of the human bodies that are by their ecotechnological actions causing probably irreversible climate change.

In this essay, beginning, on the basis of a passage from an essay by Claire Colebrook, with reflections on the phrase "material spirit," I have then shown, with Jean-Luc Nancy's help, that the Christian dogma of the incarnation is the basic form of material spirit in Western culture. I have gone on, finally, to identify, this time with help from Burke, Marx, and Derrida, the way secular ideologies are transposed forms of the linguistic structures present in wordings of the incarnation.

Notes

Introduction / Gregory C. Stallings, Manuel Asensi, and Carl Good

1. Karl Marx and Friedrich Engels, *The German Ideology,* sect. 1.4.B.

2. As is well known, the etymology of this word was in dispute from the earliest times. *Religare* is the most commonly assumed root, but Cicero held that "religion" was derived from *relegere,* "to read again."

3. Michel Foucault, "What Is Critique?," in *The Politics of Truth,* 28–30 passim.

4. John Caputo, *What Would Jesus Deconstruct? The Good News of Postmodernism for the Church.*

Eucharistic Imaginings in Proust and Woolf / Richard Kearney

I am very grateful to all my colleagues in the "Meaning and Transcendence" seminar at the Jesuit Institute at Boston College for several of the insights in this chapter, in particular those with whom I had an extensive creative correspondence: on Joyce, Proust, and Woolf, namely, Mary-Joe Hughes, Dennis Taylor, Anne Davenport, Tom Epstein, Marty Cohen, Andy Von Hendy, Vanessa Rumble, Anne Bernard, and Kevin Newmark. I am also very grateful to my assistant, Christopher Yates, for his invaluable help in editing this essay. Much of what follows in the essay represents the development of an anatheist aesthetics that I have explored elsewhere; see, for example, "Epiphanies of the Everyday: Toward a Micro-Eschatology," in *After God: Richard Kearney and the Religious Turn in Phenomenology,* ed. John Panteleimon Manoussakis (New York: Fordham University Press, 2006), and my related essays, "*Traversing the Imaginary: Epiphanies in Joyce and Proust,*" in *Traversing the Imaginary: Richard Kearney and the Postmodern Challenge,* ed.

Peter Gratton and John Panteleimon Manoussakis (Evanston, IL: Northwestern University Press, 2007), "Enabling God," in *After God,* and "Hermeneutics of the Possible God," in *Givenness and God: Questions of Jean-Luc Marion,* ed. Ian Leask and Eoin G. Cassidy (New York: Fordham University Press), 220–42.

1. Virginia Woolf, *The Letters of Virginia Woolf,* 3:457–58.

2. Paul Ricoeur, "Life in Quest of Narrative," 26, emphasis added.

3. Paul Ricoeur, *Time and Narrative,* 3:170.

4. Paul Ricoeur, *On Translation,* 23.

5. On this later point, see Julia Kristeva, *Time and Sense: Proust and the Experience of Literature,* 3–22. For a eucharistic hermeneutics of reading, see also Valentine Cunningham, *Reading after Theory,* 148ff.: "Here is a body of text and the text as body, the body of the other, the text as other, to be consumed, ingested, in a memorial act, an act of testimony, of worldly witness. . . . In holy communion the believer is blessed and graced, signed as Christ's own, marked as sanctified. In reading on this [eucharistic model], the reader is, in some way or another, also graced, blessed, marked as the text's own."

6. Søren Kierkegaard, *Repetition.*

7. "Transubstantiation," *The Oxford English Dictionary.* This definition refers especially to the doctrine of the Roman Catholic Church dating back to 1533, but it also applies with minor variations to the rites of the Greek Orthodox and Anglican churches.

8. Maurice Merleau-Ponty, *Phenomenology of Perception,* 246. I am grateful to John Manoussakis for this reference; see Manoussakis's extended discussion of this theme in *God after Metaphysics: A Theological Aesthetics.* Merleau-Ponty also has an intriguing notion of "primary faith" which operates at the most basic level of our ordinary perception and which requires an interruption of critical nonfaith or suspension if we are to return to it as an "enigma" or "wonder" after the event. See, for example, the opening section of *The Visible and the Invisible:* "We see the things themselves, the world is what we see: formulae of this kind express a faith common to the natural man and the philosopher—the moment he opens his eyes; they refer to a deep-seated set of mute 'opinions' implicated in our lives. But what is strange about this faith is that if we seek to articulate it into theses or statements, we enter into a labyrinth of difficulties and contradictions." So our world of primary perception is already, at a prereflective level of lived experience, a primary faith, which the philosophical moment of questioning interrupts. But this interruption—as formalized in Husserl's reduction and epoché for example—does not offer answers so much as invite us to think of ourselves as an "enigma" (3–4). But this enigma should not be thought of in terms of some abstract intellectual curiosity or in terms of an Oedipus riddle to be solved. Rather, it is an enigma, in the sense of a challenge to our preconceived views, an endless wrestling with the options of meaning and meaninglessness in an effort to see what seeing means, to better understand what belief believes. As such, the philosophical suspension of primary faith introduces a sense of "wonder before what is," which in turn allows for the possibility of a second faith in the wake of philosophical interrogation and poetic wonderment.

9. Merleau-Ponty, *Phenomenology of Perception,* 246.

10. These are Merleau-Ponty's words, and while agnostic they are not, I think, neutral: "The Christian God wants nothing to do with a vertical relation of subordination. . . . He is not simply a principle of which we are the consequence, a will whose instruments we are, or even a model of which human values are the only reflection. There is a sort of impotence of God without us, and Christ attests that God would not be fully God without becoming fully man. . . . Transcendence no longer hangs over man; he becomes, strangely, its privileged bearer" (*Phenomenology of Perception,* 83–84).

11. In *Strangers to Ourselves,* Kristeva strongly recommends that we surmount the theocratic dualisms of pure and impure, saved and damned, native and stranger, for, she argues, such dualisms lead to sacrificial scapegoating and war. In my interview with Kristeva in *Debates in Continental Philosophy,* she states, "The big work of our civilization is to fight this hatred—without God" ("Strangers to Ourselves: The Hope of the Singular," 166).

12. Julia Kristeva, *Time and Sense: Proust and the Experience of Literature,* 246.

13. Ibid., 3ff.

14. Ibid., 101. Kristeva comments on Proust's fascination with the Catholic Eucharist and links it with his aesthetic interest in John Ruskin:

> For Proust, who was in search of the real presence of signs, the Mass described as taking place in "the cathedrals that are the greatest and most original expression of French genius" proved to be a living example of the experience sought by his emerging aesthetic. The religion of the "living God" was thoroughly attractive, and it was the primary source of Proust's interest in Ruskin. . . . Proust was sincerely disturbed by anticlerical laws and by the general anticlericalism of governing bodies. At the same time, he recognized that the *écoles libres* held a sectarian view of freemasons and Jews and noted that clericalism itself "had completely freed itself from the dogmas of the Catholic religion. . . . The Christian spirit . . . [has] nothing to do with the partisan spirit which we seek to destroy." . . . With this in mind we see that John Ruskin (1819–1900) was the writer through whom Proust felt he could reinvigorate the religious aesthetic (or the aestheticized religion, for therein lay the entire question) in a modern and progressive fashion. (100–101)

Kristeva goes on to argue that Ruskin's seduction was "aesthetic *as well as* religious." "When Proust outlined his nascent conception of life as 'real life' and artistic experience as a real presence, as 'time embodied' and a 'transubstantiation,' he relied on this confirmed socialist, this admired or challenged modern man" (101).

15. Ibid., 23.

16. Ibid., 102, 106, 108, 133ff. passim.

17. Ibid., 106.

18. Ibid., 108. Kristeva cites this telling passage from Proust's *Contre Sainte-Beuve:* "Crossing a courtyard I came to a standstill among the glittering uneven

paving-stones. . . . In the depth of my being I felt the *flutter* of a past that I did not recognize; it was just as I set foot on a certain paving-stone that this feeling of *perplexity* came over me. I felt an invading *happiness,* I knew that I was going to be enriched by that *purely personal thing, a past impression, a fragment of life in unsullied preservation. Suddenly,* I was flooded by a stream of light. It was the sensation underfoot that I had felt on the smooth, slightly uneven pavement of the baptistery of Saint Mark's" (107). It is interesting that the other novel under consideration here also ends with a touchstone of a telling kind, the rock of the lighthouse that Mr Ramsay touches in *To the Lighthouse.*

19. Marcel Proust, *In Search of Lost Time,* vol. 7, *Time Regained,* 290.

20. Ibid., 291.

21. Ibid., 290. Gilles Deleuze makes the point in *Proust and Signs* that Proust's experience of "essences" requires the "style" of art and literature to be brought to expression. Proust speaks here of "a qualitative difference in the way that the world looks to us, a difference that, if there were no such thing as art, would remain the eternal secret of each man" (*In Search of Lost Time,* vol. 3, 895). In volume 7, *Time Regained,* Proust famously describes the move from the inner secret essence within each life to the style of literary art an act of "translation."

22. Kristeva, *Time and Sense,* 112.

23. Ibid., 112.

24. Ibid., 112.

25. Ibid., 113.

26. Ibid., 113.

27. Ibid, 3–22, 116. Kristeva also identifies nominal associations here with Marie Madeleine in the scriptures.

28. Ibid., 114.

29. Ibid., 115.

30. Ibid., 115.

31. Ibid., 116.

32. Proust, *In Search of Lost Time,* vol. 2, 23.

33. Ibid., vol. 4, 432.

34. Ibid., vol. 1, 95.

35. Walter Benjamin, "The Image of Proust," in *Illuminations,* 210.

36. Walter Benjamin, *The Arcades Project,* 69. One might also mention here John Caputo's notion of holy "quotidianism" in *The Weakness of God: A Theology of the Event,* 155–56.

37. Proust, *In Search of Lost Time,* vol. 6, 509.

38. Ibid., 509.

39. Ibid., 509.

40. Ibid., 509.

41. Ibid., 509. The point is not that epiphanies never happened before the library scene; it is that Marcel was not yet ready to see and hear them for what they really were. He had not yet, to cite Deleuze, been fully trained in his "apprenticeship to signs." And it is not until such apprenticeship is accomplished,

through his recapitulative awareness of "being-towards-death" in the library, that Marcel can finally acknowledge the preciousness of even the most banal and discarded events through the lens of time recaptured (*le temps retrouvé).* Art is less a matter of romantic creation than of epiphanic re-creation. For, as Marcel asks, "was not the re-creation by the memory of impressions which had then to be deepened, illumined, transformed into equivalents of understanding, was not this process one of the conditions, almost the very essence of the work of art as I had just now in the library conceived it?" (*In Search of Lost Time,* vol. 6, 525). Such epiphanic understanding marks the moment of *anagnorisis.* Otherwise put, time has to be lost before it can be recovered. Unless the seed dies, accidents cannot be retrieved as essences, contingencies as correspondences, obsessions as epiphanies. Only through the veil of mortality can the sacred radiate across the profane world, which the arrogant repudiate as ineligible for art. It is only after he renounces his promethean will to write that Marcel's previously unexperienced experience is reexperienced in all its neglected richness (and the greater the neglect, the greater the richness). For it is precisely the rejected and remaindered events of Marcel's existence that now return, in and through literature, as "resurrections." The three personas of Marcel—as character, as narrator, and as author—seem to crisscross here for the first time, like three Proustian magi recognizing that the deepest acts of communion are to be found in the most fortuitous acts of ordinary perception.

42. Ibid., vol. 6, 530–31. So what do these Proustian conclusions tell us about epiphany? They indicate, I suggest, that epiphany is a process that is "achieved" in a series of double moves. The first double move is that of mortality and natality. The second is that of metaphor (the translation of one thing into another) and metonymy (the disclosure of new meaning through the accidental contiguity of contingent things), and the third, that of constructing and deconstructing. It is in this last double gesture that the text surpasses itself and finally reaches out toward its future readers. For if we begin with the notion that literature "constructs" an epiphany based on the recreation of impressions recalled in involuntary memory, the literary text in turn "deconstructs" itself to allow for its re-creation by the reader. That is how Penelope's tapestry and Françoise's sewing work—stitching and unstitching, weaving and unweaving, endlessly. In a form of hermeneutic arc, the text configures an epiphany already prefigured by a life that is ultimately refigured by the reader (see Ricoeur, *Time and Narrative,* vol. 2, especially the section titled "The Traversed Remembrance of Things Past" in chapter 4). And this reader is one who not only cocreates the text with the author but re-creates it again as she returns from "text to action." So if epiphany invites a first move from life to literature, it reinvites us to come back again from literature to life. In both Proust and Woolf, it is indeed Penelope who has the last word.

43. Cited by J. Hillis Miller, "The Rhythm of Creativity: *To The Lighthouse,"* in *Tropes, Parables, Performatives: Essays in Twentieth-Century Literature,* 159.

44. Virginia Woolf, *A Room of One's Own,* 102. Cited by Miller, "The Rhythm of Creativity," 169.

45. Erich Auerbach, "The Brown Stocking," in *Mimesis: The Representation of Reality in Western Literature,* 536. See also 540 and 552.

46. Virginia Woolf, *To the Lighthouse,* 82.

47. Ibid., 83.

48. Ibid., 97.

49. Ibid., 104–5.

50. Ibid., 104.

51. Ibid., 62. The references to Lily leaping into a "gap" and finding the third, final stroke that draws the "line, there in the centre" is interesting when we consider the image of the "wedge," so intimately and recurrently associated with Mrs Ramsay. This trope carries connotations of a deep inner emptiness or nothingness, as in references to "the wedge of darkness" or "the wedge-shaped core of darkness," which holds out the possibility of some mystical fullness or completion. When we recall that Lily has been trying to compose a portrait of Mrs Ramsay and James in the form of a "purple triangle," we might be tempted to construe Lily's finishing brushstroke as the line that completes the two-sided wedge—the missing third side, so to speak. After which she can say, "it was done. . . . I have had my vision" (209). Interestingly, this vision coincides with the exact moment that the missing father, Mr Ramsay, lands on the rock of the lighthouse and finds acknowledgment in the hearts of his children, James and Cam. He is, so to speak, finally accepted back into the picture of mother and child. This is the moment that Lily, on shore in front of her painting, suddenly finds her "razor's edge" balance between "art and Mr Ramsay." The final "cut" is made, the third stroke applied to the wedge. The triangle is completed, the work done, the novel concluded. This charged figurative imagery of wedge and triangle may be read, I suggest, in aesthetic, psychoanalytic, or Trinitarian terms, or all three combined.

52. Ibid., 63–64. This approximates to the Buddhist and Hindu view that the sacred is in all sentient beings. See, for example, the teaching of Dilgo Khyentse Rinpoche in this regard: "Pure perception is to recognize the buddha-nature in all sentient beings and to see primordial purity and perfection in all phenomena" (cited in John Makransky, *Awakening Through Love,* 92). The sacramental reference for all natural things is also evidenced in certain biblical texts, such as the Song of Songs (which Mrs Ramsay's vision echoes in the final lines just cited) and in the nature visions of certain Christian mystics, such as Saint Francis and Hildegaarde of Bingen (see in particular her notion of *veriditas,* or the divine "greening" of all things), not to mention Gerard Manley Hopkins or Pierre Teilhard de Chardin. Woolf's English Protestant culture may not, however, have made her familiar with such writings. Either way, Woolf's mysticism, however "Asiatic" its allusions at times, remains nondenominational and nonconfessional, one might even say nontheistic or posttheistic—or anatheistic.

53. Virginia Woolf, *Moments of Being,* cited by Martin Corner in "Mysticism and Atheism in *To the Lighthouse,*" 43. In a diary entry of May 9, 1926, Woolf notes she had quarreled with her husband, Leonard, who "disliked the irrational Xtian in me" (Bell, *The Diary of Virginia Woolf,* vol. 3, 801).

54. The metaphor of the razor's edge is a famous verse from Katha Upanishads, 3, 16. Here is the full passage, concerning the discovery of the true mystical sense (Atman-Brahman): "Arise! Awake! Pay attention, / When you've attained your wishes! A razor's sharp edge is hard to cross— / That, poets say, is the difficulty of the path." The passage goes on: "When a man perceives it, / fixed and beyond the immense, / He is freed from the jaws of death" (verse 15). Or again, if a person "proclaims this great secret . . . during a meal for the dead, / it will lead him to eternal life" (verse 17). Eucharistic echoes abound. One might also cite here the mystical notions of immanent transcendence to be found in Hindu swamis such as Ramana and Ramakrishna or Christian Hindu sages such as Abhishiktananda, Bede Griffiths, and Sarah Grant.

55. Woolf, *To the Lighthouse,* 202.

56. Woolf, *A Writer's Diary,* cited by Martin Corner in "Mysticism and Atheism in *To the Lighthouse,*" 48.

57. Ibid.

58. See Miller, "The Rhythm of Creativity," 152–53.

59. Corner, "Mysticism and Atheism," 50.

60. Woolf, *To the Lighthouse,* 192.

61. Ibid., 161.

62. Georges Didi-Huberman, *Confronting Images.* I am grateful to my colleague, Stephen Schloesser, for this reference. See also Gaston Bachelard's notion of a similar sacramental aesthetic in his reading of "elemental participation" (based on the Greek notion of *methexis*—e.g. I Corinthians 10:16–17) over against "mimetic representation." (Bachelard, *The Poetics of Space*). His account of the material imagination paved the way for Merleau-Ponty's "flesh of the world." See Eileen Rizo-Patron, "Regressus ad Uterum: Bachelard's Alchemical Hermeneutic," and her PhD thesis, "Through the Eye of a Needle: Hermeneutics as Poetic Transformation."

63. Woolf, *To the Lighthouse,* 207.

64. Ibid., 180.

65. Cited in Corner, "Mysticism and Atheism," 51.

66. See Jean-François Lyotard's intriguing comments on "ana" and "post" in the postscript to *The Postmodern Condition.*

Impossible Confessions / Karmen MacKendrick

This essay is adapted from a presentation I gave at a conference, "The Sacred and the Debased in the Work of Georges Bataille," at Occidental College, Los Angeles, in 2008. I am grateful to Malek Moazzam-Doulat and his amazing students for the opportunity and inspiration.

1. Georges Bataille, "Discussion on Sin," in *The Unfinished System of Nonknowledge,* 73 (this work is hereafter cited in the text as DS).

2. Arthur Vermeersch, "Religious Obedience," in *The Catholic Encyclopedia.*

3. "And whereas, in project, the result alone counts, in sacrifice, it is in the act itself that value is concentrated. Nothing in sacrifice is put off until later—it

has the power to contest everything at the instant that it takes place, to summon everything, to render everything present." (Georges Bataille, *Inner Experience,* 137; this work is hereafter cited in the text as *IE*).

4. Georges Bataille, *Guilty,* 79 (this work is hereafter cited in the text as *G*).

5. A small sampling: in *Story of the Eye,* Marcelle hangs herself, and Simone kills a priest. The priest at the heart of *L'Abbé C* ends up tortured to death, but not before the destruction of his soul by his betrayal of those he loves. Of the character Dirty in *Blue of Noon,* the narrator declares, "She's too voracious to go on living. She won't live. . . . I kept thinking that . . . she would die. She disappeared with the train" (*Blue of Noon,* 149; this work is cited in the text as *BN*). The title character of *My Mother* dies, though in a rather offstage way; *The Dead Man,* as the title suggests, features a dead man, in this case at the very beginning of the story.

6. It should be noted that the destruction here attends not only the object or person sacrificed but also the one who performs the sacrifice. Jeffrey Kosky in "Georges Bataille's Religion without Religion" provides a nice summary of this point:

> Bataille maintains that the sacred breaks with the profane, workaday world of productive, economic existence by transgressing the limits of individual existence and conventional morality. Evident in "primitive" religious life with its moments of potlatch, orgy, and other forms of ritual excess, the sacred, for Bataille, culminated in sacrifice—where an individual executes a useless act of unredeemed expenditure, giving without return and so losing without gain. Sacrifice, for Bataille, is therefore always self-sacrifice insofar as the self gives without receiving anything in return and thus defies its own selfhood. (82)

7. Compare this passage from *My Mother:*

> I associated the image I still had of divinity with that, equally violent, of Hansi's voluptuousness, and both of these I associated with those abominations whose potency, whose horribleness were infinite. I had in the days of my godliness meditated upon Christ crucified and upon the ungodliness of His wounds. The torturing nausea which came from an over-indulgence in sensual pleasure had introduced me to that awful confusion in which no sensation existed without being pitched to deliriousness (117; this work is subsequently cited in the text as *MM*).

8. Bataille's lover Colette Peignot in "The Sacred" calls Christ "the eternally humiliated," adding, "The stations of the cross, the story of the spit exalts Christ" (Peignot, *Laure: The Collected Writings,* 39).

9. "I would undress and I would cry out, 'God of terror, very low dost thou bring us, very low hast thou brought us, my mother and me. . . .' I realized in the course of time that I took pride in being like this, and reminding myself that pride was the worst sin of all, I would straighten up" (*MM,* 51, ellipsis in original).

10. Simone serves this function in *Story of the Eye,* the mother in *My Mother,* Madame Edwarda in the story by that name, the Count in *The Dead Man,* Eponine in *L'Abbe C,* Dirty in *Blue of Noon,* and so on.

11. Virginia Burrus, *Saving Shame: Martyrs, Saints, and Other Abject Subjects,* 3.

12. "I persistently note, 'There is no wall between eroticism and mysticism!' It's really quite funny—since they use the same words, deal in identical images, and they refuse to recognize it!" (Bataille, *On Nietzsche,* 131; this work is subsequently cited in the text as *ON*) Again: "The saint turns from the voluptuary in alarm: she does not know that his unacknowledgeable passions and her own are really one" (Bataille, *Erotism,* 7; this work is subsequently cited in the text as *E*). What Bataille himself doesn't quite acknowledge here is that the voluptuary may be just as horrified to see in the chaste confines of the church an impulse so like his own.

13. "Only the way mystics depict their laceration can correspond to my laceration" (*G,* 78). See also the introduction to *Madame Edwarda* (140–44).

14. Michael Richardson, "Seductions of the Impossible: Love, the Erotic and Sacrifice in Surrealist Discourse," 387.

15. Michel Foucault, "Sexuality and Power," 124.

16. Ibid., 125.

17. Burrus, *Saving Shame,* 2.

18. Michel Foucault, "On the Government of the Living," 157.

19. "And so to the treatment of those faults of which we have spoken above, intercourse with other men is not merely no hindrance, but a considerable help" (Cassian, *Conference* 19, XVI).

20. John Cassian, *Conferences* 19, I.

21. *Story of the Eye,* with its various confessional scenes, tries to refuse confession's relentless demands on memory, but finds itself confessing as inadvertently as a blush: "I began writing . . . animated chiefly by a desire to forget, at least for the time being, the things that I can be or do personally. Thus, at first, I thought that the character speaking in the first person had no relation to me" (Bataille, afterword to *Story of the Eye,* 89; this work is hereafter cited in the text as *SE*). Attempting to emphasize his irreligiosity, Bataille confesses his own confessional history: "I went to a priest in August 1914; and until 1920, rarely did I let a week go by without confessing my sins! In 1920, I changed again, I stopped believing in anything but my future chances" (*SE,* 101, from 1943 preface).

22. Blushes occur throughout *My Mother* (38, 48, 68, 70—in the imperative!—97, etc.), in *Madame Edwarda* (150), and in *Story of the Eye* (12, 40, 82), just to give a few representative instances.

23. Peter Brown, *The Body and Society: Men, Women and Sexual Renunciation in Early Christianity,* 231.

24. Bataille, *Blue of Noon,* 154 (this work is hereafter cited in the text as *BN*).

25. David Brakke, "The Problematization of Nocturnal Emissions in Early Christian Syria, Egypt, and Gaul," 449, cited in Burrus, *Saving Shame,* 41.

26. Key figures for the interested would be John Cassian, in his *Conferences,* and the late anti-Pelagian writings of Augustine.

27. Foucault, "On the Government of the Living," 157.

28. See Michel Foucault, "About the Beginning of the Hermeneutics of the Self": "obedience is a permanent relationship, and even when the monk is old, even when he became, in his turn, a master, even then he has to keep the spirit of obedience as a permanent sacrifice of his own will" (174).

29. Bataille, *Theory of Religion,* 13.

The Third Life of Saint Teresa of Jesus / Manuel Asensi

1. There are multiple versions of this *villancico.* The text here follows the version in *Obras completas de Santa Teresa de Jesús* (Sígueme). The version that appears in José Manuel Blecua's anthology of Spanish Renaissance poetry, published by Clásicos Castalia, is shorter (it has 31 lines, whereas the version I am citing has 59). Furthermore, that version has variants in lines 12 and 25–31. The instability of the text—quite characteristic of Renaissance and convent writing (I am thinking of the *cuadernos de canto*)—as well as the different conception of the "author" are the result of my use of the longer variant. Antonio Prieto has underscored this instability: "The poetry of Saint Teresa, for which no author manuscript survives, is quite likely to have been dictated in some cases: poems recited for her nuns who, in turn, transcribed them, sometimes without stating the author, and then compiled them with other similar poems, a practice that has created problems for verifying authenticity" (Prieto, *La poesía española del siglo XVI,* vol. 2, *Aquel valor que respetó olvido,* 738). Other variants are also commented on in the essay.

2. Teresa of Avila, *Interior Castle,* 55–56, translation modified. (The Spanish original of this text can be found in Teresa de Jesús, *Obras completas,* 606.)

3. R. D. Laing, *The Divided Self,* 17.

4. It is striking that in some versions of the poem I have come across, for example on the Internet, the "he placed" (*puso*) is changed into "I placed" (*puse*). The change is not simply a gratuitous one, since when "I placed" is written, all the effects of being possessed and of the ventriloquism—indeed, the entire consequence of the presence of the Other inhabiting the self— are lost. That change erases one of the most interesting and important aspects of this poem, for it directly affects the poem's pronounced polyphony.

5. I will not compare the two poems following Helmut Hatzfeld's *Estudios literarios sobre mística española.* It should be remembered that he highly valued the poetic quality of Saint John of the Cross while dismissing Saint Teresa as a mere versifier.

6. Gilles Deleuze, *Francis Bacon,* 11.

7. Hélène Cixous, *The Newly Born Woman,* 99.

Renunciation and Absorption: On the Dimensionality of Baroque Asceticism / Burcht Pranger

1. Xavier Bray, ed., *The Sacred Made Real: Spanish Painting and Sculpture, 1600–1700,* 17.

2. Ibid., 160.

3. Ibid., 160.

4. Ibid., 40.

5. Ibid., 7.

6. Peter Brown, *The Body and Society: Men, Women and Sexual Renunciation in Early Christianity;* Virginia Burrus, *The Sex Lives of the Saints: An Erotics of Ancient Hagiography.*

7. That being so, I would like to argue against attempts to derive from this cognitive and visual renunciation a rapprochement of Christianity with other religions, in particular Islam and certain types of Buddhism, that have also been critical of images and in which (visual) asceticism takes pride of place. A point in case is the German theologian, philosopher, and Neoplatonist Meister Eckhart (c. 1260–c. 1327), whose radical program of *Entbildung,* or "de-imaging," has tempted many an interpreter (historians of comparative religion and specialists in mysticism and spirituality) into finding common ground where I think there is none. In my view, in comparing religions one should take the high rather than the low road. In that respect, even Eckhart's most de-imaged (*entbildet*) notion of the divine, his most radical "cognitive" withdrawal into the desert, is still governed by a *visible* presence of sorts where the difference with Zurbarán's *Christ on the Cross* is one of degree rather than kind.

8. John Calvin, *The Institutes of the Christian Religion,* vol. 4, 17, 25.

9. The *extra Calvinisticum* denotes the fact that "the Word is fully united to but never totally contained within the human nature and, therefore, even in the incarnation is to be conceived of as beyond or outside of (*extra*) the human nature" (Richard A. Muller, *Dictionary of Latin and Greek Theological Terms: Drawn Principally from Protestant Scholastic Theology,* 111). See also Edward Davis Willis, *Calvin's Catholic Christology: The Function of the So-Called Extra Calvinisticum in Calvin's Theology.*

10. The use of "absorption" in an art-historical sense has been coined by Michael Fried as "the inwardness of a painting." Fried has taken the term from Diderot, who used it in antithesis to theatricality, which he denotes as involving address by the figures in a painting to the beholder. See Fried, *Absorption and Theatricality: Painting and Beholder in the Age of Diderot.* In this article I use "absorption" in a more general sense as the transformation (almost) of one person or image into another, taking the spectator along in the process. As a result, I also use "theatricality" in a slightly less outward sense than Fried. This is not to deny the importance of Fried's notion of "absorption" and "theatricality"—on the contrary. It would be worthwhile to write an essay on my subject matter on the basis of a Friedlike approach. Such an effort should, however, be preceded by a thorough analysis of Fried's "absorption." See note 19.

11. See A. D. Nuttall, *Why Does Tragedy Give Pleasure?*

12. Bernard of Clairvaux, *In ascensione sermo* 2.34, in *Sancti Bernardi Opera,* vol. 5, 128–29.

13. Bray, *The Sacred Made Real,* 80.

14. David Davies, "Shocking the Senses to Stir the Soul," lecture, National Gallery, London, October 23, 2009.

15. See my *The Artificiality of Christianity: Essays on the Poetics of Monasticism,* esp. chap. 15, "Images of Iron: Ignatius of Loyola and Joyce."

16. Bray, *The Sacred Made Real,* 162.

17. In fact, this image of the *amplexus* goes further back to the late twelfth century (Herbert of Clairvaux's *Liber miraculorum*) and, more famously, Conrad of Eberbach's *Exordium magnum* (early thirteenth century). See James France, "The Heritage of Saint Bernard in Medieval Art."

18. Bray, *The Sacred Made Real,* 162.

19. Once more it should be pointed put that I use "theatricality" in an un-Fried-like sense as taking place within the picture/image rather than turning outward. Here we hit upon a problematic aspect in Fried's notion of "absorption" and "theatricality": how to account for theatricality *within* absorption as, for instance, the "absorbed" interaction between Christ and Bernard in Ribalta's painting? The closest Fried comes to discussing this problem is in his analysis of Caravaggio's *Narcissus* absorbed to the point of being immersed in his own image. See Fried, *The Moment of Caravaggio,* 134–39.

20. Precisely this aspect of reciprocity is ignored by art historians such as Xavier Bray and James France. France wonders why it has taken so long for the image of the *amplexus* "to find expressions in art. . . . The theme is pure Bernard, based on his theology centred on Christ's sacrifice on the cross, a corollary of Christ's full participation in our humanity, and a theme which recurs time and again in his work" ("The Heritage," 328). It would be interesting to trace how Bernard's *dynamic* presence and participation in sacred scenes has disappeared from devotional literature while persisting in art.

21. I have discussed Bérulle in more detail in my *The Artificiality of Christianity,* chap. 14, "Baroque Devotion."

22. Pierre de Bérulle, *Grandeurs de Iésus,* discours II, in *Oeuvres Complètes,* 190–91.

23. Ibid., 189–90.

"For the Life Was Manifested" / Kevin Hart

I thank Jean-Yves Lacoste, Paul Mariani, and Henry Weinfield for comments on an earlier version of this essay.

1. All quotations from the Bible are from the King James version.

2. Augustine, "First Homily," in *Homilies on the First Epistle of John,* 22.

3. I leave aside, solely for reasons of economy, the question of the role of the sacraments. Hopkins's poetry is not a sacrament and does not deal with sacraments, although there is no reason not to think of it as sacramental and as dealing with sacramentals. See my essay, "Poetry and Revelation: Hopkins, Counter-Experience and *Reductio.*"

4. See Karl Rahner, "The 'Spiritual Senses' According to Origen," and idem, "The Doctrine of the 'Spiritual Senses' in the Middle Ages"; Hans Urs von Bal-

thasar, *The Glory of the Lord,* vol. 1, *Seeing the Form,* and vol. 2, *Studies in Theological Style: Clerical Styles,* esp. 317–26. Also see Stephen Fields, "Balthasar and Rahner on the Spiritual Senses."

5. Origen, *Contra Celsum,* 44; Gregory of Nyssa, *Commentary on the Song of Songs,* 195; John of the Cross, "The Ascent of Mount Carmel," book 2, chap. 4, sect. 2. It should be recalled, though, that elsewhere in the commentary on the canticle, Gregory holds that one encounters God only in the darkness of faith.

6. For Origen, the inner person and the outer person were created separately. See his *Homilies on Genesis and Exodus* 1.13. It should also be remembered that Origen rejected Aristotle's notion of matter as the substrate of all properties, as stated in *Metaphysics* 1.3.1, along with the teaching of the eternity of matter. See *On First Principles* 4.4.7.

7. See Tatian, *Oratio ad Graecos and Fragments,* chaps. 12, 13, 30.

8. For Origen, of course, the soul had cooled down from its original warmth when close to God, and so descended to the material world. See Origen, *On First Principles* 2.8.3.

9. See, for example, Martin Heidegger, *Being and Time,* ¶10.

10. On this theme, see Ronald Bruzina, *Edmund Husserl and Eugen Fink: Beginnings and Ends in Phenomenology 1928–1938,* 6.3.1 and 6.3.2. I leave aside here a narrow discussion of the differences between Husserl and Fink regarding spirit.

11. See Husserl's quotation from Augustine's *De vera religione* at the very end of his *Cartesian Meditations: An Introduction to Phenomenology.* For Husserl on the soul, and in particular his rejection of the soul as naturalistically conceived, see his *The Crisis of European Sciences and Transcendental Phenomenology: An Introduction to Phenomenological Philosophy,* 63, 116, 118, 170, 214.

12. One influential account of the spiritual senses identifies them strictly with the intellect and excludes the imagination and even the will. See A. Poulain, *The Graces of Interior Prayer,* chap. 6.

13. Edmund Husserl, *Ideas Pertaining to a Pure Phenomenology and to a Phenomenological Philosophy: Second Book,* 100, 259.

14. See Angela Ales Bello, *The Divine in Husserl and Other Explorations,* part 1, chap. 2.

15. See Husserl, *Ideas Pertaining to a Pure Phenomenology and to a Phenomenological Philosophy: First Book,* § 58.

16. I follow the later Husserl in distinguishing the *epochē* and the reduction. See *The Crisis of European Sciences,* § 41.

17. Husserl, *Cartesian Meditations,* 46.

18. Not only the Christian, of course, though I limit myself here to that religion. It should be noted that atheists also have the supernatural attitude, but only in negative: they deny that there truly *is* such an attitude to be taken seriously. On what I have called the "supernatural attitude" see Husserl's words as recorded by Dorian Cairns in his *Conversations with Husserl and Fink,* 47.

19. See Karl Jaspers, *Philosophical Faith and Revelation.*

20. See on this topic Max Scheler, *On the Eternal in Man,* 268–69.

21. Husserl, *Ideas, Book 1,* 117.

22. Husserl, A V 21, 128a. I quote James G. Hart's translation of the passage in his "A Précis of Husserlian Phenomenological Theology," 148.

23. It is tempting to examine the relations between Husserl's view of God and experience, as expressed here, and Karl Rahner's notion of "transcendental experience." I put this aside for another occasion. I also leave aside the interesting question of whether the divine mode of presence, as entertained by Husserl in this passage, bears any resemblance to Bernard of Clairvaux's understanding of the presence of God that cannot be traced in the mind. See his *On the Song of Songs,* 4, sermon 74. 6.

24. Augustine, *The Literal Meaning of Genesis,* in *On Genesis,* 12.6.15–7.16.

25. See Bello, *The Divine in Husserl,* part 1, chap. 2, sect. 2.

26. On this issue, see Anthony J. Steinbock, *Phenomenology and Mysticism: The Verticality of Religious Experience,* esp. chaps. 1 and 5.

27. Husserl looks at the matter from the other side: for him, the one who makes the *epochē* is like a religious convert. See *The Crisis of European Sciences,* § 35.

28. Maurice Blondel, "The Letter on Apologetics," in *The Letter on Apologetics and History and Dogma,* 130.

29. See Eberhard Jüngel, *God as the Mystery of the World: On the Foundation of the Theology of the Crucified One in the Dispute between Theism and Atheism,* 32. Jüngel's sense of experiencing experience remains within the supernatural attitude, however.

30. Husserl, *Briefwechsel,* vol. 3, 454.

31. Not only Bonaventure but also Karl Barth. See his *Church Dogmatics,* vol. 1, *The Doctrine of the Word of God,* part 2, 470.

32. Husserl, *The Crisis of European Sciences,* 97.

33. See Ignatius of Loyola, "The Spiritual Exercises," in *Spiritual Exercises and Selected Works,* §§ 121–25.

34. George Herbert, "Prayer" (I), in *The Works of George Herbert,* 51.

35. Claude Colleer Abbott, ed., *The Letters of Gerard Manley Hopkins to Robert Bridges,* 56.

36. Gerard Manley Hopkins, *Poems and Prose,* 31. I have added all Hopkins's accents. All further quotations from Hopkins's poems are from this edition.

37. See Hugh of Saint Victor, "The Soul's Three Ways of Seeing," in *Selected Spiritual Writings,* 183. Also see his *Didascalicon,* 99–100.

38. See Richard of Saint Victor, *The Twelve Patriarchs, The Mystical Ark, Book Three of "The Trinity,"* 71.

39. Ignatius, "The Spiritual Exercises," 148, 149, 150.

40. Christopher Devlin, ed., *The Sermons and Devotional Writings of Gerard Manley Hopkins,* 175.

41. It should not be assumed that Hopkins's commentary on the "Spiritual Exercises" is undertaken exclusively in an Ignatian spirit. His interest in Scotus is clearly legible in his comments. However, I am more interested here in the habit

of contemplation than the Scotist inflection that Hopkins gives to his Ignatian training. See Franco Marucci, *The Fine Delight that Fathers Thought: Rhetoric and Medievalism in Gerard Manley Hopkins,* 188–98.

42. For Saint Ignatius, one contemplates the visible and meditates upon the invisible; in the monastic tradition it is usually the other way round. See David Anthony Downes, *The Ignatian Personality of Gerard Manley Hopkins,* chap. 6. For an account of contemplation as a gaze on the face of God, see Gregory the Great, *Morals on the Book of Job* 3:1, 56–57.

43. See Augustine, *De consensus evangelistarum,* I.5.8. The relevant passage reads, "*ista vero magis in fide et apud perpaucos per speculum in enigmate et ex parte in aliqua visione incommutabilis veritatis.*"

44. Richard of Saint Victor, *The Mystical Ark,* book 2, chap.12.

45. Hopkins, *The Collected Works of Gerard Manley Hopkins,* vol. 4, *Oxford Essays and Notes,* 307.

46. See, for example, *Carmen* I.iv, II.xiv, and IV.vii.

47. Yet see *Sermons and Devotional Writings,* 136–38, where the "spiritual senses" are directed to consider the fires of hell.

48. On the traces of Ruskin in this poem, see Alison G. Sulloway, *Gerard Manley Hopkins and the Victorian Temper,* 89.

49. Humphry House, ed., *The Journals and Papers of Gerard Manley Hopkins,* 289, and Claude Colleer Abbott, ed., *Further Letters of Gerard Manley Hopkins Including his Correspondence with Coventry Patmore,* 373

50. John Milton, *Paradise Lost,* ed. Alastair Fowler, 8: 257–61.

51. Paul Mariani is right to point us also to the similar rhythm in the opening line of Swinburne's "Hermaphroditus": "Lift úp thy líps, turn róund, look báck for lóve." See Mariani, *A Commentary on the Complete Poems of Gerard Manley Hopkins,* 116n55.

52. House, *The Journals and Papers of Gerard Manley Hopkins,* 204.

53. For other "phenomenological I's," see Husserl, *The Basic Problems of Phenomenology: From the Lectures, Winter Semester, 1910–1911,* § 39; idem, *Analyses Concerning Passive and Active Synthesis: Lectures on Transcendental Logic,* 52.

54. Husserl, *Phantasy, Image Consciousness, and Memory (1898–1925),* 606.

55. House, *The Journals and Papers of Gerard Manley Hopkins,* 230.

56. Ibid., 205.

57. It should be noted, though, that Husserl allows imagination to fulfill empty intentions: the meaning, not the object, has intuition. See Husserl, "Psychological Studies in the Elements of Logic," in *Early Writings in the Philosophy of Logic and Mathematics,* 150–51, and *Logical Investigations,* vol. 2, 725.

58. Hopkins, *Oxford Essays and Notes,* 313.

59. See Heidegger, *The Fundamental Concepts of Metaphysics: World, Finitude, Solitude,* part 1.

60. See Lynn Staley, trans. and ed., *The Book of Margery Kempe,* 10.

61. Theodosa Gray, trans., *The Homilies of Saint Gregory the Great on the Book of the Prophet Ezekiel,* 2.1.18. See also Gregory's similar comment in his *Morals on*

the Book of Job 3.1, 262. Gregory is not alone in this view. See, for example, Ambrose of Milan, *Exposition of the Holy Gospel According to Saint Luke,* 20, 30, and Grégoire Palamas, *Défense des saints hésychastes,* vol. 1, pp. 1, 3, 27.

62. In a different key, one that is almost Stevensian, J. Hillis Miller speaks of a "marriage of spirit and matter" in Hopkins. See his *The Disappearance of God: Five Nineteenth-Century Writers,* 290.

63. See Devlin, *The Sermons and Devotional Writings,* 151.

64. Henry D. Thoreau, *Journal,* vol. 3, 354–55. The entry was made on August 5, 1851.

65. House, *The Journals and Papers of Gerard Manley Hopkins,* 199.

66. Blondel, *Action: Essay on a Critique of Life and a Science of Practice (1893),* 198.

67. See Richard of Saint Victor, *The Mystical Ark,* book 5, chap. 4.

68. Ibid., book 6, chap. 18. In Richard's schema Hopkins the poet would be in the third stage of contemplation, with only three wings, whereas those who make spiritual leaps have six wings.

69. On anticipation, see Jean-Yves Lacoste, "La phénoménalité de l'anticipation," in *La phénoménalité de Dieu: Neuf études,* esp. 150–57.

Augustine, Rosenzweig, and the Possibility of Experiencing Miracle / Virginia Burrus

1. Augustine, *City of God,* 10.2; hereafter cited as *CG.* Quotations in Latin are from the 1965 Corpus Christianorum edition, *De civitate Dei.*

2. Franz Rosenzweig, *The Star of Redemption,* 118–19; hereafter cited as *SR.* Quotations in German are from the 1954 Verlag Lambert Schneider edition (3rd), *Der Stern der Erlösung.*

3. Francesco Paolo Ciglia, "Auf der Spur Augustins: *Confessiones* und *De civitate Dei* als Quellen des *Stern der Erlösung.*" Ciglia is not the first to remark on the significance of Augustine's *City of God* for Rosenzweig's *Star:* Amos Funkenstein argues that Rosenzweig takes crucial inspiration from Augustine's work "for his dualistic version of a profane history and a sacred non-history" (*Perceptions of Jewish History,* 298).

4. This is Rosenzweig's own description, from a letter of September 2, 1928, to Richard Koch, cited by Ciglia, "Auf der Spur Augustins," 224n2. The fuller text reads: "Nachdem ich 1913 plötzlich zum Philosophen geworden war, . . . fiel mir Ende 1916 der Plan meines 'Lebenswerks' ein. . . . Der Plan ging auf ein Buch de omnibus rebus et quibusdam aliis, wie der Stern nachher geworden ist, aber in Form eines Biblekommentars. . . . Vor nun zehn Jahren schrieb ich dan plötzlich überstürzteraber, wie sich erst später herausgestellt hat, glücklicherweise den Kommentar unter Weglassung des Texts" (Letter 526 in Franz Rosenzweig, *Briefe,* 618–20).

5. Elliot R. Wolfson, "Introduction to Barbara Galli's Translation of Rosenzweig's *Star,*" in *The Star of Redemption,* xvii.

6. Ciglia comments, "Man kann mit einigem Recht sagen, dass Rosenzweig in Augustin nie nur eine Gestalt aus längst vergangenen Tagen, sondern immer auch einen lebendigen Gesprächspartner gesehen hat, von dem man Anregungen und Denkanstösse erhhalten kann" ("Auf der Spur Augustins," 225). In the face of the paucity of explicit references to Augustine in *Star,* Ciglia uses the evidence of Rosenzweig's journals (later published as *Paralipomena*) and his letters to demonstrate that Rosenzweig was immersed in Augustine's texts starting around 1916.

7. Cited by Cigla, "Auf der Spur Augustins," 228–29). The quotation is from Rosenzweig's *Paralipomena,* and Rosenzweig's reference is to *Confessions* 12.24.

8. This point is particularly well made with regard to Augustine by M. B. Pranger, "The Unfathomability of Sincerity: On the Seriousness of Augustine's *Confessions.*" With regard to Rosenzweig, Wolfson's comments are incisive: "The interpretative act—which bespeaks the essential nature of speech-thinking, the dialogical comportment unique to the human being, in its inscripted and oral forms—affords one an opportunity to experience time, and, more specifically, the moment, which encapsulates time in its most elemental cadence, as novel repetition" ("Introduction," xix). Rosenzweig's moves to distance himself from Augustine on this and related points deserve further consideration, as we shall see.

9. Rosenzweig does not, of course, use the term "postmodern," but he positions his theory of miracle as initiating a new era of thought, following upon the third "Enlightenment" represented by nineteenth-century historicism.

10. Norbert Samuelson makes the case for Halevi as a source, simultaneously dismissing the possibility of any significant Augustinian influence: "those of us who are familiar with the writings of the Church fathers will recognize at best some slight similarities between Rosenzweig's account of miracles and the still crude conceptual appeals to miracles by the Church fathers. There is no question that Rosenzweig in fact has the theology of the Church fathers in mind as his model for appeal to miracles in theological debate. But at the state that Christian philosophy had reached at the time of these spiritual giants, the concept of miracle was not what Rosenzweig said it was" ("Halevi and Rosenzweig on Miracles," 161). Samuelson's appeal to "progress" contrasts with Rosenzweig's presentation of himself as retrieving an ancient insight that is appealing precisely because it evades modern historicism's commitment to a narrative of progress. More to the point, Samuelson does not succeed in demonstrating that Halevi's theory of miracles explains all that is in Rosenzweig's, or that Augustine's explains none of it. As Ciglia argues in "Auf der Spur Augustins," the influence of *City of God* 10, 21, and 22 is easily identifiable, for they are texts on which Rosenzweig commented in his journals.

11. Paula Fredriksen argues for the relatively benign character of Augustine's supersessionism: "By . . . embedding Jewish legal observance in history, Augustine in effect demythologized, and so secularized, its implications: carnal praxis was not a huge and enduringly indictable moral failing, but divinely mandated ac-

tion appropriate to those earlier times. Further, by understanding this practice as incarnate prophetic enactment, Augustine domesticated it for Catholic doctrine, relating ancient Jewish observances to current Christian beliefs by way of conformation rather than contrast" ("*Secundum Carnem:* History and Israel in the Theology of St. Augustine," 29). Famously, Rosenzweig very nearly embodied such a supersessionism, determining to become a (practicing) Jew so as subsequently to become a proper Christian, as he recounted to his cousin Rudolph Ehrenberg in a letter of October 31, 1913: "I declared I could turn Christian only *qua* Jew." Equally famously, he shifted his decision, so that the path to Christianity ultimately led him back to Judaism: "It no longer seems necessary to me, and therefore, being what I am, no longer possible. I will remain a Jew" (Letter 59 in Rosenzweig, *Briefe,* 71–72, translated by Nahum Glatzer in *Franz Rosenzweig: His Life and Thought,* 25, 28). In a letter to his mother written October 23, 1913, soon after his "conversion," Rosenzweig mentions both Tertullian and Augustine in the context of a scathing (and very witty) denunciation of Christian supersessionism (Letter 57 in Rosenzweig, *Briefe,* 66).

12. Following the lead of Henri Marrou, Robert Grant pronounces Augustine lamentably credulous, marveling at the church father's ability to marvel. The cause of such surprising naïveté, Grant suggests, lies not only with Augustine's literal reading of scripture but also with "the fact that natural science was moribund" in his day. Indeed, Augustine's strong emphasis on the significance of the miraculous in his later works may be seen to have hastened the demise "of ancient science and indeed of ancient civilization," Grant concludes with a flourish (*Miracle and Natural Law in Graeco-Roman and Early Christian Thought,* 216–20). Whereas Grant worries that Augustine has equated the natural with the miraculous, rendering nature merely inscrutable, John Mourant argues that Augustine increasingly dissociates miracle from nature, abandoning his theory of "seminal reasons" and coupling his long-standing emphasis on the subjective aspect of miracle with a sharper differentiation between "natural and religious miracles." "Religious miracles receive an objective validity through Scriptural revelation," notes Mourant, adding that they are distinct from natural wonders in their manifestation of divine purposefulness. He admits that Augustine may seem unduly credulous with regard to miracles reported in his own day but urges that his apparent credulity needs to be placed in context, above all the context of Augustine's own experience of "the miracle of the grace of conversion." Still, even Mourant seems to squirm a bit, noting that Augustine's "will to believe leads almost to an exaggerated credibility in the testimony of others" ("Augustine on Miracles," 122–27). Rowan Greer places Augustine's view of miracle as the culmination of a shift within Christianity away from a Platonizing cultivation of individual virtue and toward a corporate piety geared to accessing sources of divine power: for the mature Augustine, "God's will is all that remains, and it is difficult to see that 'nature' remains in any sense a meaningful concept"; echoing Grant, Greer notes, "No longer are miracles natural; nature is itself miraculous" (*The Fear of Freedom: A Study of Miracles in the Roman Imperial Church,* 176).

13. Greer, *The Fear of Freedom,* 177.

14. See especially his essay of that name: Franz Rosenzweig, *The New Thinking* (German edition: Franz Rosenzweig, *Kleinere Schriften*), 373–98.

15. Mark Vessey, "Introduction," in *History, Apocalypse, and the Secular Imagination: New Essays on Augustine's City of God,* 8.

16. See notes 4 and 7 above.

17. While serving in the military in March 1916, Rosenzweig wrote to his parents from a train on the way to the front, requesting a copy of the first of a two-volume set: "Bestellen bitte Augustin 'De civitate Dei' in Teubner *un*begunden, und zwar nur das erste Bändchen (es sind zwei), kostet vier oder fünf Mark." Two days later, he wrote to remind them again, apparently impatient that the little volume had not yet arrived: "den Augustin könnt ihr schicken" (Letters 72, 73 in Rosenzweig, *Briefe,* 93–94). The Teubner (issued in a third edition in 1908) contains books 1–13, thus conforming to neither of Augustine's own divisions!

18. Letter to Firmus, cited in the introduction to the Penguin edition of Augustine, *City of God,* xxxvi.

19. Rosenzweig, *The New Thinking,* 86.

20. As Rosenzweig writes in *The New Thinking,* 92–93: "But so the miracle remains that there is yet something that has form, and something that does not pass away. To be sure, not in the real world of the ever renewed life, where only the present is present, and the past only past, and the future only coming. But of these three, time in the most temporal sense is only the present [*ist ja Zeit im zeitlichsten Sinn nur die Gegenwart*]. And as the forms of paganism project into the present, like a bygone creation, so too is the coming redemption anticipated in eternal forms. . . . The third volume [of *Star*] deals with these."

21. Rosenzweig, *The New Thinking,* 82.

22. The preference for the lesser miracle is perhaps most famously articulated by David Hume in his 1748 *Enquiry Concerning Human Understanding;* insofar as the lesser "miracle" is almost inevitably the falsehood of the testimony of even a reliable witness, the position virtually eliminates the possibility that actual miracles take place. See the selection from Hume in Richard Swinburne, ed., *Miracles,* 23–40, as well as the several essays by contemporary philosophers engaging Hume's thought.

23. Elliot R. Wolfson, *Language, Eros, Being: Kabbalistic Hermeneutics and Poetic Imagination,* 372.

24. The discussion of love is only hinted at in the introduction to part 2, owing to its structural positioning; it seems significant, however, that it cannot quite be left out. As Eric Santner puts it, with regard to Rosenzweig's theory of miracle, "We might say that all Rosenzweig wanted to show was that truly inhabiting the midst of life . . . was actually a remarkable, even a miraculous achievement that required some form of divine support—ultimately a form of *love*—kept alive, in time, by a certain form of life" ("Miracles Happen: Benjamin, Rosenzweig, Freud, and the Matter of the Neighbor," 133).

25. Santner, "Miracles Happen," 82.

26. As noted, Robert Grant charges Augustine with dangerous disregard for the difference between miracle and created nature, thus between myth and science: "Augustine's view is not so much that miracles are natural as that nature is miraculous. To view nature from this point of view is to abandon any attempt to explain its workings" (*Miracle and Natural Law,* 217). John Mourant agrees that Augustine often claims to find all of nature subjectively wondrous and that he does not understand the miraculous as outside or in opposition to nature. However, Augustine does, according to Mourant, make objective distinctions between the miraculous and the ordinary within nature and also, especially in his later work, between natural and supernatural "religious" miracles; "religious" miracles are distinguished by their scriptural validation and manifest providential purpose ("Augustine on Miracles," 105, 122).

27. James Wetzel, *Augustine and the Limits of Virtue,* xi–xii. To be fair, Rosenzweig himself may be seen to generate considerable ambiguity with regard to the relation of miracle to creation (or indeed, the possible conflation thereof); see the discussion of Paul Mendes-Flohr, "Rosenzweig's Concept of Miracle," 62–66.

28. Francesco Paolo Ciglia, "Der Gordische Knoten der Zeit: Aspecte des Dialogs Zweischen Rosenzweig und Augustin," 323–45. See also the brief remarks on the resonance of Augustine's and Rosenzweig's theories of time (without reference to Rosenzweig's as a reader of Augustine) by Steven Kepnes, "Rosenzweig's Liturgical Reasoning as a Response to Augustine's Temporal Aporias."

29. From the *Paralipomena,* cited by Ciglia, "Der Gordische Knoten der Zeit," 330n9.

30. The *Star* also disavows its Augustinian fundaments, however. There Rosenzweig ultimately aligns Christianity with historical-political agency, contrasted with Judaism's uprootedness from history and politics: "Our life is no longer interwoven with anything external, we have taken root in ourselves, without roots in the earth, eternal wanderers therefore, yet deeply rooted in ourselves, in our own body and blood. And this rooting in ourselves and only in ourselves guarantees our eternity for us" (*SR,* 324). He explicitly associates Augustine with the (in his view, distinctly Christian) conflation of worldly politics and divine providence: "Augustine . . . now explains: for the Church . . . discord between one's own welfare and the faith that is loyal to one that is higher could not arise; for it 'salus' and 'fides' are united" (*SR,* 349). Despite Rosenzweig's strong and precise distancing of his own Jewish perspective from Augustine's Christian one with regard to eternal versus historical life, the very distinction owes much to Augustine, as Amos Funkenstein (*Perceptions of Jewish History,* 298–301) has argued: like Augustine, Rosenzweig posits a "parallel but disjoint" history of divine and earthly peoples in which the citizens of "the city of God" are dispersed as wanderers and aliens among the citizens of the world, having no real stake in the fortunes of political states but rather being rooted in a heavenly or eternal society. To put it simply, what Augustine claims for Christians, Rosenzweig claims for Jews. Too simply, perhaps, for at the same time that he appropriates an Augustinian *contemptus mundi,* Rosenzweig also appropriates and transvalues the "car-

nality" that Augustine assigns to the Jews, as Funkenstein further observes; this becomes for Rosenzweig the Jewish rootedness "in our own body and blood" (*SR,* 324).

31. James Wetzel, "Snares of Truth: Augustine on Free Will and Predestination," 136.

32. Wetzel, "Snares of Truth," 138.

33. Thomas A. Smith, "The Pleasure of Hell in *City of God* 21," 201.

34. Smith, "The Pleasure of Hell," 204.

35. Indeed, the reality of hell may be graspable only from the imagined perspective of *absolute* hindsight, a provisionally posited God's-eye view—posited merely provisionally, because hell cannot actually be posited, nor can God easily be interjected into a discussion of hell (except by falling back into voyeurism or vengeance, as Augustine occasionally does).

36. I first learned of the deep-sea, hot-water worms from the February 10, 2009, interview with Robert Ballard on the television program *The Colbert Report.* These worms are also featured, interestingly (given parallels of literary genre), on the website Science Frontiers: The Unusual & Unexplained (www.science-frontiers.com).

37. Elliot R. Wolfson, "Light Does Not Talk But Shines: Apophasis and Vision in Rosenzweig's Theopoetic Temporality."

38. Paradoxically, perhaps, as a literary performance Augustine's version of eternity is arguably the more intensely "carnal" and temporalized, if also (thereby?) more in danger of slipping out of the performative present and into an eternally deferred futurity—a danger of which Rosenzweig is sharply aware. See his critical comments on "the Christian chronology": "Not as moment therefore does the moment become the representative of eternity for the Christian, but as central point of Christian world time; and this world time, since it does not elapse but stands, consists of nothing but such 'central points'; every event stands in the center between beginning and end of the eternal way and through this central position in the temporal interval kingdom [*im zeitlichen Zwischenreich*] of eternity, is itself eternal" (*SR,* 360).

39. As Wolfson argues, with regard to Rosenzweig, in "Light Does Not Talk But Shines."

40. Funkenstein identifies the difference between Rosenzweig and Augustine thus: "Rosenzweig has no need for heaven and angels. His City of God is here on earth, already eternal in that it will be ever present" (*Perceptions of Jewish History,* 299). On one level, this is not just a fair but an extremely important distinction. On another level, it doesn't quite hold: first, the significance of Augustine's "need for heaven and angels" is less transparent than it might initially seem (correspondingly, his concept of "eternity" is more subtle than it is often taken to be, with respect to "heaven and angels"); second, Rosenzweig's own resolution of the tension between parts 2 and 3 of *Star*—between presence and eternity—is less clear than it might be. (And if the resolution is a dissolution, where does that leave his insistence on triadic irreducibility? This is the challenge issued by Wolfson in

"Light Does Not Talk But Shines"). I am suggesting there is a shared ambivalence, though one that tugs from different directions.

41. I am drawn to (without being able fully to comprehend) the critique of "objectivation" put forth by quantum physicist Erwin Schrödinger and both cited and further explicated by Shimon Malin, who notes, "we are so used to mistaking the abstract for the concrete that the fundamental fact of experiencing is excluded from scientific analysis" ("Whitehead and the Collapse of Quantum States," 79).

42. Greer, *The Fear of Freedom,* 175.

43. Karmen MacKendrick, *Word Made Skin: Figuring Language at the Surface of Flesh,* 155. The context is a discussion of scars, not miracles.

44. Wolfson, *Language, Eros, Being,* xvii.

45. Funkenstein, *Perceptions of Jewish History,* 304.

46. See Rosenzweig's comment with regard to his pre-"conversion" perspective: "I thought I had Christianized my view of Judaism, but in actual fact I had done the opposite: I had 'Judaized' my view of Christianity. I had considered the year 313 as the beginning of a falling away from true Christianity" (Letter 59 in Rosenzweig, *Briefe,* 72, trans. Glatzer, *Franz Rosenzweig,* 24). For Rosenzweig, a "Judaized" Christianity is one robbed of its rightful secularism, yet his very appropriation of Augustine's own thought for his construction of the Jews as the eternal people versus the "worldly" Christians (see Funkenstein, *Perceptions of Jewish History,* 298–301) should complicate, if not challenge, this dualism.

"Come forth into the light of things": Material Spirit as Negative Ecopoetics / Kate Rigby

1. A critical historiography of the symbolism of light has been undertaken by Geoffrey Berry in the context of his doctoral research in the Centre for Comparative Literature and Cultural Studies at Monash University ("Under the Dominion of Light: An Ecocritical Mythography"). I am indebted to him for alerting me to the ecophilosophical ramifications of this trope. See also Berry, "Maneuvering Light: Utopian Urbanity and Its Ecological Cost."

2. Kate Rigby, "Earth, World, Text: On the (Im)possibility of Ecopoiesis."

3. Bertholt Brecht, "An die Nachgebornen," in *Gesammelte Werke.* Unless otherwise indicated all translations from German are my own.

4. The title of Michael Bennett's valuable plaidoyer for a more urban-oriented ecocriticism, focusing on issues of social justice, "From Wide Open Spaces to Metropolitan Places: The Urban Challenge to Ecocriticism," tends in this direction. It should be noted, however, that he ends his article by calling for an ecocritical linking of "deep" and "social ecology" rather than an outright suppression of the former in favor of the latter. On this question, see also my "Ecocriticism."

5. Val Plumwood, "Shadow Places and the Politics of Dwelling."

6. Joni Adamson, Mei Mei Evans, and Rachel Stein, eds., *The Environmental Justice Reader.*

7. Hans Magnus Enzensberger. "Weiterung," in *Die Gedichte,* 204.

8. Hans Magnus Enzensberger, "Zwei Fehler," in *Die Gedichte,* 206.

9. Recalling Marx's observation in *The Holy Family* that the private property relation "alienates not only the individuality of human beings but also that of things," Bloch argues in *The Principle of Hope* that under capitalism, nature appears exclusively in the mode of *natura dominata,* being valued solely in instrumental terms as a means to an end, subject to human control and exploitation. Reviving the concept of nature as productive process rather than static mechanism, as posited in the *Naturphilosophie* of Hegel and above all Schelling, Bloch holds to the hope that the emancipatory transformation of human relations would also restore nature to the status of *natura naturans,* a subject in its own right. Thus recognizing the independent agency and coproductivity of nature, he suggests, necessitates the development of new forms of technology, based on the principle of alliance rather than domination. Bloch, *The Principle of Hope,* vol. 2, 690–91.

10. Raymond Williams, *The Country and the City,* 271.

11. Theodor Adorno, *Prisms,* 34.

12. Elaine Martin, "Re-reading Adorno: The 'After Auschwitz' Aporia," 11.

13. George Steiner, *Language and Silence: Essays on Language, Literature and the Inhuman,* ix.

14. Val Plumwood, "Nature as Agency and the Prospects for a Progressive Naturalism."

15. See my "Writing in the Anthropocene: Idle Chatter or Ecoprophetic Witness?"

16. For example, Scott Slovic, *Seeking Awareness in American Nature Writing,* and Lawrence Buell, *The Environmental Imagination: Thoreau, Nature Writing, and the Formation of American Culture.*

17. Lance Newman, *Our Common Dwelling: Henry Thoreau, Transcendentalism and the Class Politics of Nature.* See also Mark Cladis's excellent discussion of religion, ecology, and democracy with respect to the contemporary nature writers Annie Dillard, Barry Lopez, and Terry Tempest Williams in "Stone-Throwers with Excellent Aim: Waking up to an Environmental Democratic Vision."

18. The most trenchant critique of ecocritical and ecopoetic mimeticism from a poststructuralist perspective to date is Morton's *Ecology Without Nature,* but the restrictiveness of privileging nonfiction nature writing was also targeted previously by Dominic Head ("The (Im)possibility of Ecocriticism"), and the preference for realism roundly rejected by Dana Phillips (*The Truth of Ecology: Nature, Culture and Literature in America*).

19. For example, William Cronon, "The Trouble with Wilderness; or, Getting Back to the Wrong Nature," in *Uncommon Ground: Rethinking the Human Place in Nature.*

20. See my "Writing after Nature."

21. Adorno, *Aesthetic Theory,* 108.

22. Ibid., 97.

23. Mary Oliver, *Blue Iris: Poems and Essays,* 53.

24. Oliver, "The Sunflowers," in *Blue Iris,* 2.

25. Yves Bonnefoy, "Lifting Our Eyes from the Page."

26. Lawrence Buell, *The Future of Environmental Criticism,* 33.

27. The uncovering of its materialist moiety has been a primary concern of ecocritical Romanticism studies (as reviewed in, for example, Kevin Hutchings, "Ecocriticism in British Romanticism Studies") and is centralized in Onno Oerlemans, *Romanticism and the Materiality of Nature.*

28. William Wordsworth, "The Tables Turned," in *Lyrical Ballads, and Other Poems, 1797–1800,* 108–9.

29. Adam Potkay, "Wordsworth and the Ethics of Things."

30. Blackston cited in Potkay, "Wordsworth and the Ethics of Things," 394.

31. Potkay, "Wordsworth and the Ethics of Things," 395.

32. Ibid., 392.

33. Sylvia Benso, *The Face of Things: A Different Side of Ethics,* xxxii.

34. Ibid., xxix–xxx.

35. Potkay, "Wordsworth and the Ethics of Things," 396 (the original source of the quotation is Sylvia Benso, *The Face of Things,* xxxi).

36. Denis Edwards, *Ecology at the Heart of Faith: The Change of Heart That Leads to a New Way of Living on Earth,* 58–60.

37. In my earlier work I have interpreted the religious orientation of Wordsworth's early verse as closer to panentheism (and hence to physic-theology, Neoplatonism, and German *Naturphilosophie*) than to Spinozan "pantheism" (see my *Topographies of the Sacred,* 47–48). However, recent research by Marjorie Levinson ("A Motion and a Spirit: Romancing Spinoza") indicates that the significance of Spinoza for Wordsworth and other English Romantic era poets was probably greater and more direct than has hitherto been recognized.

38. Freya Mathews, *For Love of Matter: A Contemporary Panpsychism,* 351. See also Bill Brown, "Thing Theory."

39. Mathews, *For Love of Matter,* and idem, *Reinhabiting Reality: Towards a Recovery of Culture.*

40. See also Stacey Alaimo and Susan Hekman, *Material Feminisms;* Jane Bennett, "The Force of Things: Steps Toward an Ecology of Matter"; and Diana Coole and Samantha Frost, eds., *New Materialisms.* This new materialist turn is also entering ecocriticism, notably through the work of Serenella Iovino and Serpil Oppermann ("Material Ecocriticism: Materiality, Agency, and Models of Narrativity"), who are currently editing a volume for Indiana University Press on material ecocriticism.

41. Benso, *The Face of Things,* 150.

42. Ibid., 147.

43. Ibid., 150.

44. Jean-Luc Marion, *Being Given: Toward a Phenomenology of Givenness,* 159. It might be noted that "luminosity" is a key term for another recent work of theologically inclined phenomenology, as in David Walsh's *Modern Philosophical Revolution: The Luminosity of Existence,* which nonetheless oddly declines conversation with Marion.

45. Wordsworth, "Nutting," in *Lyrical Ballads,* 218–20.

46. Edwards, *Ecology at the Heart of Faith,* 110.

47. The question of the materiality of the text is addressed along ecocritical lines, and with reference to the text of the Bible in particular, by Anne Elvey in *The Matter of the Text: Material Engagements between Luke and the Five Senses.*

48. James Phillips, "Wordsworth and the Fraternity of Joy."

49. William Wordsworth, *Poems, In Two Volumes, and Other Poems, 1800–1807,* 207.

50. Alison Calder, introduction to *Desire Never Leaves: The Poetry of Tim Lilburn,* ix. Hugh Dunkerley also discusses Lilburn's ecopoetics of the *via negativa* in his "Poetry and Unknowing."

51. Tim Lilburn, *Living in the World As If It Were Home,* 22.

52. Lilburn, "In the Hills, Watching," in *Living in the World As If It Were Home,* 18.

53. Lilburn, "There Is No Presence," in *Desire Never Leaves,* 25.

54. Lilburn, *Living in the World As If It Were Home,* 35.

55. Ibid., 18.

56. Ibid., 61.

57. Ibid., 21.

58. Lilburn, "There Is No Presence," in *Desire Never Leaves,* 27.

59. Lilburn, "Pumpkins," in *Desire Never Leaves,* 5.

60. For an excellent introduction to biosemiotics oriented towards ecocritical studies, see W. Wheeler, *The Whole Creature: Complexity, Biosemiotics and the Evolution of Culture.*

61. Cited in Mark Tredinnick, *The Land's Wild Music: Encounters with Barry Lopez, Peter Matthiessen, Terry Tempest Williams and James Galvin,* 211.

62. See my article "Writing in the Anthropocene: Idle Chatter or Ecoprophetic Witness?"

63. John Clare, "The Mores," in *Selected Poems,* 89–91.

The Angel and the Storm: "Material Spirit" in the Era of Climate Change / Tom Cohen

1. Bruno Latour, "An Attempt at a 'Compositional Manifesto,'" 485–86.

2. Robert S. Lehman, "Allegories of Rending: Killing Time with Walter Benjamin," 247.

3. Beatrice Hansen, *Walter Benjamin's Other History: Of Stones, Animals, Human Beings, and Angels.*

4. Walter Benjamin, "Theses on the Philosophy of History," in *Illuminations,* 257–58. Subsequent page references to this work appear in the text.

5. This angel has an affinity not to divinity but to "natural history," in Benjamin's vocabulary, which again is neither natural nor historial as such. "Natural history" is elicited, rather, as an *interruption* of artefacted times before different temporal metrics oblivious to human time.

6. Benjamin's "natural history" situates a *so-called* materiality of the earth's chance eons at a non-site braided with alloarchival and trace events. It cannot be anthropomorphized at all, as its metrics alone assures (neither turned into Gaia, a nurturing mother, or more interestingly in Peter Ward's counterstrike, Medea, a destroying mother—both still human metaphors and *maternal* myths, the first tirelessly "organic"). Only here the caesura arrives *as if* from without, depersonified. It impinges on political imaginaries and economic regimes, social contracts, and so on, as it stands to override their parentheses. This opens a reading of "nature" as a parallel and interwoven scene of mnemonic process and proto-mimetic atelic "evolutionary" wars penetrating chemical and molecular zones and interfaced with human *animation.* And it is not because "nature" envelops all, but because proactive and mimetic technicities permeate the living and inorganic systems—of which human language (which Benjamin considers nonhuman) is a special mnemonic instance, with its limiting compulsion to repeat, create imaginary reserves, hypostasize passing effects as stable signifiers, group icons, package anteriorities, and so on. It brings a question of *inscriptions* again to the fore, only balanced against irreversible terrestrial or ecographic processes in backloops removed from zombied perceptual and semantic programs.

7. Jacques Derrida, *Specters of Marx: The State of the Debt, the Work of Mourning and the New International,* 58. Subsequent page references to this work appear in the text.

8. One should not give Benjamin all the credit for his fable since it is itself a reading of Klee's graphic figure—the sensuous-mouthed if childish wire-form of some skinny Terminator *avant la lettre,* stripped of fleshy cover.

9. What we call *archive* names the mnemonic networks of anteriority as such and the inscriptions from which presents are generated. Yet it is active, can mutate, erase its programs, veer into temporal accelerations, self-cancelling loops, fevered ills, time bubbles. It may even flip its perpetual focus on anteriority, as it does today, when calculable "futures" saturate a present in advance. Some of these represent cancelled or consumed "futures," predicted extinction events and population culling. In such instances the desire for preemption arises, which seems to accelerate the effect it wished to deter. This logic of temporal control of disastrous futures is parodied in the Bush doctrine. One cannot stop discussing, trying to preempt, forestall, or derealize certain *things*—the material consequences of the hypercarbon era. But the prospect of bursting our "time bubble" opens a series of questions. And there is no angel of history here.

10. Nothing in the trope of a "democracy to come" that is spectral, nothing in its literalizations, accords with the likely "futures" unfolding today. The era of democracy appears closing, its closure rehearsed by the Bush kleptomediacratic state. "Deconstruction," if it (still) exists, took its compass point from a nonanthropic *trace.* The geomorphic *caesura* for humans may appear instantaneous (like the nuclear blast or the meteor strike) or stretch the figure of the interval to encompass a nonhuman duration, like the mere hundred years to coastal inundation. It may be today, with our addiction to and banalization of "shock," cinematic and

otherwise, what is suppressed is any metrics for the event that arrives in differing durations.

11. The big bang, the nuclear blast, the comet impact that extincts dinosaurs, the terrorist strike or blow, revolution, the trauma as anteriority—all hypostasize the counter-instant as the perceptual marker to negotiate around.

12. Again and again, today, a critical border in contemporary criticism seems gestured to and then folded back into a humanistic structure. One could apply this to the recent deployments of "biopolitics" triggered by Agamben: in *Homo Sacer,* however, Agamben's recirculation of Foucault's term turns on a humanistic and eurocentric circuit—the excavation of a minor Roman law as a preoriginary inscription, the European blind of viewing the Holocaust as a unique and penultimate case (as it would not be to Asia or even Russia), the reduction of the "biopolitical" to a human-upon-human practice still (the *Homo sacer*). Each still operates to guard an anthropic, and here eurocentric, circuit that the figure itself would exceed. One could say the same of the fascination with the "state of exception" and sovereignty, which presumes the suspension of a (democratic) bureaucratic managerial contract in the name of preserving the *people.*

13. A "materiality of inscription" is de Man's proleptic term for what Derrida, in his very different mode, will conjure as the non-site of *khora.* As sheer anteriority and as technic, such accords perhaps less with the stone face than with the atomized grain of sand or mud. De Man, who seemed to veer repeatedly into the site of the speaking dead (that redounds to the reader), or the precession of face in prosopopoeia—and, hence, the side of inscription—seemed drawn across this screen. Nanological, to disinscribe a perceptual regime suggests not the violent exposure of another truth or any possible erasure (short of a totalitarian burning of archives and eradication of populations) but the precession of the preoriginary status of the inscription or its technological base—a precession, say, of word by the letter, alphabeticism by trace. The movement, as Benjamin understood, is structurally suicidal, since its success would imply the erasure of its own "present" as a structure (or the past that defined it). It could also be called suicidal in structure in that it expends itself on arriving at the "irreversible" border of a mutation, a permanent exodus, that can only be affirmed from another, at the other side, at which point his labor is erased. This is the non-site that the materialistic historiographer would awaken to with his shocks, blasting, and allochronic gambles. But in Benjamin's "Theses," one could say, he is indiscreetly pulled away.

14. It is interesting to reflect on how premier critical styles entering the twenty-first century strangely accompanied, with no interventionist power, the entry into the Bush regime's auto-da-fé. It is the more fascinating to consider the current disorientation before a dawning of "climate change," which has rearranged through force imaginary contracts with time (or time-space)—that is, with the latter's unequivocal rupture of the representational membrane as if from without.

15. From such a perspective, the rhetorical premises of ecocriticism, of environmentalism, of green politics as such (sustainability, mitigation, essentially maintenance regimes) are variations on the angelicism that accelerates the expo-

nential curve of autodispossession. Ecological thought tends to return to the same organicist models as would be implicated in hyperconsumption itself, and the maintenance of the *oikos.*

16. Carrying over his analytic of the temporal nonpresent into a critique of Francis Fukuyama's "end of history" allowed him to miss a looming out-of-jointness of fantastic proportion that would, if anything, represent more of a blow to anthropomorphism than deconstruction and Marx combined. That would have been the geomorphic irruptions we call climate change. Its temporal ruptures are multiple, and multiply embedded in innumerable systems. It is extended to a rupture of human temporalities altogether, with the proliferation of other geomorphic time-lines ("global warming," mass extinctions, dying seas, resource depletion, biodiversity collapse).

17. The "materiality of inscription," if one cared for this term, involves no tangible materiality, since it precedes phenomenality and represents the fusion of mnemonics and the orders of world, perception, and act that emerge and occur—no more, that is, than an *inscription* accords with a thing, an object, *hylē,* and so on, outright. What it pretends to name, out of the draft of anteriority, penetrates the interpretation of perception and the generation of value, fetish, and so on, at the crease of where "spirit" and "matter" form a band, or ribbon, in the faux moebius fashion named (by contrast, the materialism of the Marxian model, cast by the opposition of labor and capital, maintains a mind-matter or body-spirit dichotomy even as "materiality" embraces an abstract domain). An inscription would never be manifest as such but rather dispersed amid the symptomatics of decision, perceptual memory, hermeneutics, rhetorical machines.

18. An example would be the insistence, readily literalized, of the injunction against "futures" so as to keep such properly open—even, that is, when the monstrous future is incalculable and turns against that move itself, as today, when the absence of address of climate change in Derrida disappoints and appears "damaging" (Timothy Clark).

19. He is a dissimulating "angel," which is to say costumed. This is already apparent in Klee's painting, where the wired image emits the torsion of a broken if sensuous demonic doll, a sort of antimetaphysical Chuckie.

The Material Working of Spirit / J. Hillis Miller

1. C. P. Cavafy, "It Must Have Been the Spirits."

2. Claire Colebrook, "Matter Without Bodies," 15.

3. Jacques Derrida, "Psyche: Invention of the Other," 1; *Psyché: Inventions de l'autre,* 11.

4. Ibid.

5. J. L. Austin, *How to Do Things with Words.*

6. Jacques Derrida, *Spectres de Marx: L'état de la dette, le travail du deuil, et la nouvelle Internationale* (1993); *Specters of Marx: The State of the Debt, the Work of Mourning, and the New International* (1994).

7. Derrida, “Psyche: Invention of the Other,” 1; *Psyché: Inventions de l’autre,* 11.

8. Jean-Luc Nancy, *La Déclosion: Déconstruction du Christianisme,* 125; *Dis-Enclosure: The Deconstruction of Christianity,* 81.

9. Nancy, *Dis-Enclosure,* 81–82, trans. modified.

10. Ibid., 82.

11. See the first three lines of “Ribh denounces Patrick”:

An abstract Greek absurdity has crazed the man,
A Trinity that is wholly masculine. Man, woman, child (daughter or son),
That’s how all natural or supernatural stories run.
William Butler Yeats, *The Poems: A New Edition,* 284

12. Nancy, *La Déclosion,* 125; *Dis-Enclosure,* 81.

13. G. S. Kirk and J. E. Raven, *The Presocratic Philosophers: A Critical History with a Selection of Texts,* 199.

14. Martin Heidegger, “Anaximander’s Saying,” 265; “Der Spruch des Anaximander,” 325. (All the Greek words are in Greek letters in Heidegger’s essay.)

15. Gerard Manley Hopkins, *Poems,* 105–6.

16. Hopkins, “The Wreck of the Deutschland,” in *Poems,* 59.

17. Ibid., 61.

18. For two out of many definitions of “God-terms” in Burke’s work, see Burke, *A Grammar of Motives,* 74–77; idem, *A Rhetoric of Motives,* 110–14. In the former passage, Burke defines “God-terms” as “names for the ultimates of motivation.” In the latter passage “honor” is given as an example of a possible God-term within a certain sociolinguistic system.

19. De Man is citing and translating Rousseau, *Oeuvres Complètes.*

20. Paul de Man, “Textual Allegories,” 134.

21. Jacques Derrida, “Faith and Knowledge: The Two Sources of ‘Religion’ at the Limits of Reason Alone,” 87; “Foi et savoir: Les deux sources de la ‘religion’ aux limites de la simple raison,” 68–69.

22. See http://en.wikipedia.org/wiki/Ecotechnology (accessed June 22, 2011).

23. Jean-Luc Nancy, *Corpus,* 78; *Corpus* (English translation), 89.

24. For the *sídhe,* see the Wikipedia entry “Aos Sí” at http://en.wikipedia.org/wiki/Sídhe#The_s.C3.ADdhe:_abodes_of_the_aes_s.C3.ADdhe (accessed June 22, 2011).

25. For a learned and provocative exploration of what might be called a pan-technology, with an emphasis on sign systems, see Louis Armand, *Literate Technologies: Language, Cognition, Technicity.*

26. Henri Bergson, *Oeuvres,* 1245, my translation.

27. For example, Derrida, “Faith and Knowledge,” 87; “Foi et savoir,” 68–69.

28. Paul de Man, *The Resistance to Theory,* 11.

29. Ibid., 88.

30. Ibid., 11.

31. Ibid.

32. Ibid.

33. Ibid.

34. Derrida, *Specters of Marx,* 144; *Spectres de Marx,* 229. Subsequent page references to this work are provided parenthetically in the text; page numbers of the French version follow in brackets.

Works Cited

Abbott, Claude Colleer, ed. *Further Letters of Gerard Manley Hopkins Including His Correspondence with Coventry Patmore.* 2nd ed. London: Oxford University Press, 1956.

Abbott, Claude Colleer, ed. *The Letters of Gerard Manley Hopkins to Robert Bridges.* Oxford: Oxford University Press, 1955.

Adamson, Joni, Mei Mei Evans, and Rachel Stein, eds. *The Environmental Justice Reader.* Tucson: University of Arizona Press, 2002.

Adorno, Theodor. *Aesthetic Theory.* Translated by C. Lenhardt. Edited by Gretel Adorno and Rolf Tiedemann. London and New York: Routledge and Kegan Paul, 1984.

———. *Prisms.* Translated by Samuel and Shierry Weber. Cambridge, MA: MIT Press, 1981.

Adorno, Theodor, and Max Horkheimer. *Dialectic of Enlightenment.* Translated by John Cumming. London: Verso, 1979.

Alaimo, Stacey, and Susan Hekman. *Material Feminisms.* Bloomington: Indiana University Press, 2008.

Ambrose of Milan. *Exposition of the Holy Gospel According to Saint Luke.* Translated by Theodosia Tomkinson. Etna, CA: Center for Traditionalist Orthodox Studies, 2003.

Armand, Louis. *Literate Technologies: Language, Cognition, Technicity.* Prague: Litteraria Pragensia, 2006.

Auerbach, Erich. "The Brown Stocking." In *Mimesis: The Representation of Reality in Western Literature.* Princeton, NJ: Princeton University Press, 1968.

Augustine. *City of God.* Translated by Henry Bettenson. New York: Penguin, 1984.

———. *De civitate Dei.* Corpus Christianorum, Series Latina. Turnhout, Belgium: Brepols, 1965.

———. "First Homily." In *Homilies on the First Epistle of John.* Translated and with an introduction and notes by Boniface Ramsey. Edited by Daniel E. Doyle and Thomas Martin. New York: New City Press, 2008.

———. *The Literal Meaning of Genesis.* In *On Genesis.* Translated and with an introduction and notes by Edmund Hill. Edited by John E. Rotelle. The Works of Saint Augustine. Hyde Park, NY: New City Press, 2002.

Austin, J. L. *How to Do Things with Words.* 2nd ed. Edited by J. O. Urmson and Marina Sbisà. Oxford: Oxford University Press, 1980.

Bachelard, Gaston. *The Poetics of Space.* Boston: Beacon Press, 1994.

Balthasar, Hans Urs von. *The Glory of the Lord.* Vol. 1, *Seeing the Form.* Translated by Erasmo Leiva-Merikakis. San Francisco: Ignatius Press, 1982.

———. *The Glory of the Lord.* Vol. 2, *Studies in Theological Style: Clerical Styles.* Translated by Andrew Louth et al. San Francisco: Ignatius Press, 1984.

Barth, Karl. *Church Dogmatics.* Vol. 1, *The Doctrine of the Word of God.* Edited by G. W. Bromiley and T. F. Torrance. Translated by G. T. Thomson and Harold Knight. Edinburgh: T. and T. Clark, 1956.

Bataille, Georges. *Blue of Noon.* Translated by Harry Matthews. London: Marion Boyars, 1986.

———. "Discussion on Sin." In *The Unfinished System of Nonknowledge.* Translated by Stuart Kendall and Michelle Kendall. Minneapolis: University of Minnesota Press, 2004.

———. *Erotism: Death and Sensuality.* Translated by Mary Dalwood. San Francisco: City Lights, 2001.

———. *Guilty.* Translated by Bruce Boone. Culver City, CA: Lapis Press, 1988.

———. *Inner Experience.* Translated by Leslie A. Boldt. Albany: State University of New York Press, 1988.

———. *L'Abbé C.* Translated by Philip Facey. London: Marion Boyars, 1989.

———. *My Mother, Madame Edwarda, and The Dead Man.* Translated by Austryn Wainhouse. London: Marion Boyars, 1995.

———. *On Nietzsche.* Translated by Bruce Boone. Paragon House, 1994.

———. *Story of the Eye.* Translated by Joachim Neugroschel. San Francisco: City Lights, 2001.

———. *Theory of Religion.* Translated by Robert Hurley. New York: Zone Books, 1992.

Bello, Angela Ales. *The Divine in Husserl and Other Explorations.* Analecta Husserliana 98. Dordrecht: Springer-Verlag, 2009.

Benjamin, Walter. *The Arcades Project.* Translated by Kevin McLoughlin. Cambridge, MA: Harvard University Press, 1999.

———. "The Image of Proust." In Walter Benjamin, *Illuminations.* Translated by Harry Zohn. Edited by Hannah Arendt, 201–16. New York: Schocken Books, 1968.

———. "Theses on the Philosophy of History." In *Illuminations.* Translated by Harry Zohn. Introduction by by Hannah Arendt. New York: Random House, 1969.

Bennett, Jane. "The Force of Things: Steps Toward an Ecology of Matter." *Political Theory* 32, no. 3 (June 2004): 347–72.

Bennett, Michael. "From Wide Open Spaces to Metropolitan Places: The Urban Challenge to Ecocriticism." *ISLE* 8, no. 1 (2001): 31–52.

Benso, Sylvia. *The Face of Things: A Different Side of Ethics.* Albany: SUNY, 2000.

Bergson, Henri. *Oeuvres.* Paris: Presses Universitaires de France, 1959.

Bernard of Clairvaux, *In ascensione sermo.* In *Sancti Bernardi Opera,* vol. 5. Edited by Jean Leclerq. Rome: Editiones Cistercienses, 1966.

———. *On the Song of Songs,* vol. 4 of *Sancti Bernardi Opera.* Translated by Irene Edmonds. Introduction by Jean Leclercq. Kalamazoo, MI: Cistercian Publications, 1980.

Berry, Geoff. "Maneuvering Light: Utopian Urbanity and its Ecological Cost." *Double Dialogues* 8 (Summer 2007–8). http://www.doubledialogues.com/archive/issue_eight/berry.html.

———. "Under the Dominion of Light: An Ecocritical Mythography." PhD thesis, Monash University, 2009.

Bérulle, Pierre de. *Grandeurs de Iésus,* discours 2. In *Oeuvres Complètes.* Edited by P. Gibieuf. Paris, 1644. Photo-mechanically reprinted in 2 vols. Montsoult: Maison d'Institutition de l'Oratoire, 1960.

Bloch, Ernst. *The Principle of Hope.* Translated by Neville Plaice, Stephen Plaice, and Paul Knight. 3 vols. Cambridge, MA: Harvard University Press, 1995.

Blondel, Maurice. *Action: Essay on a Critique of Life and a Science of Practice.* Translated by Oliva Blanchette. South Bend, IN: Notre Dame University Press, 1984. First published 1893.

———. "The Letter on Apologetics." In *The Letter on Apologetics and History and Dogma.* Translated by Alexander Dru and Illtyd Trethowan. Grand Rapids, MI: Eerdmans, 1994. First published 1964.

Bonnefoy, Yves. "Lifting Our Eyes from the Page." *Critical Inquiry* 16 (Summer 1990): 794–806.

Brakke, David. "The Problematization of Nocturnal Emissions in Early Christian Syria, Egypt, and Gaul." *Journal of Early Christian Studies* 3, no. 4 (1995): 419–60.

Bray, Xavier, ed. *The Sacred Made Real: Spanish Painting and Sculpture 1600–1700.* London: National Gallery Company / Yale University Press, 2009.

Brecht, Bertholt. *Gesammelte Werke.* Frankfurt a.M.: Surhkamp, 1967.

Brown, Bill. "Thing Theory." *Critical Inquiry* 28, no. 1 (2001): 1–22.

Brown, Peter. *The Body and Society: Men, Women and Sexual Renunciation in Early Christianity.* New York, Columbia University Press, 1988.

Bruzina, Ronald. *Edmund Husserl and Eugen Fink: Beginnings and Ends in Phenomenology 1928–1938.* New Haven, CT: Yale University Press, 2004.

Buell, Lawrence. *The Environmental Imagination: Thoreau, Nature Writing, and the Formation of American Culture.* Cambridge, MA: Cambridge University Press, 1995.

———. *The Future of Environmental Criticism.* London: Blackwell, 2005.

Burke, Kenneth. *A Grammar of Motives.* New York: Prentice-Hall, 1945.

———. *A Rhetoric of Motives.* New York: Prenctice-Hall, 1950.

———. *The Rhetoric of Religion: Studies in Logology.* Berkeley and Los Angeles: University of California Press, 1970.

Burrus, Virginia. *Saving Shame: Martyrs, Saints and Other Abject Subjects.* Philadelphia: University of Pennsylvania Press, 2007.

———. *The Sex Lives of Saints: An Erotics of Ancient Hagiography.* Philadelphia: University of Pennsylvania Press, 2004.

Cairns, Dorian. *Conversations with Husserl and Fink.* The Hague: Martinus Nijhoff, 1976.

Calder, Alison. Introduction to *Desire Never Leaves: The Poetry of Tim Lilburn,* by Tim Lilburn. Edited by Alison Calder. Waterloo, ON: Wilfred Laurier University Press, 2007.

Calvin, John. *The Institutes of the Christian Religion,* vol. 4. Translated by Henry Beveridge. Grand Rapids, MI: Eerdmans, 1953.

Caputo, John. *The Weakness of God: A Theology of the Event.* Bloomington: Indiana University Press, 2006.

———. *What Would Jesus Deconstruct? The Good News of Postmodernism for the Church.* Grand Rapids, MI: Baker Academic, 2007.

Cassian, John. *Conferences.* Translated and with notes by Edgar C. S. Gibson. A Select Library of Nicene and Post-Nicene Fathers of the Christian Church, 2nd ser., vol. 11. New York, 1894. http://www.osb.org/lectio/cassian/conf/.

Cavafy, C. P. "It Must Have Been the Spirits." Translated by Daniel Mendelsohn. *New York Times,* January 26, 2009, 28.

Chrétien, Jean-Louis. *The Call and the Response.* Translated by Anne A. Davenport. New York: Fordham University Press, 2004.

Ciglia, Francesco Paolo. "Auf der Spur Augustins: *Confessiones* und *De civitate Dei* als Quellen des *Stern der Erlösung.*" In *Rosenzweig als Leser: Kontextuelle Komentare zum "Stern der Erlösung."* Edited by Martin Brasser, 223–44. Tübingen: Max Niemeyer Verlag, 2004.

———. "Der Gordische Knoten der Zeit: Aspecte des Dialogs Zweischen Rosenzweig und Augustin." In *Franz Rosenzweigs "Neues Denken" Internationaler Kongress Kassel 2004, 1. Band: Selbstbegrenzendes Denken—in Philosophos,* ed. Wolfdietrich Schmied-Kowarzik, 323–45. Freiburg-München: Karl Alber Verlag, 2006.

Cixous, Hélène. *The Newly Born Woman.* Translated by Betsy Wing. Minneapolis: University of Minnesota Press, 1986.

Cladis, Mark. "Stone-throwers with Excellent Aim: Waking up to an Environmental Democratic Vision," *Religion and Literature* 40, no. 1 (2008): 81–102.

Clare, John. *Selected Poems.* Edited by Jonathan Bate. London: Faber and Faber, 2004.

Colebrook, Claire. "Matter Without Bodies." *Derrida Today* 4, no. 1 (2011): 1–20.

Coole, Diana, and Samantha Frost, eds. *New Materialisms.* Durham, NC: Duke University Press, 2010.

Corner, Martin. "Mysticism and Atheism in *To the Lighthouse.*" In *Virginia Woolf's To the Lighthouse,* ed. Harold Bloom. London: Chelsea House Publishers, 1988.

Cronon, William. "The Trouble with Wilderness; or, Getting Back to the Wrong Nature." In *Uncommon Ground: Rethinking the Human Place in Nature,* ed. W. Cronon, 69–90. New York: Norton, 1995.

Cunningham, Valentine. *Reading after Theory.* Oxford: Blackwell, 2002.

de Man, Paul. "Textual Allegories." Manuscript, 1973.

———. *The Resistance to Theory.* Minneapolis: University of Minnesota Press, 1986.

Deleuze, Gilles. *Francis Bacon: The Logic of Sense.* Translated by Daniel W. Smith. Minneapolis: University of Minnesota Press, 2003.

———. *Proust and Signs.* London: Athlone Press, 2000.

Derrida, Jacques. *The Animal That Therefore I Am.* Translated by David Wills. Edited by Marie-Louise Mallet. New York: Fordham University Press, 2008.

———. "Faith and Knowledge: The Two Sources of 'Religion' at the Limits of Reason Alone." Translated by Samuel Weber. In *Acts of Religion,* ed. Gil Anidjar, 42–101. New York: Routledge, 2002.

———. "Foi et savoir: Les deux sources de la 'religion' aux limites de la simple raison." In *La religion,* ed. Jacques Derrida and Gianni Vattimo, 9–86. Paris: Seuil, 1996.

———. "Psyche: Invention of the Other." In *Psyche: Inventions of the Other,* ed. Peggy Kamuf and Elizabeth Rottenberg, vol. 1, 1–47. Stanford, CA: Stanford University Press, 2007.

———. *Psyché: Inventions de l'autre.* Paris: Galilée, 1987.

———. *Specters of Marx: The State of the Debt, the Work of Mourning and the New International.* Translated by Peggy Kamuf. New York: Routledge 1994.

———. *Spectres de Marx: L'état de la dette, le travail du deuil et la nouvelle Internationale.* Paris: Galilée, 1993.

Devlin, Christopher, ed. *The Sermons and Devotional Writings of Gerard Manley Hopkins.* Oxford: Oxford University Press, 1959.

Didi-Huberman, Georges. *Confronting Images.* University Park, PA: Penn State University Press, 2005.

Downes, David Anthony. *The Ignatian Personality of Gerard Manley Hopkins.* New York: University Press of America, 1990.
Dunkerly, Hugh. "Poetry and Unknowing." Manuscript, 2008.
Edwards, Denis. *Ecology at the Heart of Faith: The Change of Heart That Leads to a New Way of Living on Earth.* Maryknoll, NY: Orbis Books, 2006.
Elvey, Anne F. *The Matter of the Text: Material Engagements between Luke and the Five Senses.* Sheffield: Sheffield Phoenix Press, 2011.
Enzensberger, Hans Magnus. *Die Gedichte.* Frankfurt a.M: Suhrkamp, 1983.
Fields, Stephen. "Balthasar and Rahner on the Spiritual Senses." *Theological Studies* 57 (1996): 224–41.
Foucault, Michel. "About the Beginning of the Hermeneutics of the Self." In *Religion and Culture,* ed. Jeremy Carrette, 156–81. Manchester, UK: Manchester University Press, 1999. First published 1978.
———. "On the Government of the Living." In *Religion and Culture,* ed. Jeremy Carrette, 154–57. Manchester: Manchester University Press, 1999. Lecture given in 1980.
———. "Sexuality and Power." In *Religion and Culture,* ed. Jeremy Carrette, 115–30. Manchester: Manchester University Press, 1999. Lecture given in 1980.
———. "What Is Critique?" In *The Politics of Truth.* Translated by Lysa Hochroth. Edited by Sylvère Lotringer and Lysa Hochroth, 41–82. New York: Semiotext(e), 1997.
France, James. "The Heritage of Saint Bernard in Medieval Art." In *A Companion to Bernard of Clairvaux,* ed. Brian Patrick McGuire, 305–46. Leiden: Brill, 2010.
Fredriksen, Paula. "*Secundum Carnem:* History and Israel in the Theology of St. Augustine." In *The Limits of Ancient Christianity: Essays on Late Antique Thought and Culture in Honor of R. A. Markus,* ed. William E. Klingshirn and Mark Vessey, 26–41. Ann Arbor: University of Michigan Press, 1999.
Fried, Michael. *Absorption and Theatricality: Painting and Beholder in the Age of Diderot.* Berkeley and Los Angeles: University of California Press, 1980.
———. *The Moment of Caravaggio.* Princeton, NJ: Princeton University Press, 2010.
Funkenstein, Amos. *Perceptions of Jewish History.* Berkeley: University of California Press, 1993.
Glatzer, Nahum. *Franz Rosenzweig: His Life and Thought.* Indianapolis, IN: Hackett Publishing Co., 1998.
Grant, Robert M. *Miracle and Natural Law in Graeco-Roman and Early Christian Thought.* Amsterdam: North-Holland Publishing Co., 1952.
Gray, Theodosa, trans. *The Homilies of Saint Gregory the Great on the Book of the Prophet Ezekiel.* Introduction by Bishop Chrysostomos. Etna, CA: Center for Traditionalist Orthodox Studies, 1990.
Greer, Rowan A. *The Fear of Freedom: A Study of Miracles in the Roman Imperial Church.* University Park, PA: Penn State University Press, 1989.

Gregory of Nyssa. *Commentary on the Song of Songs.* Translated and with an introduction by Casimir McCambley. Preface by Panagiotes Chrestou. Brookline, MA: Hellenic College Press, 1987.

Gregory the Great. *Morals on the Book of Job.* Translated by members of the English Church. A Library of Fathers of the Holy Catholic Church. Oxford: John Henry Parker, 1847.

Hägglund, Martin. *Radical Atheism: Derrida and the Time of Life.* Stanford, CA: Stanford University Press, 2008.

Hansen, Beatrice. *Walter Benjamin's Other History: Of Stones, Animals, Human Beings, and Angels.* Los Angeles: University of California Press, 2000.

Hart, James G. "A Précis of Husserlian Phenomenological Theology." In *Essays in Phenomenological Theology.* Edited by Steven W. Laycock and James G. Hart. Albany: State University of New York Press, 1986.

Hart, Kevin. "Poetry and Revelation: Hopkins, Counter-Experience and *Reductio.*" *Pacifica: Australian Theological Studies* 18 (2005): 259–80.

Hartman, Geoffrey H. *Wordsworth's Poetry, 1787–1814.* Cambridge, MA: Harvard University Press, 1987.

Hatzfield, Helmut. *Estudios literarios sobre mística española.* Madrid: Gredos, 1955.

Head, Dominic. "The (Im)possibility of Ecocriticism." In *Writing the Environment: Ecocriticism and Literature,* ed. Richard Kerridge and Neil Sammells, 27–39. London: Zed Books, 1998.

Heidegger, Martin. "Anaximander's Saying." In *Off the Beaten Track.* Translated by Julian Young and Kenneth Haynes, 242–81. Cambridge: Cambridge University Press, 2002.

———. *Being and Time.* Translated by John Macquarrie and Edward Robinson. Oxford: Basil Blackwell, 1973.

———. "Der Spruch des Anaximander." In *Holzwege,* 296–343. Frankfurt a.M.: Vittorio Klostermann, 1972.

———. *The Fundamental Concepts of Metaphysics: World, Finitude, Solitude.* Translated by William McNeill and Nicholas Walker. Bloomington: Indiana University Press, 1995.

Herbert, George. "Prayer." In *The Works of George Herbert,* vol. 1. Edited by F. E. Hutchinson. Oxford: Clarendon Press, 1945.

Hopkins, Gerard Manley. *The Collected Works of Gerard Manley Hopkins.* Vol. 4, *Oxford Essays and Notes.* Edited by Lesley Higgins. Oxford: Oxford University Press, 2006.

———. *Poems.* 4th ed. Edited by W. H. Gardner and N. H. MacKenzie. London. Oxford University Press, 1967. http://www.lib.latrobe.edu.au/AHR/archive/Issue-September-2006/rigby.html.

———. *Poems and Prose.* Edited by W. H. Gardner. Harmondsworth: Penguin, 1953.

House, Humphry, and Graham Storey, eds. *The Journals and Papers of Gerard Manley Hopkins.* London: Oxford University Press, 1959.

Hugh of Saint Victor. "The Soul's Three Ways of Seeing." In *Selected Spiritual Writings.* Introduction by Aelred Squire. New York: Harper and Row, 1962.

———. *Didascalicon.* Translated by Jerome Taylor. New York: Columbia University Press, 1991.

Husserl, Edmund. *Analyses Concerning Passive and Active Synthesis: Lectures on Transcendental Logic.* Translated by Anthony J. Steinbock. Edmund Husserl Collected Works, vol. 9. Dordrecht: Kluwer Academic Publishers, 2001.

———. *The Basic Problems of Phenomenology: From the Lectures, Winter Semester, 1910–1911.* Translated by Ingo Farin and James G. Hart. Edmund Husserl Collected Works. Dordrecht: Springer-Verlag, 2006.

———. *Briefwechsel.* Edited by Elizabeth and Karl Schuhmann. 10 vols. Dordrecht: Kluwer, 1994.

———. *Cartesian Meditations: An Introduction to Phenomenology.* Translated by Dorian Cairns. The Hague: Martinus Nijhoff, 1977.

———. *The Crisis of European Sciences and Transcendental Phenomenology: An Introduction to Phenomenological Philosophy.* Translated and with an introduction by David Carr. Evanston, IL: Northwestern University Press, 1970.

———. *Ideas Pertaining to a Pure Phenomenology and to a Phenomenological Philosophy: First Book.* Translated by F. Kersten. Edmund Husserl Collected Works, vol. 2. Boston: Kluwer Academic Publishers, 1998.

———. *Ideas Pertaining to a Pure Phenomenology and to a Phenomenological Philosophy: Second Book,* trans. Richard Rojecewicz and André Schuwer. Edmund Husserl Collected Works, vol. 3. Boston: Kluwer Academic Publishers, 1989.

———. *Logical Investigations.* Translated by J. N. Findlay. 2 vols. London: Routledge and Kegan Paul, 1970.

———. *Phantasy, Image Consciousness, and Memory (1898–1925).* Translated by John B. Brough. Edmund Husserl Collected Works, vol. 11. Dordrecht: Springer-Verlag, 2005.

———. "Psychological Studies in the Elements of Logic." In *Early Writings in the Philosophy of Logic and Mathematics.* Translated by Dallas Willard. Dordrecht: Kluwer Academic Publishers, 1994.

Hutchings, Kevin. "Ecocriticism in British Romanticism Studies." *Literature Compass* 41, no. 1 (2007): 172–202.

Ignatius of Loyola. "The Spiritual Exercises." Translated by George E. Ganss. In *Spiritual Exercises and Selected Works.* Edited by George E. Ganss. Mahwah, NJ: Paulist Press, 1991.

Iovino, Serenella and Serpil Opperman. "Material Ecocriticism: Materiality, Agency, and Models of Narrativity." *Ecozon@* 3 no. 1 (2012): 75–91.

Jaspers, Karl. *Philosophical Faith and Revelation.* Translated by E. B. Ashton. London: Collins, 1967.

John of the Cross. "The Ascent of Mount Carmel." In *The Collected Works of St John of the Cross.* Translated by Kieran Kavanaugh and Otilio Rodriguez. Washington, DC: ICS Publications, 1979.

Jüngel, Eberhard. *God as the Mystery of the World: On the Foundation of the Theology of the Crucified One in the Dispute between Theism and Atheism.* Translated by Darrell L. Guder. Grand Rapids, MI: Eerdmans, 1983.

Kepnes, Steven. "Rosenzweig's Liturgical Reasoning as a Response to Augustine's Temporal Aporias." In *Liturgy, Time, and the Politics of Redemption,* ed. Randi Rashkover and C. C. Pecknold, 112–23. Grand Rapids, MI: Eerdmans, 2006.

Kierkegaard, Søren. *Repetition.* Princeton, NJ: Princeton University Press, 1941.

Kirk, G. S. and J. E. Raven. *The Presocratic Philosophers: A Critical History with a Selection of Texts.* Cambridge: Cambridge University Press, 1966.

Kosky, Jeffrey. "Georges Bataille's Religion without Religion: A Review of the Possibilities Opened by the Publication of *The Unfinished System of Nonknowledge.*" *Journal of Religion* 84, no. 1 (2004): 78–87.

Kristeva, Julia. *Strangers to Ourselves.* Translated by Leon Roudiez. New York: Colombia University Press, 1991.

———. "Strangers to Ourselves: The Hope of the Singular." Interview with Richard Kearney. In Richard Kearney, *Debates in Continental Philosophy,* 159–166. New York: Fordham University Press, 2004.

———. *Time and Sense: Proust and the Experience of Literature,* trans. Ross Guberman. New York: Columbia University Press, 1996.

Lacoste, Jean-Yves. "La phénoménalité de l'anticipation." In *La phénoménalité de Dieu: Neuf études.* Paris: Éditions du Cerf, 2008.

Laing, R. D. *The Divided Self.* 1960. London, Penguin Books, 1990.

Latour, Bruno. "An Attempt at a 'Compositionist Manifesto.'" *New Literary History* 41, no. 3 (Summer 2010): 471–490.

Lehman, Robert S. "Allegories of Rending: Killing Time with Walter Benjamin." *New Literary History* 39 (2008): 233–250.

Levinson, Marjorie. "A Motion and a Spirit: Romancing Spinoza." *Studies in Romanticism* 46, no. 4 (Winter 2007): 367–408.

Lilburn, Tim. *Desire Never Leaves: The Poetry of Tim Lilburn.* Edited and with an introduction by Alison Calder. Waterloo, ON: Wilfred Laurier University Press, 2007.

———. *Living in the World As If It Were Home.* Dunvegan, ON: Cormorant, 1999.

Lyotard, Jean-François. Postscript to *The Postmodern Condition.* Translated by Geoffrey Bennington. St. Paul, MN: University of Minnesota Press, 1984.

MacKendrick, Karmen. *Word Made Skin: Figuring Language at the Surface of Flesh.* New York: Fordham University Press, 2004.

Makransky, John. *Awakening Through Love.* Boston: Wisdom Publications, 2007.

Malin, Shimon. "Whitehead and the Collapse of Quantum States." In *Physics and Whitehead: Quantum, Process, Experience,* ed. Timothy E. Eastman and Hank Keeton, 74–83. Albany: State University of New York Press, 2004.

Manoussakis, John. *God after Metaphysics: A Theological Aesthetics.* Bloomington: Indiana University Press, 2007.

Mariani, Paul. *A Commentary on the Complete Poems of Gerard Manley Hopkins.* Ithaca, NY: Cornell University Press, 1970.
Marion, Jean-Luc. *Being Given: Toward a Phenomenology of Givenness.* Translated by Jeffrey L. Kosky. Stanford, CA: Stanford University Press, 2002.
Martin, Elaine. "Re-reading Adorno: The 'After Auschwitz' Aporia." *Forum* 2 (Spring 2006). http://forum.llc.ed.ac.uk/issue2/martin.pdf.
Marucci, Franco. *The Fine Delight that Fathers Thought: Rhetoric and Medievalism in Gerard Manley Hopkins.* Washington, DC: The Catholic University Press, 1994.
Marx, Karl and Friedrich Engels. *The German Ideology.* Online edition, Marxists.org. http://www.marxists.org/archive/marx/works/1845/german-ideology/ch03.htm.
Mathews, Freya. *For Love of Matter: A Contemporary Panpsychism.* Albany: State University of New York Press, 2003.
———. *Reinhabiting Reality: Towards a Recovery of Culture.* Albany: State University of New York Press, 2005.
Mendes-Flohr, Paul. "Rosenzweig's Concept of Miracle." In *Jüdisches Denken in einer Welt ohne Gott: Festshcrift für Stéphane Mosès,* ed. Jens Mattern, Gabriel Motzkin, and Shimon Sandbank, 53–66. Berlin: Verlag Vorwerk 8, 2000.
Merleau-Ponty, Maurice. *Phenomenology of Perception.* London: Routledge, 2002.
———. *The Visible and the Invisible,* trans Alfonso Lingis. Evanston, IL: Northwestern University Press, 1968.
Miller, J. Hillis. *The Disappearance of God: Five Nineteenth-Century Writers.* Cambridge, MA: Harvard University Press, 1963.
———. "The Rhythm of Creativity: *To the Lighthouse.*" In *Tropes, Parables, Performatives: Essays in Twentieth-Century Literature.* Durham, NC: Duke University Press, 1991.
Milton, John. *Paradise Lost.* Edited by Alastair Fowler. London: Longman, 1968.
Morton, Timothy. *Ecology without Nature: Rethinking Environmental Aesthetics.* Cambridge, MA: Harvard University Press, 2007.
Mourant, John A. "Augustine on Miracles." *Augustinian Studies* 4 (1973): 103–27.
Muller, Richard A. *Dictionary of Latin and Greek Theological Terms: Drawn Principally from Protestant Scholastic Theology.* Grand Rapids, MI: Baker, 1985.
Naess, Arne. "The Shallow and the Deep, Long-Range Ecology Movement: A Summary." *Inquiry* 16, no. 1 (1973): 95–100.
Nancy, Jean-Luc. *Corpus.* Translated by Richard A. Rand. New York: Fordham University Press, 2008.
———. *Corpus.* Paris: Éditions Métailié, 2006.
———. *Dis-Enclosure: The Deconstruction of Christianity.* Translated by Bettina Bergo, Gabriel Malenfant, and Michael B. Smith. New York: Fordham University Press, 2008.

———. *La Déclosion: Déconstruction du christianisme, 1.* Paris: Galilée, 2005.

Newman, Lance. *Our Common Dwelling: Henry Thoreau, Transcendentalism and the Class Politics of Nature.* New York: Palgrave Macmillan, 2005.

Nutall, A. D. *Why Does Tragedy Give Pleasure?* Oxford: Oxford University Press, 1996.

Oerlemans, Onno. *Romanticism and the Materiality of Nature.* Toronto: University of Toronto Press, 2002.

Oliver, Mary. *Blue Iris: Poems and Essays.* Boston: Beacon Press, 2004.

Origen. *Contra Celsum.* Translated and with an introduction and notes by Henry Chadwick. Cambridge: Cambridge University Press, 1965.

———. *Homilies on Genesis and Exodus.* Edited by Richard E. Heine. Washington, DC: Catholic University of America Press, 1982.

———. *On First Principles.* Translated and with notes by G. W. Butterworth. Introduction by Henri de Lubac. Gloucester, MA: Peter Smith, 1973.

Palamas, Grégoire. *Défense des saints hésychastes.* 2nd ed. Translated and edited by Jean Meyendorff. 2 vols. Leuven: Spicilegium Sacrum Lovaniense, 1973.

Peignot, Colette. *Laure: The Collected Writings.* San Francisco: City Lights, 2001.

Phillips, Dana. *The Truth of Ecology: Nature, Culture and Literature in America.* Oxford: Oxford University Press, 2003.

Phillips, James. "Wordsworth and the Fraternity of Joy." *New Literary History* 41, no. 3 (Summer 2010): 613–32.

Plumwood, Val. "Nature as Agency and the Prospects for a Progressive Naturalism." *Capitalism, Nature, Socialism* 12, no. 4 (December 2001), 3–32.

———. "Shadow Places and the Politics of Dwelling." Eco-Humanities Corner of AHR, 44, 2008. http://www.australianhumanitiesreview.org/archive/Issue-March-2008/plumwood.html.

Potkay, Adam. "Wordsworth and the Ethics of Things." *PMLA* 123, no. 2 (March 2008): 390–404.

Poulain, Augustin. *The Graces of Interior Prayer.* Translated by Leonora L. Yorke Smith with a preface by D. Considine. London: Kegan Paul, Trench, Trubner and Co., 1921.

Pranger, M. B. "The Unfathomability of Sincerity: On the Seriousness of Augustine's *Confessions*." In *Actas Do Congresso Internutional As Confissoes de Santo Agostinho 1600 Anos Depois: Presenca e Actualidade,* 193–242. Lisbon: Universidade Catolica Editora, 2002.

———. *The Artificiality of Christianity: Essays on the Poetics of Monasticism.* Stanford, CA: Stanford University Press, 2003.

Prieto, Antonio. *La poesía española del siglo XVI.* Vol. 2, *Aquel valor que respetó olvido.* Madrid, Cátedra, 1998.

Proust, Marcel. *In Search of Lost Time,* 7 vols. Translated by C. Scott Moncrieff (vols. 1–6) and Terence Kilmartin and Andreas Mayor (vol. 7). New York: Modern Library Paperback, 1999.

Rahner, Karl, "The Spiritual Senses According to Origen." Translated by David Morland. In *Theological Investigations.* Vol. 16, *Experience of the Spirit: Source of Theology,* 81–103. New York: Seabury Press, 1983.

———. "The Doctrine of the 'Spiritual Senses' in the Middle Ages." Translated by David Moreland. In *Theological Investigations.* Vol. 16, *Experience of the Spirit: Source of Theology,* 104–34. New York: Seabury Press, 1983.

Richard of St. Victor, *The Twelve Patriarchs, The Mystical Ark, Book Three of "The Trinity."* Translated and with an introduction by Grover A. Zinn. Preface by Jean Châtillon. New York: Paulist Press, 1979.

Richardson, Michael. "Seductions of the Impossible: Love, the Erotic and Sacrifice in Surrealist Discourse." *Theory, Culture, & Society* 15, nos. 3–4 (1998): 375–92.

Ricoeur, Paul. "Life in Quest of Narrative." In *On Paul Ricoeur,* ed. David Wood. London: Routledge, 1991.

———. *On Translation.* Translated by Eileen Brennan. New York: Routledge, 2006.

———. *Time and Narrative.* Translated by Kathleen McLaughlin and David Pellauer. 3 vols. Chicago: University of Chicago Press, 1988.

Rigby, Kate. "Earth, World, Text: On the (Im)possibility of Ecopoiesis." *New Literary History* 35, no. 3 (2004): 427–42.

———. "Ecocriticism." In *Literary and Cultural Criticism at the Twenty-First Century,* ed. Julian Wolfreys, 151–78. Edinburgh: Edinburgh University Press, 2002.

———. "Writing in the Anthropocene: Idle Chatter or Ecoprophetic Witness?" *Australian Humanities Review* 47 (November 2009). http://www.australianhumanitiesreview.org/archive/Issue-November-2009/rigby.html.

———. "Writing After Nature." *Australian Humanities Review* 39–40 (September 2006): 1–15.

———. *Topographies of the Sacred: The Poetics of Place in European Romanticism.* Charlottesville: University of Virginia Press, 2004.

Rizo-Patron, Eileen. "Regressus ad Uterum: Bachelard's Alchemical Hermeneutic." *Philosophy Today* 52 (2008): 21–30.

———. "Through the Eye of a Needle: Hermeneutics As Poetic Transformation." PhD diss., State University of New York, 2006.

Rosenzweig, Franz. *Briefe.* Edited by Edith Rosenzweig. Berlin: Schocken Verlag, 1935.

———. *Der Stern der Erlösung.* 3rd ed. Heidelberg: Verlag Lambert Schneider, 1954. First published 1921.

———. *Kleinere Schriften.* Berlin: Schocken Verlag, 1937.

———. *The New Thinking.* Translated by Alan Udoff and Barbara E. Galli. Syracuse, NY: Syracuse University Press, 1999.

———. *The Star of Redemption.* Translated by Barbara Galli. Madison: University of Wisconsin Press, 2005.

Rousseau, Jean-Jacques. *Oeuvres Complètes,* vol. 4. Edited by Bernard Gagnebin and Marcel Raymond. Èditions de la Pléiade. Paris: Gallimard, 1969.

Samuelson, Norbert. "Halevi and Rosenzweig on Miracles." In *Approaches to Judaism in Medieval Times,* ed. David R. Blumenthal, 157–73. Chico, CA: Scholars Press, 1984.

Santner, Eric L. "Miracles Happen: Benjamin, Rosenzweig, Freud, and the Matter of the Neighbor." In *The Neighbor: Three Inquiries in Political Theology,* ed. Slavoj Žižek, Eric L. Santner, and Kenneth Reinhard, 76–133. Chicago: University of Chicago Press, 2006.

Scheler, Max. *On the Eternal in Man.* Translated by Bernard Noble. Hamden, CT: Archon Books, 1972.

Slovic, Scott. *Seeking Awareness in American Nature Writing.* Salt Lake City: University of Utah Press, 1992.

Smith, Thomas A. "The Pleasure of Hell in *City of God* 21." In *History, Apocalypse, and the Secular Imagination: New Essays on Augustine's* City of God, ed. Mark Vessey, Karla Pollmann, and Allan D. Fitzgerald, 195–204. Bowling Green, OH: Philosophy Documentation Center, 1999.

Staley, Lynn, trans. and ed. *The Book of Margery Kempe.* New York: W. W. Norton, 2001.

Steinbock, Anthony J. *Phenomenology and Mysticism: The Verticality of Religious Experience.* Bloomington: Indiana University Press, 2008.

Steiner, George. *Language and Silence: Essays on Language, Literature and the Inhuman.* London: Yale University Press, 1970.

Sulloway, Alison G. *Gerard Manley Hopkins and the Victorian Temper.* London: Routledge and Kegan Paul, 1972.

Swinburne, Richard, ed. *Miracles.* New York: Macmillan, 1989.

Tatian. *Oratio ad Graecos and Fragments.* Translated and edited by Molly Whittaker. Oxford: Clarendon Press, 1982.

Teresa de Jesús. *Obras completas de Santa Teresa de Jesús.* Edited by Maximiliano Herráiz. Salamanca: Ediciones Sígueme, 1997.

Teresa of Avila, *Interior Castle.* Translated by Kieran Kavanaugh and Otillo Rodriguez. Mahwah, NJ: Paulist Press, 1979.

Thoreau, Henry D. *Journal.* Vol. 3, 1848–1851. General editor, John C. Broderick; volume editors Robert Sattelmeyer et al. Princeton, NJ: Princeton University Press, 1990.

Tredinnick, Mark. *The Land's Wild Music: Encounters with Barry Lopez, Peter Matthiessen, Terry Tempest Williams and James Galvin.* San Antonio, TX: Trinity University Press, 2005.

Vermeersch, Arthur. "Religious Obedience." In *The Catholic Encyclopedia,* vol. 11. New York: Robert Appleton Company, 1911. http://www.newadvent.org/cathen/11182a.htm.

Vessey, Mark. "Introduction." In *History, Apocalypse, and the Secular Imagination: New Essays on Augustine's City of God,* ed. Mark Vessey, Karla Pollmann, and

Allan D. Fitzgerald, 1–26. Bowling Green, OH: Philosophy Documentation Center, 1999.
Walsh, David. *The Modern Philosophical Revolution: The Luminosity of Existence.* Cambridge: Cambridge University Press, 2008.
Wetzel, James. "Snares of Truth: Augustine on Free Will and Predestination." In *Augustine and His Critics,* ed. Robert Dodaro and George Lawless, 124–41. London: Routledge, 2000.
———. *Augustine and the Limits of Virtue.* Cambridge: Cambridge University Press, 1992.
Wheeler, W. *The Whole Creature: Complexity, Biosemiotics and the Evolution of Culture.* London: Lawrence & Wishart, 2006.
Williams, Raymond. *The Country and the City.* London: Hogarth Press, 1985.
Willis, Edward Davis. *Calvin's Catholic Christology: The Function of the So-Called Extra Calvinisticum in Calvin's Theology.* Leiden: Brill, 1966.
Wolfson, Elliot R. "Introduction to Barbara Galli's Translation of Rosenzweig's *Star.*" In *The Star of Redemption,* by Franz Rosenzweig. Translated by Barbara Galli, xvii–xx. Madison: University of Wisconsin Press, 2005.
———. *Language, Eros, Being: Kabbalistic Hermeneutics and Poetic Imagination.* New York: Fordham University Press, 2005.
———. "Light Does Not Talk But Shines: Apophasis and Vision in Rosenzweig's Theopoetic Temporality." In *New Directions in Jewish Philosophy,* ed. Aaron W. Hughes and Elliot R Wolfson. Bloomington: Indiana University Press, 2010.
Woolf, Virginia. *A Room of One's Own.* London: Hogarth Press, 1929.
———. *A Writer's Diary.* Edited by Leonard Woolf. New York: Houghton Mifflin Harcourt, 2003.
———. *The Diary of Virginia Woolf.* Edited by Anne Olivier Bell. 5 vols. New York: Harcourt, Brace Jovanovich, 1977–1984.
———. *The Letters of Virginia Woolf.* Edited by Nigel Nicholson and Joanne Trautmann. 6 vols. New York: Harcourt Brace Javonovich, 1977.
———. *Moments of Being.* New York: Harcourt Brace & Co., 1985.
———. *To the Lighthouse.* London: Harcourt Press, 1927.
Wordsworth, William. *Lyrical Ballads, and Other Poems, 1797–1800.* Edited by J. Butler and K. Green. Ithaca, NY: Cornell University Press, 1992.
———. *Poems, In Two Volumes, and Other Poems, 1800–1807.* Edited by Jared Curtis. Ithaca, NY: Cornell University Press, 1983.
Yeats, William Butler. *The Poems: A New Edition.* Edited by Richard J. Finneran. New York: Macmillan, 1983.

Contributors

Manuel Asensi is professor and chair of the Department of Literary Theory at the University of Valencia, Spain. His work focuses on literary theory, literature, film studies, and mystical poetry. He is the author of numerous books of criticism, including *Crítica y sabotaje* (Anthropos/Siglo XXI, 2011) (currently being translated into English as *Sabotage Critique*), *Los años salvajes de la teoría: Philippe Sollers, Tel Quel y la génesis del pensamiento post-estructural francés* (The Savage Years of Theory: Sollers, Tel Quel and the Genesis of French Poststructuralism) (Tirant lo Blanch, 2004), *J. Hillis Miller or Boustrophedonic Reading/Others* (with J. Hillis Miller, Stanford University Press, 1999), and *Literatura y filosofía* (Literature and Philosophy) (Síntesis, 1995). He has also written a three-volume history of literary theory, published by Editorial Tirant lo Blanch, and several monographs on Cervantes, Derrida, Hitchcock, and early German Romanticism.

Virginia Burrus is the Bishop W. Earl Ledden Professor of Religion at Syracuse University. Her teaching and research interests in the field of ancient Christianity include gender, asceticism, constructions of orthodoxy and heresy, and the history of theology. She is currently president of the North American Patristics Society and co-editor of the University of Pennsylvania Press series Divinations: Rereading Late Ancient Religion. She is the author of six books, including *Seducing Augustine: Bodies, Desires, Confessions* (Fordham University Press, 2010), co-written with Mark Jordan and Karmen MacKendrick; and *Sex Lives of Saints: An Erotics of Ancient Hagiography* (University of Pennsylvania Press, 2004). She is also co-editor, with Catherine Keller, of *Toward a Theology of Eros: Transfiguring Passion of the Limits of Discipline* (Fordham University Press, 2006).

Tom Cohen is professor of English at the University at Albany. His work focuses on literary theory and cultural politics and traverses a number of disciplines, including cinema studies, digital thought, biopolitics, and climate change. He has published broadly on American authors as well as on Greek and continental philosophy and film. His five books include *Theory and "The Future": On de Man, on Benjamin* (co-authored with Claire Colebrook and J. Hillis Miller, Routledge, forthcoming); *Hitchcock's Cryptonymies 1: Secret Agents* (University of Minnesota Press, 2005); *Hitchcock's Cryptonymies 2: War Machines* (University of Minnesota Press, 2005); *Ideology and Inscription: "Cultural Studies" after Benjamin, de Man, and Bakhtin* (Cambridge University Press, 1998), and *Anti-Mimesis from Plato to Hitchcock* (Cambridge University Press, 1994).

Carl Good is a freelance translator who lives in Chicago. He formerly taught in the Spanish departments of Emory University and Indiana University, Bloomington. He has edited the collection *The Effects of the Nation: Mexican Art in an Age of Globalization* (Temple University Press, 2001) and has published numerous articles on Hispanic American literature and literary theory. He serves as co-editor of the journal *Discourse: Journal for Theoretical Studies in Media and Culture.*

Kevin Hart is Edwin B. Kyle Professor of Christian Studies at the University of Virginia, Charlottesville and Eric D'Arcy Professor of Philosophy at the Australian Catholic University. His research focuses on systematic theology and the phenomenology of the Christian faith, as well as on religion and literature, including Christian theology and poetry. He is the author of numerous books of criticism, including *Clandestine Encounters: Philosophy in the Narratives of Maurice Blanchot* (Notre Dame University Press, 2010), *The Dark Gaze: Maurice Blanchot and the Sacred* (University of Chicago Press, 2004), and *The Trespass of the Sign: Deconstruction, Theology, and Philosophy* (Cambridge University Press, 1989). He has edited numerous volumes, including Jean-Luc Marion's *The Essential Writings* (Fordham University Press, 2013) and *The Power of Contestation: Perspectives on Maurice Blanchot* (with Geoffrey Hartman, Johns Hopkins University Press, 2005).

Richard Kearney holds the Charles B. Seelig Chair of Philosophy at Boston College and has served as visiting professor at University College Dublin, the University of Paris (Sorbonne), and the University of Nice. He is the author of more than twenty books on European philosophy and literature and has edited or co-edited fourteen more. As a public intellectual in Ireland, he was involved in drafting a number of proposals for a Northern Irish peace agreement. He has presented five series on culture and philosophy for Irish or British television. His recent publications include *Debates in Continental Philosophy* (Fordham University Press, 2004) and a three-volume work, *Philosophy at the Limit* (various publishers, 2001–2003).

Karmen MacKendrick is Professor of Philosophy at Le Moyne College. Her multidisciplinary research addresses questions of language, corporeality, and temporality, primarily in relation to theology and religious studies. She is the author of *Divine Enticement* (Fordham University Press, 2013), *Fragmentation and Memory* (Fordham University Press, 2008), *Word Made Skin* (Fordham University Press, 2004), *Immemorial Silence* (SUNY Press, 2001), and (with Virginia Burrus and Mark D. Jordan) *Seducing Augustine* (Fordham University Press, 2010).

J. Hillis Miller is UCI Distinguished Research Professor of Comparative Literature and English, Emeritus, at the University of California at Irvine. He has published many books and articles on nineteenth- and twentieth-century literature and on literary theory. His latest books include *For Derrida* (Fordham University Press, 2009); *The Medium Is the Maker* (Sussex Academic Press, 2009); *The Conflagration of Community: Fiction Before and After Auschwitz* (University of Chicago Press, 2011); and *Theory and the Disappearing Future: On de Man, On Benjamin* (Routledge, 2012), with Tom Cohen and Claire Colebrook. He is a Fellow of the American Academy of Arts and Sciences and a member of the American Philosophical Society.

Burcht Pranger is professor and chair of the Department of the History of Christianity at the University of Amsterdam. His work focuses on medieval theology, literature and religion, and theology and music. He is author of *The Artificiality of Christianity: Essays on the Poetics of Monasticism* (Stanford University Press, 2003) and *Bernard of Clairvaux and the Shape of Monastic Thought* (Brill, 1994).

Kate Rigby is associate professor and director of the Centre for Comparative Literature and Cultural Studies at Monash University, Australia. Her primary research interest is German studies, with a focus on the literature and philosophy of the age of Goethe; German thought in the twentieth century (especially German critical theory and phenomenology); and ecological humanities. She is the author of three books: *Topographies of the Sacred: The Poetics of Place in European Romanticism* (University of Virginia Press, 2004), *Transgressions of the Feminine: Tragedy, Enlightenment and the Figure of Women in Classical German Drama* (Reihe Siegen, 1996), and (with Silke Beinssen-Hesse) *Out of the Shadows: Contemporary German Feminism* (Melbourne University Press).

Gregory C. Stallings is associate professor of Spanish at Brigham Young University. He has published articles on (in various configurations) poetry, fiction, philosophy, jazz, and film. He is the author of *Jazz y literatura* (Tirant lo Blanch, 2009) and is currently at work on a manuscript on phenomenology and neomysticism in twentieth-century Spanish literature.

Index

Perspectives in Continental Philosophy
John D. Caputo, series editor

John D. Caputo, ed., *Deconstruction in a Nutshell: A Conversation with Jacques Derrida.*

Michael Strawser, *Both/And: Reading Kierkegaard—From Irony to Edification.*

Michael D. Barber, *Ethical Hermeneutics: Rationality in Enrique Dussel's Philosophy of Liberation.*

James H. Olthuis, ed., *Knowing* Other-*wise: Philosophy at the Threshold of Spirituality.*

James Swindal, *Reflection Revisited: Jürgen Habermas's Discursive Theory of Truth.*

Richard Kearney, *Poetics of Imagining: Modern and Postmodern.* Second edition.

Thomas W. Busch, *Circulating Being: From Embodiment to Incorporation—Essays on Late Existentialism.*

Edith Wyschogrod, *Emmanuel Levinas: The Problem of Ethical Metaphysics.* Second edition.

Francis J. Ambrosio, ed., *The Question of Christian Philosophy Today.*

Jeffrey Bloechl, ed., *The Face of the Other and the Trace of God: Essays on the Philosophy of Emmanuel Levinas.*

Ilse N. Bulhof and Laurens ten Kate, eds., *Flight of the Gods: Philosophical Perspectives on Negative Theology.*

Trish Glazebrook, *Heidegger's Philosophy of Science.*

Kevin Hart, *The Trespass of the Sign: Deconstruction, Theology, and Philosophy.*

Mark C. Taylor, *Journeys to Selfhood: Hegel and Kierkegaard.* Second edition.

Dominique Janicaud, Jean-François Courtine, Jean-Louis Chrétien, Michel Henry, Jean-Luc Marion, and Paul Ricoeur, *Phenomenology and the "Theological Turn": The French Debate.*

Karl Jaspers, *The Question of German Guilt.* Introduction by Joseph W. Koterski, S.J.

Jean-Luc Marion, *The Idol and Distance: Five Studies.* Translated with an introduction by Thomas A. Carlson.

Jeffrey Dudiak, *The Intrigue of Ethics: A Reading of the Idea of Discourse in the Thought of Emmanuel Levinas.*

Robyn Horner, *Rethinking God as Gift: Marion, Derrida, and the Limits of Phenomenology.*

Mark Dooley, *The Politics of Exodus: Søren Kierkegaard's Ethics of Responsibility.*

Merold Westphal, *Overcoming Onto-Theology: Toward a Postmodern Christian Faith.*

Edith Wyschogrod, Jean-Joseph Goux, and Eric Boynton, eds., *The Enigma of Gift and Sacrifice.*

Stanislas Breton, *The Word and the Cross.* Translated with an introduction by Jacquelyn Porter.

Jean-Luc Marion, *Prolegomena to Charity.* Translated by Stephen E. Lewis.

Peter H. Spader, *Scheler's Ethical Personalism: Its Logic, Development, and Promise.*

Jean-Louis Chrétien, *The Unforgettable and the Unhoped For.* Translated by Jeffrey Bloechl.

Don Cupitt, *Is Nothing Sacred? The Non-Realist Philosophy of Religion: Selected Essays.*

Jean-Luc Marion, *In Excess: Studies of Saturated Phenomena.* Translated by Robyn Horner and Vincent Berraud.

Phillip Goodchild, *Rethinking Philosophy of Religion: Approaches from Continental Philosophy.*

William J. Richardson, S.J., *Heidegger: Through Phenomenology to Thought.*

Jeffrey Andrew Barash, *Martin Heidegger and the Problem of Historical Meaning.*

Jean-Louis Chrétien, *Hand to Hand: Listening to the Work of Art.* Translated with an introduction by Stephen E. Lewis.

Jean-Louis Chrétien, *The Call and the Response.* Translated with an introduction by Anne Davenport.

D. C. Schindler, *Han Urs von Balthasar and the Dramatic Structure of Truth: A Philosophical Investigation.*

Julian Wolfreys, ed., *Thinking Difference: Critics in Conversation.*

Allen Scult, *Being Jewish/Reading Heidegger: An Ontological Encounter.*

Richard Kearney, *Debates in Continental Philosophy: Conversations with Contemporary Thinkers.*

Jennifer Anna Gosetti-Ferencei, *Heidegger, Hölderlin, and the Subject of Poetic Language: Toward a New Poetics of Dasein.*

Jolita Pons, *Stealing a Gift: Kierkegaard's Pseudonyms and the Bible.*

Jean-Yves Lacoste, *Experience and the Absolute: Disputed Questions on the Humanity of Man.* Translated by Mark Raftery-Skehan.

Charles P. Bigger, *Between* Chora *and the Good: Metaphor's Metaphysical Neighborhood.*

Dominique Janicaud, *Phenomenology "Wide Open": After the French Debate.* Translated by Charles N. Cabral.
Ian Leask and Eoin Cassidy, eds., *Givenness and God: Questions of Jean-Luc Marion.*
Jacques Derrida, *Sovereignties in Question: The Poetics of Paul Celan.* Edited by Thomas Dutoit and Outi Pasanen.
William Desmond, *Is There a Sabbath for Thought? Between Religion and Philosophy.*
Bruce Ellis Benson and Norman Wirzba, eds., *The Phenomenology of Prayer.*
S. Clark Buckner and Matthew Statler, eds., *Styles of Piety: Practicing Philosophy after the Death of God.*
Kevin Hart and Barbara Wall, eds., *The Experience of God: A Postmodern Response.*
John Panteleimon Manoussakis, *After God: Richard Kearney and the Religious Turn in Continental Philosophy.*
John Martis, *Philippe Lacoue-Labarthe: Representation and the Loss of the Subject.*
Jean-Luc Nancy, *The Ground of the Image.*
Edith Wyschogrod, *Crossover Queries: Dwelling with Negatives, Embodying Philosophy's Others.*
Gerald Bruns, *On the Anarchy of Poetry and Philosophy: A Guide for the Unruly.*
Brian Treanor, *Aspects of Alterity: Levinas, Marcel, and the Contemporary Debate.*
Simon Morgan Wortham, *Counter-Institutions: Jacques Derrida and the Question of the University.*
Leonard Lawlor, *The Implications of Immanence: Toward a New Concept of Life.*
Clayton Crockett, *Interstices of the Sublime: Theology and Psychoanalytic Theory.*
Bettina Bergo, Joseph Cohen, and Raphael Zagury-Orly, eds., *Judeities: Questions for Jacques Derrida.* Translated by Bettina Bergo and Michael B. Smith.
Jean-Luc Marion, *On the Ego and on God: Further Cartesian Questions.* Translated by Christina M. Gschwandtner.
Jean-Luc Nancy, *Philosophical Chronicles.* Translated by Franson Manjali.
Jean-Luc Nancy, *Dis-Enclosure: The Deconstruction of Christianity.* Translated by Bettina Bergo, Gabriel Malenfant, and Michael B. Smith.
Andrea Hurst, *Derrida Vis-à-vis Lacan: Interweaving Deconstruction and Psychoanalysis.*
Jean-Luc Nancy, *Noli me tangere: On the Raising of the Body.* Translated by Sarah Clift, Pascale-Anne Brault, and Michael Naas.
Jacques Derrida, *The Animal That Therefore I Am.* Edited by Marie-Louise Mallet, translated by David Wills.
Jean-Luc Marion, *The Visible and the Revealed.* Translated by Christina M. Gschwandtner and others.
Michel Henry, *Material Phenomenology.* Translated by Scott Davidson.
Jean-Luc Nancy, *Corpus.* Translated by Richard A. Rand.
Joshua Kates, *Fielding Derrida.*
Michael Naas, *Derrida From Now On.*

Shannon Sullivan and Dennis J. Schmidt, eds., *Difficulties of Ethical Life.*

Catherine Malabou, *What Should We Do with Our Brain?* Translated by Sebastian Rand, Introduction by Marc Jeannerod.

Claude Romano, *Event and World.* Translated by Shane Mackinlay.

Vanessa Lemm, *Nietzsche's Animal Philosophy: Culture, Politics, and the Animality of the Human Being.*

B. Keith Putt, ed., *Gazing Through a Prism Darkly: Reflections on Merold Westphal's Hermeneutical Epistemology.*

Eric Boynton and Martin Kavka, eds., *Saintly Influence: Edith Wyschogrod and the Possibilities of Philosophy of Religion.*

Shane Mackinlay, *Interpreting Excess: Jean-Luc Marion, Saturated Phenomena, and Hermeneutics.*

Kevin Hart and Michael A. Signer, eds., *The Exorbitant: Emmanuel Levinas Between Jews and Christians.*

Bruce Ellis Benson and Norman Wirzba, eds., *Words of Life: New Theological Turns in French Phenomenology.*

William Robert, *Trials: Of Antigone and Jesus.*

Brian Treanor and Henry Isaac Venema, eds., *A Passion for the Possible: Thinking with Paul Ricoeur.*

Kas Saghafi, *Apparitions—Of Derrida's Other.*

Nick Mansfield, *The God Who Deconstructs Himself: Sovereignty and Subjectivity Between Freud, Bataille, and Derrida.*

Don Ihde, *Heidegger's Technologies: Postphenomenological Perspectives.*

Françoise Dastur, *Questioning Phenomenology.* Translated by Robert Vallier.

Suzi Adams, *Castoriadis's Ontology: Being and Creation.*

Richard Kearney and Kascha Semonovitch, eds., *Phenomenologies of the Stranger: Between Hostility and Hospitality.*

Michael Naas, *Miracle and Machine: Jacques Derrida and the Two Sources of Religion, Science, and the Media.*

Alena Alexandrova, Ignaas Devisch, Laurens ten Kate, and Aukje van Rooden, *Re-treating Religion: Deconstructing Christianity with Jean-Luc Nancy.* Preamble by Jean-Luc Nancy.

Emmanuel Falque, *The Metamorphosis of Finitude: An Essay on Birth and Resurrection.* Translated by George Hughes.

Scott M. Campbell, *The Early Heidegger's Philosophy of Life: Facticity, Being, and Language.*

Françoise Dastur, *How Are We to Confront Death? An Introduction to Philosophy.* Translated by Robert Vallier. Foreword by David Farrell Krell.

Christina M. Gschwandtner, *Postmodern Apologetics? Arguments for God in Contemporary Philosophy.*

Ben Morgan, *On Becoming God: Late Medieval Mysticism and the Modern Western Self.*

Neal DeRoo, *Futurity in Phenomenology: Promise and Method in Husserl, Levinas, and Derrida.*

Sarah LaChance Adams and Caroline R. Lundquist eds., *Coming to Life: Philosophies of Pregnancy, Childbirth, and Mothering.*

Thomas Claviez, ed., *The Conditions of Hospitality: Ethics, Politics, and Aesthetics on the Threshold of the Possible.*

Roland Faber and Jeremy Fackenthal, eds., *Theopoetic Folds: Philosophizing Multifariousness.*

Jean-Luc Marion, *The Essential Writings.* Edited by Kevin Hart.

Adam S. Miller, *Speculative Grace: Bruno Latour and Object-Oriented Theology.* Foreword by Levi R. Bryant

Jean-Luc Nancy, *Corpus II: Writings on Sexuality.*

David Nowell Smith, *Sounding/Silence: Martin Heidegger at the Limits of Poetics.*

Claude Romano, *Event and Time.* Translated by Stephen E. Lewis.

Frank Chouraqui, *Ambiguity and the Absolute: Nietzsche and Merleau-Ponty on the Question of Truth.*

Gregory C. Stallings, Manuel Asensi, and Carl Good, eds., *Material Spirit: Religion and Literature Intranscendent.*